Table of **CONTENTS**

6 **CHAPTER 1:**
HIT THE OPEN ROAD!
Ready for the adventure of your life? Read how these folks hit the road, roaming across North America, driving up to Alaska and traveling down to Mexico. These trips are sure to impress!

30 **CHAPTER 2:**
HAVE CAR, WILL TRAVEL
The automobile created a quick, comfortable way for folks to set out for adventure. Whether we were driving across the country or simply enjoying a Sunday drive, wheels kept us on the move.

50 **CHAPTER 3:**
THE GREAT OUTDOORS
From the mountains to the prairies, North America hosts a variety of breathtaking scenic marvels. Travel from coast to coast without stepping out your door with the memories found here.

76 **CHAPTER 4:**
ROADSIDE WONDERS
The world's largest rocking chair and a two-headed cow...these are just two of the roadside spectacles tourists might visit during a road trip. This chapter features popular attractions like these and stories from the "Mother Road," Route 66.

94 **CHAPTER 5:**
TICKET TO FUN
The need for high-flying fun knows no age limit. From vintage boardwalks to popular amusement parks, these magical spots inspire the kid in everyone. Revisit the carnivals, arcades and other eye-opening destinations we loved to visit.

108 CHAPTER 6:
LIFE'S A BEACH
What better away to escape life's hectic pace than
with a shoreside getaway? Grab your swimsuit and
beach towel, because these sunny stories spotlight
stories from ocean lovers.

128 CHAPTER 7:
BACKTRACKIN'
Automobiles aren't the only way folks saw the
sights. Here, read heartwarming stories from those
who traveled the country on trains, buses, bicycles
and canoes, as well as blimps and roller skates!

148 CHAPTER 8:
BIG-CITY ADVENTURES
Skyscrapers, subways and bustling streets have
always fascinated us. Share the excitement as
road trippers are awestruck by larger-than-life
architecture, impressive social scenes and more!

164 CHAPTER 9:
MILES OF SMILES
Readers reminisce about favorite hideaways,
money-saving tactics and the kindness of strangers
in a cheery chapter that's sure to bring a smile.

184 CHAPTER 10:
ARE WE THERE YET?
Muddy roads, flat tires, broken axles and
inadequate directions were only a few of the
issues that complicated road trips. Take a look
back at some comical mishaps weary travelers
encountered en route to their destinations.

EDITORIAL

EDITOR-IN-CHIEF Catherine Cassidy
CREATIVE DIRECTOR Howard Greenberg
EDITORIAL OPERATIONS DIRECTOR Kerri Balliet
MANAGING EDITOR/PRINT & DIGITAL BOOKS Mark Hagen
ASSOCIATE CREATIVE DIRECTOR Edwin Robles Jr.
EDITOR Amy Glander
CONTRIBUTING EDITORS Molly Jasinski, Michelle Rozumalski, Russ Maki
ART DIRECTOR Raeann Sundholm
LAYOUT DESIGNER Catherine Fletcher
CONTRIBUTING LAYOUT DESIGNERS Jill Banks, Matt Fukuda, Mélanie Lévesque
EDITORIAL PRODUCTION MANAGER Dena Ahlers
COPY CHIEF Deb Warlaumont Mulvey
COPY EDITORS Joanne Weintraub, Mary-Liz Shaw, Dulcie Shoener
BUSINESS ANALYST Kristy Martin
BILLING SPECIALIST Mary Ann Koebernik
EDITOR, REMINISCE Marija Potkonjak Andric
ASSOCIATE CREATIVE DIRECTOR Sharon K. Nelson
ART DIRECTOR, REMINISCE Gretchen Trautman

BUSINESS

VICE PRESIDENT, CHIEF SALES OFFICER Mark S. Josephson
VICE PRESIDENT, BUSINESS DEVELOPMENT & MARKETING Alain Begun
VICE PRESIDENT, PUBLISHER Russell S. Ellis
VICE PRESIDENT, DIGITAL EXPERIENCE & E-COMMERCE Jennifer Smith
VICE PRESIDENT, DIRECT TO CONSUMER MARKETING Dave Fiegel

THE READER'S DIGEST ASSOCIATION, INC.

PRESIDENT AND CHIEF EXECUTIVE OFFICER Robert E. Guth

VICE PRESIDENT, CHIEF OPERATING OFFICER, NORTH AMERICA Howard Halligan
PRESIDENT & PUBLISHER, BOOKS Harold Clarke
VICE PRESIDENT, NORTH AMERICAN OPERATIONS Philippe Cloutier
VICE PRESIDENT, CHIEF MARKETING OFFICER Leslie Doty
VICE PRESIDENT, NORTH AMERICAN HUMAN RESOURCES Phyllis E. Gebhardt, SPHR
VICE PRESIDENT, CHIEF TECHNOLOGY OFFICER Rob Hilliard
VICE PRESIDENT, CONSUMER MARKETING PLANNING Jim Woods

PICTURED ON THE FRONT COVER:

BOYS IN CAR SuperStock
MOUNT RUSHMORE A.M. Wettach-RDAEB

DID SOMEBODY SAY **ROAD TRIP?**

Aah, vacation—there's nothing like that blissful intermission from the daily grind. Given a week away from our responsibilities, what's the first thing we do? Pack up the car and barrel down the interstate. Reaching our destination involves uncovering everything from nature's wonders to roadside attractions, from small-town charm to big-city splendor—all from behind the wheel of the family car.

With *Reminisce Family Road Trips*, however, you can take a nostalgic tour down memory lane with more than 400 memorable firsthand accounts and personal snapshots that document an array of wild, wacky, hilarious and heartwarming vacation stories from the folks who experienced them.

Are you a nature junkie? Read the stories of road trippers who flocked to North America's most celebrated natural attractions: the desert vistas of the Grand Canyon, the rugged wilderness of Yosemite and Yellowstone, the great carvings of Presidents George Washington, Thomas Jefferson, Abraham Lincoln and Theodore Roosevelt on Mount Rushmore, and more.

If you're in an urban frame of mind, enjoy the citified pleasures of Chicago's soaring skyline, the patriotic appeal of Washington, D.C., or the sheer wonder of Lady Liberty's gilded torch. Or perhaps the sunglasses and beach chairs of Miami or Atlantic City are more your style? If so, stories of sand and surf will put you in a vacation frame of mind.

We also have chapters devoted to weekend jaunts to amusement parks, roadside oddities and other offbeat curiosities, all within easy reach of interstate exits. Tired of being behind the wheel? Discover the thrill of riding the rails and the many other unique modes of transportation folks employed in the early days of leisure travel.

You'll also find personal accounts of travelers who drove the famed "Mother Road," Route 66, and tales of those who discovered hidden corners of our great country. And if all this doesn't ignite your wanderlust, you'll be in stitches when you read stories of hapless tourists, campers and hitchhikers who survived mishap and misfortune only to come home with a bank of adventure-filled memories.

Whether you're a die-hard road tripper or an armchair explorer, *Reminisce Family Road Trips* is your round-trip ticket to some of the most enduring memories of hitting the open road with the family in tow. So grab the picnic basket and jump in the car—we promise you a journey that's unparalleled and unforgettable!

Best to you all,
The editors of *Reminisce* magazine

ILLINOIS

I'M A TRAVELIN' MAN
JUST PASSIN THRU

SPASMODIC GEYSER

THIS GEYSER HAS SEVERAL VENTS, INCLUDING TWO LARGE CRATERS. IT MAY PLAY FROM ANY OR ALL OF THESE SIMULTANEOUSLY. ITS ERUPTIONS RESEMBLING THOSE OF THE NEARBY SAWMILL GEYSER, AND OCCUR-RING SEVERAL TIMES A DAY AT IRREGULAR INTERVALS. WATER IS THROWN ONLY A FEW FEET HIGH FOR A PERIOD OF 20 TO 60 MINUTES.

66 You're off to Great Places! Today is your day! Your mountain is waiting. So...get on your way! 99

—Dr. Seuss

CHAPTER 1

Hit the
OPEN ROAD!

Whether you've road-tripped a dozen times or are one of the uninitiated, you'll surely agree seeing America from the road is an experience unlike any other. Because it's not just the destination that will be burned in your memory—it's the interesting places and sweeping panoramas you see along the way.

"In the summer of 1926, my family made the trip of a lifetime—we moved from Ben Avon, Pennsylvania, to Los Angeles," recalls Joseph Bragdon of Salinas, California. "We shipped our household items and made the road trip in a 1925 Nash seven-passenger sedan pulling an Auto-Kamp trailer.

"The camper was the forerunner of the foldout camping trailer common today. It had two double beds, but as there were six of us, my brother and I slept outside under one of the beds on folding cots next to the muddy wheels. Camping trailers were rare in those days, and people stared wherever we went. In campgrounds, a crowd always gathered to watch my dad and older brother set up the rig and to ask questions.

"We spent six weeks on the roads, many of them unpaved, and zigzagged across the country, visiting national parks and historic sites in 13 states.

"I was only 10, but the trip stands out in my mind. The easy pace of yesteryear gave the traveler a chance to enjoy the countryside."

Ready for the adventure of a lifetime? Read how these folks hit the road, roaming across North America, driving up to Alaska and traveling down to Mexico. You'll see that getting there was half the fun!

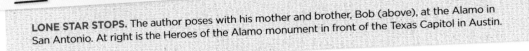

Caverns, Cannons
& CRICKETS

A prewar family trip through the American Southwest stirred a young man's wanderlust and appreciaton for nature. J.R. "BILL" BAILEY • NEW IBERIA, LOUISIANA

My family had settled in New Iberia, Louisiana, after the Texas Co. (later Texaco) transferred my father there in 1935. My parents, my older brother, Bob, and I set out from there, crossed the Sabine River into Texas and eventually arrived in Austin, where we visited the state Capitol building. On the grounds were monuments to Texas history, such as the heroes of the Alamo and Terry's Texas Rangers.

Just north of Fredericksburg, we marveled at Balanced Rock, a red granite boulder measuring 12 feet high and 10 feet in diameter, perched on two tiny points.

In San Antonio, we made sure to stop at the Alamo. The thing that impressed me the most was an old cannon on display outside the mission.

After leaving San Antonio, we drove through Hondo, where we saw a sign that had been erected by the Lions Club in 1930. It said: "Welcome. This is God's country. Don't drive thru it like hell." This was quite an unusual sign for those times!

We crossed the bridge over the Pecos River and arrived in Langtry, the home of "Judge" Roy Bean. Though actually a justice of the peace, he appointed himself a judge in the late 1800s, called himself "The Law West of the Pecos" and presided over many trials in his popular saloon.

Continuing west, we were caught in the middle of a cricket storm. Leaving the car, we heard the snap, crackle and pop that came from stepping on all

IN THE HEART OF TEXAS. Road signs (right) and AT-6A "Texan" trainers (below right) at Randolph Field in San Antonio fascinated the author's family. He's shown at Roy Bean's (below) with his brother, their mom, and the caretaker.

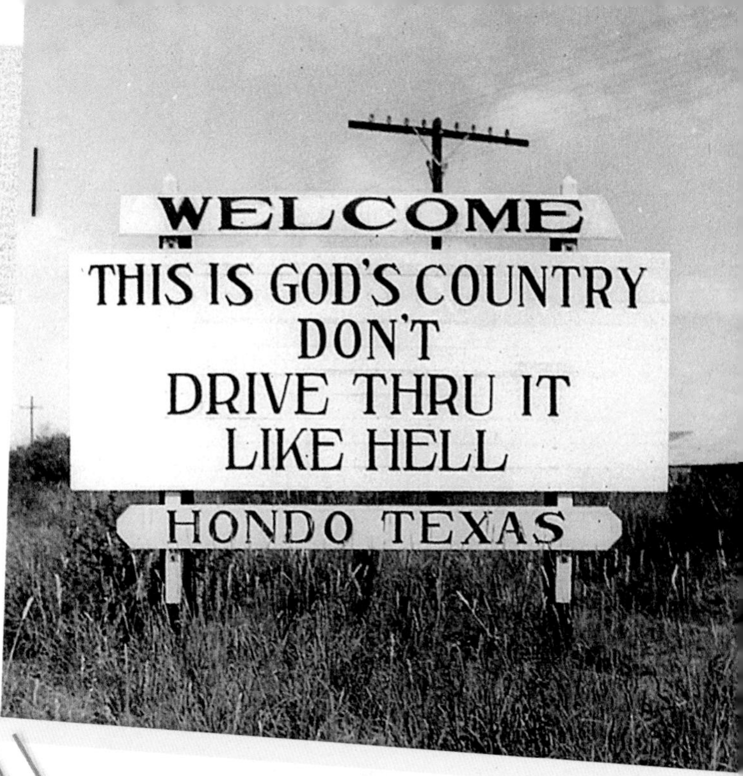
WELCOME
THIS IS GOD'S COUNTRY
DON'T
DRIVE THRU IT
LIKE HELL
HONDO TEXAS

those insects. That night we stopped at a tourist court, and Bob and I were entertained all night long by the sound of crickets flying into the blades of our window fan.

We arrived in El Paso, where we had a chance to cross into Juarez, Mexico. I was impressed by the sight of an old hitching post and a horse-watering trough, but the Mexican jumping beans were an even greater fascination.

The adventure continued as we headed for Carlsbad Caverns in New Mexico. The underground attraction was indescribably beautiful, with huge stalactites hanging overhead and stalagmites growing from the floor of the cavern. With the temperature at 56 degrees inside, I was cold, and Dad had to carry me most of the way.

From New Mexico, we headed for home. The attack on Pearl Harbor came just a few months later, so our family would not take another vacation until 1951, when we visited Bob and his family in San Bruno, California.

Along with confirming that there were hills higher than the ones ants live in, I saw at least one sight that no longer exists. In 1986, vandals destroyed Balanced Rock by dynamiting it off its base, depriving future generations of the opportunity to see what was a truly wonderful geological phenomenon.

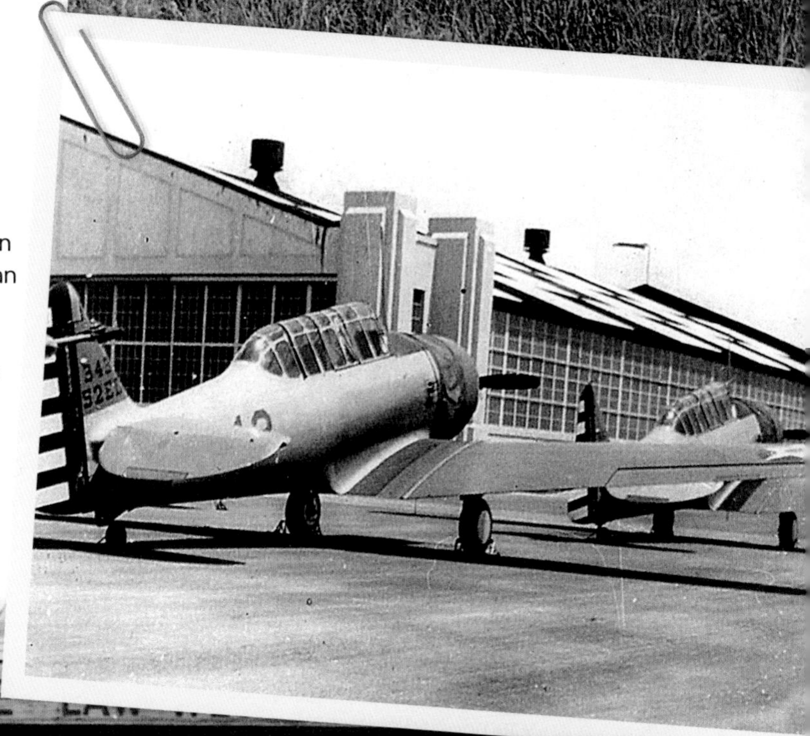

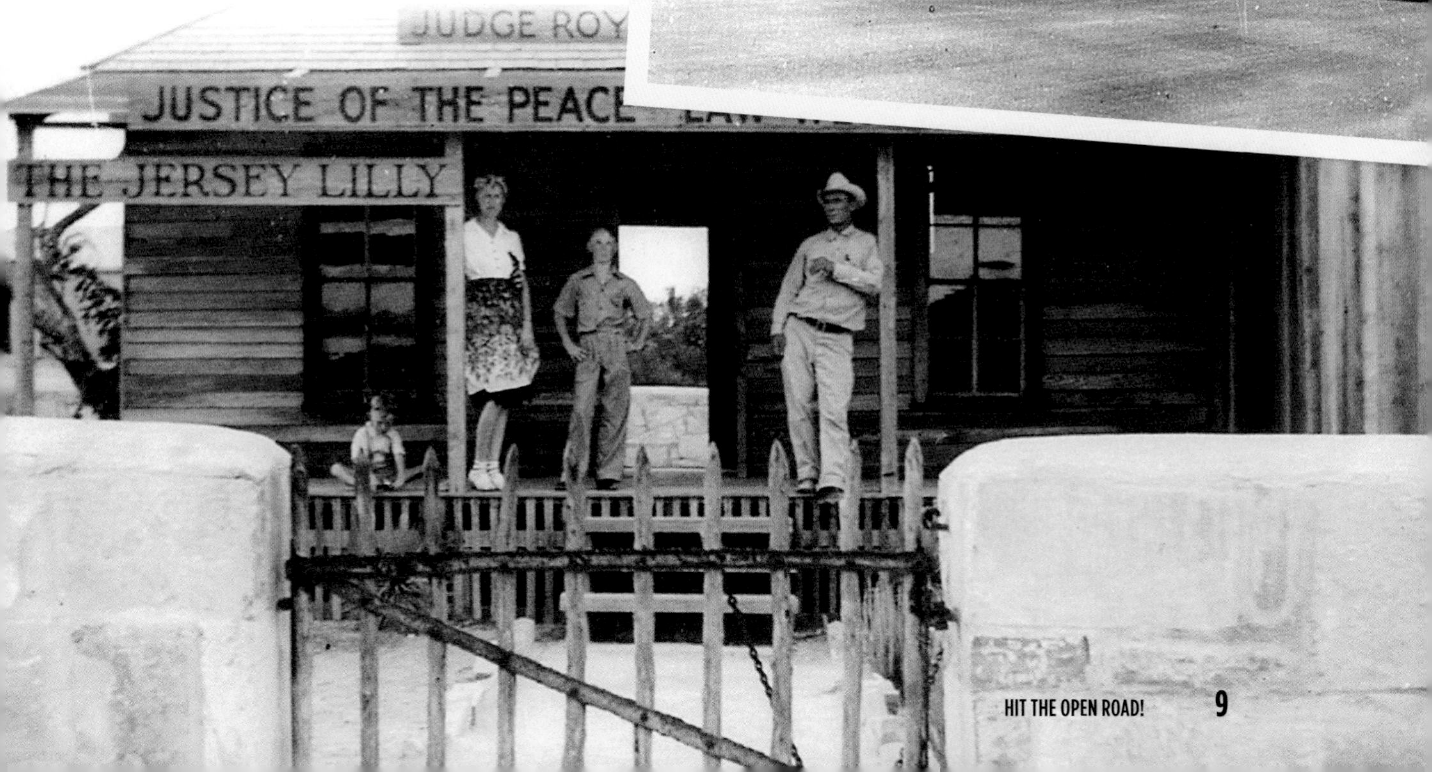
JUDGE ROY
JUSTICE OF THE PEACE
THE JERSEY LILLY

LEFT BEHIND

One of our favorite family rituals was a driving trip every summer. Our 1958 Rambler station wagon had front and back seats that folded down, creating a flat surface from the tailgate to the dashboard. It was just enough room for my parents, my older brother and me to sleep in.

On one trip, when I was about 7, we pulled into a gas station somewhere in Wyoming. While the attendants were filling the gas tank, washing the windows and checking the oil and tire pressure (remember when they did all that?), Mom, my brother and I scattered to go to the restrooms, get a drink of water and look around a bit. After a few minutes, I headed back toward the car, only to see it driving off over the crest of the hill.

I don't quite remember how I felt, except that I know I didn't panic. Sure enough, a few minutes later, the Rambler came back over the hill to my rescue. My father was livid, and my brother was trying desperately not to laugh.

I found out the others had all piled back into the car while I was still in the restroom. Without looking behind him, my dad asked, "Are you boys in?" My brother, who was about 11 at the time, answered, "Yes, we're both in," knowing full well that I was not—and off they went.

I think my father was more angry about having to waste time coming back to get me than about my mischievous brother trying to abandon me!

PAUL SOLEM • LOVELAND, COLORADO

SEEING THE SIGHTS. Road trippin' was a blast in the 1958 Rambler wagon (top). Above, author Paul and brother Tim watch a geyser at Yellowstone. Below, Mom strikes a silly pose for the camera.

SPASMODIC GEYSER

CORA

PIONEER CAMPERS. Judith Rast's grandparents set up camp at Rock Creek, California, in 1933. "Touring" and camping were novel then, and campers attracted attention.

When Touring
WAS A NOVELTY

My grandfather, Wesley Davis, loved to take his car "touring" in the early days of auto travel. He claimed to have driven over 460,000 miles between 1914 and 1934.

The following excerpt from his memoirs describes one of his trips in the mid-1920s:

"When my wife, Edith, and I began touring, there was little choice of accommodations. That changed when campgrounds for tourists began springing up like mushrooms.

"The more luxurious campgrounds offered a cabin or two and had signs touting the latest in conveniences—usually a few tables with seats attached and one or two outdoor iron stoves to be used communally. Often the tourist camp was fenced like a zoo.

"When a municipal campground opened in Portland, Oregon, curious townspeople thronged to the grounds. The onlookers stood about singly and in groups, watching our cooking and eating activities, some audibly commenting upon the procedure. Others pulled back our tent flaps and peered inside.

"Everyone wanted to know where we were going and where we'd come from. I remained as courteous as possible, though my patience was sorely tried. One day, before a particularly large audience, our little boy chalked 'Omigosh' across the side of our auto.

"Soon an apparently self-appointed guide among the onlookers was explaining to her friends that pennants and license plates on motorcars indicated where travelers were from.

"Reaching our car, she read aloud, 'Omigosh. Oh, yes—that's in California...near Pasadena.' "

JUDITH RAST • DIBOLL, TEXAS

ACROSS THE
USA ON MY BSA

A new "sickle" and 10 days of freedom were irresistible to a daring 19-year-old in 1950.

LEE SLAUGHTER • FRONT ROYAL, VIRGINIA

For some time I'd toyed with the idea of a motorcycle trek from my home outside Washington, D.C., to Yellowstone National Park in Wyoming. But my World War II Army surplus Harley-Davidson just wasn't up to the task.

Then, in the spring of 1950, when I was 19 (at right), I bought a new BSA motorcycle. With a dependable "sickle" and a 10-day leave from my job at the Department of Agriculture, I could fulfill my dream of traveling to the Wild West.

Reluctant to tell my folks about my grandiose plan, I merely said I was going for a "little ride." Four hundred mountainous miles later, I checked into a $2 motel in Ohio.

My folks didn't know where I was until they started received penny postcards. By the time I returned home, they were so relieved that they said very little.

My second and third days across the flatter Midwest improved my mileage—although I had to keep an eye out for any local sheriff eager to introduce a speeding biker to his justice of the peace.

Midmorning of the fourth day found me hopelessly lost in downtown Denver. While I pondered which way was "out," a big Harley "74" motorcycle suddenly roared up alongside me, the springs on its banana seat bottomed out by a 250-pound female biker—a novel sight in those days!

"Ya lost?"

I nodded timidly.

"Then follow me, Shorty," she shouted, thundering off. Her reckless riding made that option undesirable, but at least she showed me the proper direction: north. By sunset, I was at a filling station in Rawlins, Wyoming. "There ain't nothin' for 120 miles," the attendant advised.

It was all open range, and darkness

caught me midway—but not before I raced some pronghorn antelope at 60 mph until they found a higher gear and proved who was swiftest.

The next 60 miles were really spooky. Riding alone in the desert darkness 2,000 miles from home with no traffic gave me plenty of time to think, *What if...?* Seeing the lights of Lander, Wyoming, brought an emotional conclusion to a very tiring day.

I got my first silver dollars in change when I bought a chocolate malt at the Lander drugstore soda fountain. My guest room even had a mason jar full of dried rattlesnake rattles!

At Jackson Hole, the spectacular mountain peaks of the Grand Tetons loomed into view. When I finally arrived at Yellowstone, there was still snow on the ground in the shady places.

I found a string of primitive cabins that rented for $1 each, and for three glorious days, I motored to all of Yellowstone's famous sights.

At the old log visitors lodge, a genuine deerskin "Buffalo Bill" jacket (opposite page, below) that was for sale caught my eye. It cost $34—a full week's pay.

It was painful to leave my new flame—the West—and face the arduous 2,400-mile journey home. But I had a steady job waiting for me. Pushing myself to the limit, I covered the entire distance in three grueling days. The last one is a day I shall never forget—24 hours "in the saddle."

I spent much of it in pouring rain and darkness, riding through the narrow switchbacks of the Alleghenies. I got through on bottled Cokes, Baby Ruths and Amoco white gas.

Close to home, unable to keep my bloodshot eyes open one more instant, I stopped and lay down on a wet park bench. Almost instantly, a policeman was tapping my feet with his "billy," and I rode the last dozen miles home.

It's been said that you can't go back, but I can sure reminisce each summer by donning my old buckskin and riding into the Virginia high country.

When I'm laying the bike over on a sharp mountain curve, I recall how it was during my trip in 1950. The memories of that time are still as clear and crisp as the air of Yellowstone.

READY TO RIDE! These three young men were on a cross-country trip when the photo above was taken in 1927. The trio was somewhere in Oklahoma at the time. Reader Bill Pitts of Santa Rosa, California, shared the photo; his father's the one in the center.

Take 14 Boys on a
TWO-WEEK TRIP?

One brave dad packed them all into a station wagon in 1936 for an adventure across the Southwest.

HORACE FRANTZ • MENLO PARK, CALIFORNIA

When I helped organize a boys club in the early 1930s, I never thought that 14 of us would take the auto trip of a lifetime across the American Southwest.

I grew up on a large trout farm my dad owned in Salida, Colorado. In the summer of 1936, he had to take a business trip to Flagstaff, Arizona. He agreed to take along all the boys who could fit in his Ford station wagon!

We decided we'd all dress alike and chose black corduroy trousers, maroon shirts and yellow ties. In the photo above, I'm at the far left and my father is on the far right.

Each boy contributed $7 toward expenses and had to bring his own bedroll and a change of clothes. My father had a tent made that would

attach to the station wagon, and he removed the car's rear seats. We sat on our bedrolls, and the tailgate was lowered so four of the boys could ride there. A sturdy rope ran across the back of the vehicle.

Early one morning, we left—all 14 of us, ages 8 to 14, and my father. At that time, most of the boys had never been more than 50 miles from their homes.

We traveled south through Taos and Santa Fe to Albuqueruqe. Hot and dusty, we found a public beach and swam in the then-unpolluted Rio Grande.

The next stop along Route 66 was Flagstaff, where we rented a couple of hotel rooms to clean up while my father took care of business.

Then it was on to the Grand Canyon—golly, what a gulley!—before we arrived at Needles, California, and the desert. After nightfall, we stretched out our bedrolls on a rise next to the highway. We were jarred awake by a close passing train. We had camped on the elevated rise next to the tracks!

In California, we pitched our tent on the lawn of my grandmother's home. We visited a movie studio and Venice Amusement Park, riding on a roller coaster for the first time, then traveled south to Del Mar and Rancho Santa Fe, where we camped in an orange grove that belonged to my aunt.

Next we drove to San Diego, where ships of the Pacific fleet were in the harbor. My father visited the naval commander, an officer he'd known during World War I, and we were taken by launch to visit several large ships. We ended up aboard the *U.S.S. Nautilus* and got to have lunch on the ship.

When we got back to my aunt's beachfront home in Del Mar, we swam in the Pacific.

Made the News

In Los Angeles, a newspaper photographer took our picture (left) and there was a story about us in the paper. Everywhere we went, people paused and stared as 15 of us emerged from the station wagon.

On the way back home, we stopped at the recently completed Boulder Dam, now called Hoover Dam, and were able to tour the dam and powerhouses.

After swimming in Lake Mead, several in the group got severely sunburned. One of the boys had to be hospitalized in Las Vegas, and my father and one other boy were ordered to rest at a hotel. I was left in charge. We found a tourist camp with a swimming pool and put up our tent.

When everyone had recovered, we traveled to the Saltair Resort at the Great Salt Lake, where we swam and enjoyed all the amusement rides. We saw the Mormon Temple and the Tabernacle.

We arrived back home two weeks after leaving with so many stories to tell.

We all graduated from high school during World War II and went into the service, scattering across the U.S,. After the war, we settled over a wider part of the country than other classes had before us.

Perhaps our early travel adventure had whetted our appetites for more.

CROWDED CHEVY

We were so thrilled to get our first new car, a 1952 four-door Chevrolet, that we decided to take a trip with our three small children, ages 6, 4 and 2.

From Horicon, Wisconsin, we traveled to La Crosse to visit my husband's sister and family. We spent the night, then decided to go to Waterloo, Iowa, to visit another of my husband's sisters.

My sister-in-law decided to come along, too, bringing her three small children and Grandma. Now there were 10 of us in that car—four adults and six kids!

It was July, it was hot, and the car, of course, had no air conditioning.

In Iowa, we bought an entire case of oleomargarine (not sold in the Dairy State of Wisconsin at the time). The case became a seat for one of the children.

Next, we decided to head west to visit the Corn Palace in South Dakota. We spent three days in that state, there taking in all the sights—the Badlands, Wall Drug, Mount Rushmore and Crystal Cave.

We had a great time in that crowded Chevrolet, but were mighty relieved to drop off our five extra passengers in La Crosse before heading back home.

VELMA SPLINTER • HORICON, WISCONSIN

1962

NORTHERN EXPOSURE. The King family packed up and headed north to Alaska. There were many photo ops along the way for taking in the sights.

ALASKA OR BUST!

In May 1969, my husband, James, and I left Offutt Air Force Base in Nebraska for his next tour of duty, with our four children and a 19-foot trailer in tow. Our destination was Eielson Air Force Base near Fairbanks, Alaska.

We drove the rustic Alaska Highway—then known as the Alaska-Canadian or Alcan Highway—through the spring rain and snow, camping along the way. The campgrounds didn't have many amenities, but the wood-burning stoves and restrooms with running water seemed like luxuries to us and our kids, ages 6 to 13.

The night we spent at British Columbia's Liard River Hot Springs was especially memorable. That's where we saw our first moose, as well as many wild caribou and horses in that wide open, majestic land.

It wasn't until June that we reached Fairbanks, grateful we'd had a safe journey and were all still speaking to one another!

After James' assignment at Eielson, we again drove the Alcan, which was in much better condition than when we'd first traveled it two years before. This time our destination was something quieter: retirement from military service and a new civilian life back in our home state of Texas.

DORIS K. KING • GEORGETOWN, TEXAS

DAYS ON THE **DUNES**

There were two nights a year I had trouble sleeping when I was a child in the 1930s—Christmas Eve and the night before we left on our two-week camping trip to the "thumb" area of Michigan.

The day of the trip, we were awakened at dawn and told to get dressed. I would be shivering from excitement and the early-morning coolness.

Our dad and mom, Harry and Elsie Daniels, had packed our Plymouth the day before. The car's trunk and running boards were full, as was the carrier attached to the rear bumper.

My sister, Inez, and I, sat in the backseat with our cocker spaniel, Tippy, and our calico cat, Mickey. The seat was packed level with the top of the front seats.

Our destination was Albert E. Sleeper State Park on Lake Huron, near Caseville, 150 miles from our home in Detroit.

As soon as we arrived, we headed for our favorite spot, at the end of the park. It had a small sand dune between us and the beach, which we learned was good protection from storms.

Daddy and Mother set up the tent and attached the homemade screened-in kitchen, which had curtains fashioned from mosquito netting and flour sacks.

Inside the kitchen was a picnic table and cabinets made from crates. We happily spent our days playing in the lake, fishing and building sand castles. We also took hikes and rode in the car for some sightseeing.

It was a happy time in our lives, and I now can appreciate what our mother endured by leaving all the conveniences of home behind to enjoy roughing it in a tent on vacation.

BARBARA SNODGRASS • BLUE RIDGE, GEORGIA

PICNIC TIME. You can almost smell the hot dogs cooking at the cozy campsite shown here. Bruce Thompson of Waukesha, Wisconsin, took this classic summer vacation photograph in 1958. That's his wife, Joyce, at the picnic table, keeping an eye on the kids.

Onward to Adventure!

ALASKA BOUND. That's what was written on the doors of this 1928 Model A (above) in 1949 when three veterans drove it from Ohio to Alaska, Robert Wagner (left) writes from Bellevue, Ohio. Robert and his friends Maurice Gardner (center) and Richard Hertzer were on their summer break from college.

FUN VISIT. Virginia Heksel (at right, in car) and her best friend, Carol Richards, shared good times in Denver, Colorado, when Carol headed west from Milwaukee to visit Virginia in the summer of 1953.

PACKIN' UP THE PACKARD. It was time to ready the old touring car for the road when this photo was taken in 1937. Charles Brown, now of Oak Harbor, Washington, fondly recalls the vacations his family took in New Hampshire. Here they're shown strapping on the tent.

LAUNCH DAY. "We moved to Grants Pass, Oregon, in 1959, right after my graduation from high school," says Jay Finlay of Redding, California. "This picture was taken there. I'm on the left and my mom, Phyllis Merrill, is on the right. My dad, Richard, used the 1956 Chevrolet station wagon for his sign-painting business, as you can see from the sign on the door."

TOURING TIME. "My wife's family took a trip to Pikes Peak in 1928, when she was just 3 years old," writes Wallace McElyea of Las Vegas, Nevada. "My wife, Tonkajo, and her parents, Mima and Tempel Mills, are shown in the back of the car with a friend, Russell Lake. Russell's wife and son, Sarah and Wendell, are in the middle seat, but I don't know who the people in the front were. The Lakes and Millses lived in Lake City, Kansas, at the time."

Pop Needed His 'QUIET TIME'

When Dad slid behind the wheel of his trusty '26 Olds, total silence was the rule.

RUDY HORN • STEVENS POINT, WISCONSIN

Pop was 53 years old in 1927, when he bought his first (and last) car—a used 1926 Oldsmobile. My older brothers could have provided driving instructions, but Pop taught himself in our yard in Fraser, Michigan.

On his first auto excursion away from home, my 7-year-old brother and I accompanied him. I was 9 at the time. Pop sat erect, firmly gripping the wheel as he eyed the 2-foot slope that led from our driveway up to a narrow dirt road.

Revving the motor, he released the brake, let the clutch fly out…and stalled the engine. Back for a running start, we tried again. Another stall.

As we prepared for a third attempt, my brother and I glimpsed a cloud of dust far down the road. "Don't try it now, Pop! You'll never make it!"

"Quiet!" he ordered. Pop loved to talk and was a great storyteller, but when he was driving, he was a man of few words.

We waited for the car to chug past, then tried again and made it. Pop drove us all around the square, a mile in each direction. He wasn't ready to try turning around in anyone's yard.

All this was part of a plan. My father was among a number of Notherners to respond to glowing advertisements offering land for sale:

"Come to Texas! Raise oranges and grapefruit in your own orchard!"

Texas, Here We Come

Pop took out a $3,000 mortgage and bought 15 acres of year-old fruit trees. One night in late September of 1927, we piled eight family members and lots of household stuff into the Olds and my brother's 1924 Dodge roadster.

We left at midnight to get through Detroit before the city streets were filled with morning traffic. Four hours later, we were negotiating the unfamiliar streets of Toledo, Ohio.

Suddenly Pop's half-drowsing passengers were jolted awake. *Ker-bang! Ker-bang!* No roads were smooth then, but this was really bumpy. Then we saw we were driving on railroad tracks!

Apparently the road had taken a sharp turn—which we'd missed, thanks to the Olds' poor headlamps. "Gee, Pop, where are you going?"

"Quiet!"

Backing up, we rejoined the Dodge and continued south. At about 25 mph, the trip took two weeks. With a good straight stretch of road and no other cars in sight, the speedometer might hit 35. "You're going pretty fast, Pop!"

"Quiet!"

Our route through Iowa, Kansas and Oklahoma was slow and tedious, but there were frequent breaks. We kids ran around getting exercise while Pop and our older brothers patched flat tires.

We Made It!

Somehow or other, that faithful touring car got us to Texas in one piece, then back to Michigan the following spring. For several years, it reliably carried us back and forth.

Finally—after the orchards froze and the "bank holiday" of 1933 swallowed all of Pop's savings—the trusty Olds took us back to Michigan for good.

Pop converted it into a tractor, and it served us in that capacity for many more years. As they say, "They just don't build 'em like that anymore!"

NO TALKING! When Rudy Horn's father (above) learned to drive, he needed passengers to be quiet so he could concentrate, whether he was driving through the city, in the country or even, accidentally, on railroad tracks.

PIT STOP, PLEASE! The Calhoun family learned the value of a pit stop—not only for rest and refueling, but to take in the sights. Shown above right (clockwise from left) are Stevie, dad Donald, Brian, mom Marilyn and Gary.

Keeping to Dad's **SCHEDULE**

Today it's called "quality time," but I don't think we called it that when I was growing up. Still, my parents recognized its importance and spent lots of it with my two brothers and me in the '50s and '60s, especially on road trips across the country every summer.

Our dad dedicated at least two weeks to our driving vacations, though he still demanded we keep to a schedule, going from scenic wonder to historical landmark as efficiently as possible.

He had a rule: Once the car was on the move in the morning, it kept going until we either needed gas or had reached our next milestone. We always had a cooler with bologna, crackers and Coca-Cola so we could eat on the go.

One morning, shortly after heading out for the day, we were driving on a almost impassable mountain road when my older brother, Stevie, said he had to go to the bathroom. Unfortunately, as Mom and I knew, this was not in Dad's schedule, so Stevie would just have to hold it.

As the morning dragged on, each pothole on the narrow mountain road increased Stevie's discomfort until he finally announced he would explode if we didn't stop. Undeterred, Dad told him to use the empty Coke bottle on the floor.

I was the designated bottle holder. Long story short, I let go of the bottle.

After that trip, my dad still believed in keeping to a schedule, but he also recognized that you could spare the time to pull over!

GARY CALHOUN • ARGOS, INDIANA

Cross-Country
ADVENTURE

In 1947, my friend Elvine Jones (Jonesy for short) and I were stationed at the U.S. Naval Hospital in Newport, Rhode Island. After our discharges in June, Jonesy and I decided to go west.

We went to the Quonset Point Naval Air Station and hitched a ride on a plane going to Washington, D.C. From there, we got another ride to Montgomery, Alabama, then another to Fort Worth, Texas. After leaving Fort Worth, the pilot decided it was time for lunch, so we flew in to the Air Force base in Tucson, Arizona. After that, we continued west and finally reached our destination, Travis Air Force Base in Fairfield, California.

Upon arrival at the base, I contacted a Marine friend I knew when I'd been stationed at the Naval Dispensary at the Marine Air Station at Cherry Point, North Carolina.

Jonesy and I felt fortunate that my friend, Mary

Ruth Barton, had a vehicle and could pick us up. But it was hardly a luxurious ride. The car had a broken front bumper, which drooped so much we had to stop now and then to tie it back in place.

When the engine got too hot, we removed the hood and put it on the floor in the back seat—an unwelcome companion for any passengers who were back there.

The three of us started making plans to travel around California when another friend, Rosemarie Topper, received her discharge from Newport and decided to join us. Mary quit her job, and we hit the open road. We went from the Redwood forests down to San Diego and then down into Mexico.

After several months of traveling, we felt we'd seen enough—and spent enough—so we decided to head home before we were completely broke. "Home" meant Fort Myers, Florida, for Jonesy;

SANTA CRUZ COUNTY
BIG TREES
PARK

WELCOME TO
UTAH
CENTENNIAL YEAR 1847-1947
UTAH STATE ROAD COMMISSION
PLEASE DRIVE CAREFULLY

Bronx, New York, for Rosemarie; Boonville, Indiana, for Mary; and Dorchester, Massachusetts, for me.

We started out from Merced, California, and went into Nevada and on to Reno, where we had our first (and only) serious car trouble. Fortunately, it was easy to repair. Soon we were back on the road and in Utah, where we took a swim in the Great Salt Lake.

Those were the days of tourist cabins, which we stayed in only as a last resort. We preferred to drive through the night and nap in the car.

As we went through Wyoming, then Nebraska, we tried to replenish our meager supply of cash by asking for work at farms we passed. No one ever hired us.

At the Mississippi River, we got stuck briefly. There was a 10-cent toll to cross and none of us wanted to pay it. At last, Mary broke down and coughed up the dime.

Finally we reached Mary's family's farm in Boonville, where we learned how to milk cows, feed pigs and do laundry in a washtub with a scrubbing board.

Very soon after that, we went our separate ways. Sadly, we lost touch over the years.

But I will never forget the great adventure we all shared that summer long ago.

PEGGY ELLIOTT • LIMERICK, PENNSYLVANIA

THE WEST IS BEST. The western United States offered endless natural beauty and urban landscapes for the travelers. Their many stops included San Francisco's famed Golden Gate Bridge (top right) and Utah's Great Salt Lake (right).

THE FEINBERGS (from left, Lynne, Susan, mom Lila, dad Isaac, Alan and Charles) hopped on this donkey cart for a snapshot in Mexico—the only photographic evidence of their 1963 road trip.

Hitting the Road for
FAMILY FUN!

PICTURE THIS: NO CAMERA

It's hard to believe that after eight weeks and more than 11,000 miles on the road, my family had just one picture of our North American adventure.

It was our first major trip together, and my wife, Lila, our four kids and I hoped to circle the U.S. and spend a little time in Mexico and Canada. The long-planned journey began on the last day of June 1963. By then, our oldest, Lynne, was 12, and our youngest, Charles, was 4—just old enough to know what was going on.

Leaving Brooklyn, New York, in our Rambler station wagon, we headed for Interstate 80 and followed it west to Utah. Within three days, I'd lost our camera! During a short hike at Indiana Dunes State Park, I set it down on a rock while I tied Charles' shoelaces, then left it there. Our budget didn't allow for another camera, so on we went without a way of documenting our trip in pictures.

Six days later, we reached Salt Lake City. We headed south to Utah's Bryce Canyon and Zion national parks, then to Nevada's Lake Mead and Las Vegas. After two more stops, at the Grand Canyon and Phoenix, Arizona, we were ready to hit the coast.

We headed for Calexico, a California border town, and spent the night. The next morning, we crossed into Mexico and followed what seemed to be the only sign in sight pointing toward Tijuana. We zigzagged through the Sierra de Juárez on a 12-mile climb, stopping for a picnic lunch before descending into the city.

We toured Tijuana in short order, and had our one photo taken there, thanks to a street vendor who corralled us into his donkey cart and gave us silly sombreros to wear.

That donkey photo from Mexico has graced each of our homes for 50 years now. It was a better souvenir of our great family adventure than a shoe box full of prints ever could have been.

ISAAC FEINBERG • LANTANA, FLORIDA

EAGLE ON MY SHOULDER

I had just graduated from high school in 1946, and two friends, Joyce and Betty Shinn, were visiting me. Somehow we talked my mother into taking us to the Carlsbad Caverns in New Mexico.

This was not long after World War II ended, and our tires weren't very good. We ended up with three flats during our trip, so we stopped at filling stations to get them fixed.

At one gas station, we discovered a small zoo of sorts. The owner suggested I come into a cage with him to see the eagle he kept there. He put the eagle on my shoulder and my mother took my picture.

I had forgotten about it for years but remembered when I saw then-President George W. Bush release an eagle at a ball game after Sept. 11, 2001. I'm happy I got to have an eagle on my shoulder for that photo.

PATRICIA BLAKENEY SMITH • AUSTIN, TEXAS

RIDING IN GRANDPA'S VELIE

In 1923, our family drove my grandfather's 1923 Velie touring car from New Hampshire to Florida. That's me (above) in a black taffeta dress with my grandparents and Grandpa's car, which had isinglass windows that could be rolled up and down.

Our route through Georgia was difficult. The roads were being paved by men from local prisons who were wearing black and white-checked uniforms and chains around their ankles.

In Bradenton, Florida, I accidentally caused a little extra excitement. Grandfather and I were driving on a bridge over the Manatee River and I leaned against the passenger door, which flew open. I swung back and forth, and Grandpa was not able to reach me until we got across the bridge and he could stop.

BELLE "BILLIE" ELLIOTT
CHAPEL HILL, NORTH CAROLINA

ROOT BEER OASIS

When I was a girl of about 10, in the 1940s, our family decided to take a summer vacation from our home in Nebraska to California.

Of course, our Dodge had no air conditioning, and I can still remember how hot it was driving across the desert from Needles to Barstow. My face felt like shoe leather with the hot wind blowing on it.

The part of the trip I remember best is driving into Barstow on Route 66 after thinking we'd never see another living soul.

The first thing we saw in Barstow was an A&W Root Beer stand. We pulled in, and each of us had two root beers in big frosted mugs, brought to us by a cheery lady with a tray that she attached right to the window.

Nothing in the world has ever tasted as good as that frosted root beer—or ever will.

BARBARA LINDBERG • SANTA YNEZ, CALIFORNIA

Road TRIPPIN'

FAMILY ROAD TRIP

At the end of World War II, many servicemen and women were discharged from the military on the coast of California. Instead of going back home, some sent for their families to join them in the Golden State.

My dad was one of these servicemen. My mother, who rode the train from Arkansas with three small children, told me she was lucky to get a little bit of help from other military families who were headed to California.

Because we had left two sets of grandparents, two sets of great-grandparents, aunts, uncles and a slew of cousins back home, it became our summer ritual to go back for vacation. The five of us would climb into the car and set out across Arizona, New Mexico, Texas and Oklahoma to see our kinfolk.

It was a miserable trip, with no air conditioning and three sweaty, whiny kids complaining in the backseat, but my parents were determined! We never stopped to spend the night in a motel. Mother and Dad took turns at the wheel—one would sleep while the other drove.

Sleeping was a nightmare for us kids. I got the floor; Mother tried to make a pallet on the floorboard to make the hump bearable. Our old sedan had a space under the back window where a small child—my brother was the youngest and smallest—could fit. My older sister got the entire backseat since she was the oldest—and crabbiest.

The highlight of those long journeys was to come upon a new series of Burma-Shave signs. The billboards were spaced far enough apart so that you could read the words on each one you passed. Sometimes they were very funny.

We were always thrilled to pile out of the car once we arrived at our destination. Then reality would hit us—our relatives had no air conditioning and no running water or indoor plumbing, just outhouses. Oh, the joys of country living!

We'd visit my Dad's parents first. Grandma Wright would be so happy to see us. I would watch in horror as she got out in the yard to chase down a chicken! When she caught it, she would kill it, clean it, cook it and then put it in front of us to eat. It was also common for a family member to milk the cow and set the bucket of warm milk right on the table to pour into glasses. I don't think so! My milk had to be cold, thank you.

My Grandpa Wright raised his eight children to help him grow watermelons, cantaloupes and cotton. He was so hard of hearing that you had to stand beside him and yell in his ear to have a conversation. It became a tradition for my dad to surprise him with a new pair of slippers every time we made the trip. Dad would buy them in California, then wear them as we were driving so they would be broken in and comfortable for Grandpa.

We always made it a point to see my mother's brother and his wife, too. My uncle would pile us in the back of his pickup truck and take us to the lake, where he taught us to water-ski. He also showed me

ON THE ROAD AGAIN. The Wright family made an annual trek to Arkansas to visit relatives. This photo taken in the summer of 1950 shows (clockwise from left, back row) dad Oscar, mom Christine, older sister Shirley, author Delma and younger brother Gary.

FROM SEA TO SHINING SEA. From hiking mountain summits in Washington (above) to eating watermelon in Tennessee (right), pals Mary Engel, Irene Blatt, Phyllis Becher and author Arlene Doerrman had the trip of a lifetime.

how potatoes grow. Until then I'd always thought they grew on a tree, like the oranges in California.

Both sets of my great-grandparents lived in the Ozark Mountains, and we were lucky enough to visit with them, too. One of them had a well on the front porch. It was so much fun to drop the bucket down and then wind it back up to get a cool drink of water out of the ladle.

Even though we always enjoyed seeing our relatives, we were usually happy to pile back in that hot sedan to return to beautiful California. Those were the days, and I miss them.

DELMA GUNNELS • JACKSON, MISSOURI

> ❝ *We travel not to escape life, but for life not to escape us.* ❞
> —*Anonymous*

GIRLS ON THE ROAD

In 1953, three friends and I took the granddaddy of all road trips across the United States. We were all in our 20s, schoolteachers, and we wanted to make the most of the summer before we had to go back to work in the fall. This was long before the days of GPS, so we relied on AAA maps to get us through 33 states and parts of Canada and Mexico over the course of seven weeks.

We piled into my 1950 Plymouth and hit the road. Most nights we pitched a tent and cooked by campfire. Once in South Dakota, we stretched the tent right across the top of the car to give us more room.

Being teachers, we wanted to be sure to hit hot spots that offered high educational value. We visited the stockyards in Chicago, the historic French Quarter in New Orleans, the Petrified Forest and Painted Desert in Arizona, Yosemite, Yellowstone, Mount Rainier, Redwood National Park, and the Great Smoky Mountains. We saw many memorable sights along the way: caught a live performance by Nat King Cole; went to a bullfight in Mexico; and kept our distance while a black bear raided a trash can near us in the mountains.

We're in our 80s now, but memories of that trip will always be with us.

ARLENE DOERRMAN
READING, PENNSYLVANIA

HONEYMOON IN
PARADISE

My most memorable road trip was in August of 1949. I had just married the love of my life, Miss Dorine Sesterhenn, at St. Alphonsus Church on Chicago's north side.

Our journey actually began 12 years earlier. Dorine and I were both students at St. Al's grade school. She was in sixth grade and starred as the Indian princess in the seventh-grade play. I was one of the Indian dancers who accompanied her float onstage in the performance.

Eleven years later, after my return home from the war, my dad had me drive him to a picnic in Niles. Inevitably, I found my way to the dance floor and spotted a face I had not seen in several years. I said, "Weren't you the Indian princess in a play at St. Al's in '37?" Some pickup line! It turned out that Dorine and her family had just moved back into the city to an apartment one block away from mine!

Fate won out, and just four months later we were engaged. Ten months after that we walked down the aisle, and then were on our way to Canada as husband and wife for our honeymoon.

Our trip took us from northern Illinois through Wisconsin to our honeymoon destination in the Canadian backwoods. My 1936 Olds burned so much oil—a quart every 30 miles, in fact—that we had to pack our luggage in the back seat. The trunk was full of oil cans!

In those days, a trip to Canada was a big deal, and we were both anxious to go. Besides, we were newlyweds! We did not have a lodging reservation, so we were not assured of finding a nice place to stay. Out of nowhere, we came upon a mansion with a Tourists Welcome sign and took a room for the short time we were there.

As it turned out, we spent almost all of our time driving, stopping only to eat and sleep at little motor inns and cottages—and, of course, to put oil in the car. Looking back now, I think we would have had a better time driving the much shorter distance to Lake Geneva, Wisconsin, instead!

GERARD J. BUNGERT • MORTON GROVE, ILLINOIS

Curbside Cafe

In the summer of 1962, we stopped for lunch in Glacier Park as we traveled from our home in Glasgow to eastern Montana for a family reunion. Pictured (from left) are my sister Julie, me, my sisters Sharlee and Doris and our mother, Millie Knight. With that many girls in one vehicle, our luggage didn't fit in the car so we rented a U-Haul carrier.

LAURA HAEFER • BILLINGS, MONTANA

CHAPTER 2

Have Car, WILL TRAVEL

The invention of the automobile produced a dandy means of getting from here to there comfortably and speedily. Replacing the horse-drawn carriage, it became the magic carpet for rich and poor alike, allowing travelers to pack up at a moment's notice and ride the breeze.

No matter what obstacles were on the journey ahead, nothing could hinder the determined traveler.

"My in-laws had never owned a car in the early 1900s, but they finally purchased one after they got the vacation bug so they could take a trip," writes Roger Cornell of Hamilton, Ohio.

"One afternoon, my wife's father and grandfather were practicing driving around the barnyard. After figuring they'd learned all there was to learn about driving a car, they decided to put it into the barn for the night.

"Grandpa was behind the wheel, and with his son reminding him just how far into the barn he needed to go, he forgot how to stop the car. He drove right through the double doors at the back of the barn—and right out a 20-foot drop to a manure pile below!

"Fortunately, he wasn't injured, but we eventually had to hitch up a team of horses to pull him off that manure pile."

Whether we set out across the country to see the Golden Gate Bridge or just out for a leisurely Sunday drive with the entire clan—and, in some cases, a rather *large* clan—our wheels kept us on the move.

4,000 Miles in a
FORD MODEL A

Two high-school buddies save their money, pack their gear and take the cross-country trip of a lifetime, returning with valuable life lessons and heartwarming memories.

HOLLY PLAHUTA • RANDOLPH, WISCONSIN

My grandpa Dick Myers was 16 years old in 1936, and the school year in Rochester, New York, was winding down. His friend Bill Weber sat in front of him at school, and one day Bill turned around and said out of the blue, "Let's hitchhike to California."

"OK," Grandpa replied. It was an outrageous idea—two 16-year-olds who'd never been far from home, roaming the country just for the fun of it. Their concerned parents wouldn't agree to let them hitchhike but said they could make the trip by car.

Grandpa worked after school and on Saturdays at a grocery store called Loblaw's. By the end of the school year he had about $125 saved, and Bill had saved up a similar amount to finance their trip.

Their Ford Model A was a two-seater with a rumble seat. It needed new tires and a new canvas top—additions that cost the two more than the price of the auto itself. Grandpa and Bill also bought a tent. Soon they were ready to hit the road!

With about $20 left between them, the friends began their journey the day after school let out in spring. They planned to sleep in the tent every night, but quickly discovered that pitching a tent was hard work, so they ended up only using it twice.

On the second evening, looking for a spot to spend the night, the boys pulled the car off into a cornfield and unrolled their sleeping bags. Later they awoke to a bright light—a policeman was standing over them with his flashlight blazing.

"Do you know you're trespassing on this farmer's property?" the officer asked them. "You'd better come with me to the police station." The boys obediently followed, though they were shaking in their boots.

When they got to the station, the policeman pointed to the building's courtyard. "You can sleep there," he said.

Grandpa and Bill were thankful for a place to rest, and they made sure not to sleep on private property again.

They drove in the summer heat through Arizona's Yuma Desert. One scorching day, they passed a truck, and the driver waved and yelled to the boys. At first they thought he was just being friendly, so they waved back. Then the truck passed them, and the driver motioned for them to stop.

They were wary of pulling over for a stranger, but the driver seemed insistent, so they decided to follow his lead. The man asked them to come around to the back of his truck, where he opened the door to reveal a cargo of Good Humor ice cream! What a treat that was in the sweltering desert!

Grandpa and Bill reached San Diego in about a month. On the return trip, they traveled through Wyoming, Montana and the Dakotas. As they approached Wyoming's Yellowstone National Park, one of the wheels came off the car. They spent the afternoon searching for the lost wheel and eventually found it at the bottom of a hill. Then they had to find the lug nuts—no easy task.

Throughout that summer, the two of them visited fairs, played carnival games and collected pennants. They made it back home the day before school started. Grandpa kept the tent and Bill claimed the pennants.

Today, Grandpa is retired from managing a grocery business and lives in Florida. Though his road trip ended more than 75 years ago, he still remembers what it taught him.

"I learned that people really are very compassionate and friendly," he says. "My friendship with Bill became very strong, and we learned, too, in spite of some small differences, that with a little effort and thought we could solve anything."

OLD LIZZIE

I'll always have fond memories of packing up "Old Lizzie" for our family's annual two-week summer vacation at our log cabin in Idaho.

We loaded Lizzie with everything we needed to eat, drink and wear for the duration. We also carried tools, spare tires, a lantern and even a rocking chair.

It was about a 50-mile trip over awful roads, so numerous flat tires were to be expected. Luckily, my father was a former blacksmith turned mechanic, and we were well prepared for a breakdown—and believe me, Old Lizzie broke down in just about every way that was possible!

FREDA JACKSON • SPOKANE, WASHINGTON

> **Not all those who wander are lost.**
> —J.R.R. Tolkien

Ol' Betsy RIDES AGAIN

Raising cattle on a South Dakota ranch in the 1920s wasn't a profitable profession for a couple with six children. My parents wanted all of us to have an education, so they decided to move off the ranch and head west in search of a better life.

Dad bought a 1926 Model T sedan and practiced driving it over the local hills until he felt confident enough to make the long trip from South Dakota to Oregon.

We packed what belongings we could on the outside of the Model T, and all eight of us piled inside. With a total of $160, we left for the biggest adventure of our lives!

We followed the Yellowstone Trail through the wide-open spaces of Wyoming, Montana and Idaho. Along the way, we stayed in parks or in camps where, for $1.25 a night, we got a cabin with a bed, table, two chairs, a stove and fuel.

To set up camp, we three boys helped Dad pitch our leaky tent while the girls brought out the food and built a fire for the evening meal. Supper was simple, usually wienies and onions, or spuds and beans or kraut.

With Ol' Betsy purring along at a top speed of 25 mph, we averaged 100 miles a day on the 1,100-mile trip. As she crawled over the Rockies, we often had to get out and walk beside her.

But the biggest challenge was driving in the slick mud. One day when Dad tried to get out of some deep ruts, Ol' Betsy veered off to the right and crashed through a farmer's fence.

When we got to Oregon, we followed the crops and picked hops, berries, apples and plums for eight hours a day. Altogether we earned less than $10 a

RUNNING BOARD LUNCH. Nearly 50 years after this family's tough trip west, they retraced their route—in the same Model T.

AUD BUTTE
FIRE DEPT.

ROOM FOR SIX. Merle Haskins drove Ol' Betsy with his siblings (above) on the trip east. An old Model T is a tight squeeze for six adults—it was easier when they were kids! At right, Merle puts the finishing touches on Ol' Betsy's engine before taking her cross-country.

day, but that was enough for food and school clothes.

A particular delight was being able to swim after chores. (Mother never did get used to how the girls wore bathing suits that actually showed their legs!) Our life was hard, but despite the inconveniences, we were never happier.

Dad was proud of that old Model T that carried us to a new life. He kept it for 23 years and sold it in 1950, a year before he passed away.

In 1975, I visited the area where Dad was living when he died and found Ol' Betsy in a neighbor's yard. She still looked good! The owner agreed to sell her to me for $500, and we towed her to my home in Los Angeles.

I immediately began restoring the 50-year-old car. It wasn't difficult since there are a number of Model T clubs in Southern California, and parts are easy to find.

Restoring Ol' Betsy gave me the idea of retracing our family's trip in reverse. I contacted my five sisters and brothers, and they loved the idea. Mother had kept a meticulous diary, so it was possible to retrace our journey along the exact route we'd taken 48 years earlier.

Within six months, we were on our way east to South Dakota—in Ol' Betsy! Other relatives came along in modern cars to help carry luggage and provide help if we broke down.

The trip, which only took seven days this time, was relatively trouble-free, although we did have to soak the wooden wheel rims at night so the tires wouldn't fall off!

Whenever we needed a new coil, we could always locate one among the piles of rusting equipment at farms along the way. Out on the road, younger drivers whizzed past us, but the older folks honked and waved, probably recalling their own experiences long ago.

When we reached the ranch we'd left nearly 50 years before, there was a big reunion of aunts, uncles and cousins. After her 1,580-mile journey, Ol' Betsy was the subject of several newspaper and radio stories. And of course, everyone had to have a ride.

Today Ol' Betsy rests in my son's garage in California, retired but ready to roll. Who knows, there may be another adventure still left in the old girl!

BARBARA HASKINS • SANTA ROSA, CALIFORNIA

The Pedal of LAST RESORT

Sometimes it was hard to get a Ford Model T to stop, as my family discovered many years ago when we moved to Houston, Texas, from Spokane, Washington.

We made the trip in a 1926 Model T touring car that my father, J. W. Hodges, bought in 1927 or '28. It's hard to believe, but we crammed our whole family into that car—Mom, Dad, me and my four siblings—plus all our belongings.

To drive the four-cylinder Model T, you used three foot pedals: one that operated the clutch, one that engaged the reverse, and a third pedal that was used for braking. Cloth belts actually connected the pedals to the transmission.

On the driver's extreme left was a hand brake. If you pulled it halfway up, it threw the car out of gear and into neutral, which caused it to slow down and eventually stop. If you pulled it all the way back, it fully engaged the emergency brake.

At the time, the best route from Washington to Houston was down the California coastline, and then over the mountains to the east.

One morning, we headed up a mountain near Bakersfield, California. After about an hour of climbing, the old Model T just came to a stop. Dad told all of us to get out of the car. Then he turned it around and slowly headed up the rest of the way in reverse, with all of us walking behind!

Once we reached the top of the mountain, we all got back in the car and headed down the other side. That was a terrifying experience I never want to repeat!

You see, Dad couldn't slow the car down, even when he pushed the brake pedal all the way to the floor. So he put the car in reverse, which slowed us down somewhat. When that stopped working, he reached for the pedal of last resort: the clutch. By repeatedly putting the car in and out of low gear, he was able to slow us down so we could reach the bottom safely.

But before we could continue, though, Dad had to find a repair shop and have all three of the belts replaced!

JAMES HODGES • ARLINGTON, TEXAS

PEDAL TO THE METAL. Dad's clever "clutch driving" helped the family make the incredible trek to from Washington to Texas in a 1926 Model T Ford.

CRUISIN'. Top: Franklin and Gertie on a date in 1961. Bottom: The couple take the convertible for a spin on a summer day.

THEN AND
NOW

Back in 1961, I loved cruising the back roads of Door County, Wisconsin, in my 1956 Chevrolet Bel Air convertible with my best girl Gertie beside me. That was more than 50 years ago, and we're still happily driving along together.

There was a time when we drove it every day because it was our only car. When I retired in 2000, it needed some restoration. I worked on it for two years, replacing worn parts. Now it's just like brand new.

Gertie and I still drive those same Wisconsin back roads. Sometimes we load up a few of our 10 grandchildren and motor along with them. It's fun!

FRANKLIN OTRADOVEC • KEWAUNEE, WISCONSIN

> **"I travel for travel's sake. The great affair is to move."**
> —Robert Louis Stevenson

BAKER'S DOZEN. This family could hardly fit into the photograph, let alone a small automobile! Standing, from left, are Ellen, Catharine, Philip, Eileen and Agnes. Seated are John, Anne, Mom with Jere, Dad with Jo, author Julia and Bill.

Fit 13 in a **MODEL A?**

The parish picnic was days away—and this family found itself in a tight predicament.

JULIA BARRY REIFEL • PORT ORCHARD, WASHINGTON

When Dad's old Model T gave out in the '30s, he traded the shell for a small Model A. This prompted people to ask Dad why he got such a little car when he had so many children.

"Eleven isn't so large," he'd reply, "It's just right! Besides, if we had a car that could carry the whole family, the kids would get spoiled thinking they had a ride everywhere they went."

Things got sticky, though, when our church in Lakeview, Oregon, decided to have the parish picnic at a county park—17 miles from our home in Lakeview! Our priest asked the congregation

members to offer transportation to anyone needing it. Our family certainly did!

Mom Thought Fast

After Mass, a big shot in town decided he'd make brownie points with the three older girls in my family by offering to drive them to the picnic.

Dad said it'd be fine, but final permission had to come from Mom. Well, she knew all about this bachelor's ego—and that he was known to drink hard liquor. It took all of two seconds for her to say "No!"

Now, this man had a position of power in

town and was known to use it when his feelings were hurt. That's why Mom came up with an excuse, saying she needed the older girls to take care of the younger children on the way to the park, so riding with him wasn't an option.

The problem now was that all of us would have to drive in the same car to the picnic!

Mom figured out a way to get all 13 of us into the Model A. First, she had Dad remove the lid from the trunk. Then she found two apple boxes that fit within the trunk quite nicely.

The plan was that Mom and Dad would ride in front with baby Jere and 2-year-old Jo. I was 8 at the time and would sit with John, 6, Ellen, 10, and Agnes, 11, on the apple boxes with the food in the crates underneath them.

The next row was made of tomato crates where Catharine, 18, watched over Anne, 4, and Bill, 5.

Philip, 17, and our tomboy, Eileen, 16, were allowed to sit on the floor of the trunk with their feet hanging out the back. They were given firm warnings that if their shoes were dragged on the roadway, the culprits would be wearing last year's shoes to school!

With an arrangement like that, Mom truly was in need of supervisory help, so the excuse that got us into this predicament wasn't entirely false.

As we headed out to the picnic, we quickly discovered that our overworked engine wasn't capable of moving at more than 15 mph. If the roads hadn't been flat, we might never have made it.

Had a Blue-Ribbon Day

The picnic was fun, with everybody sharing food, exchanging recipes and winning lots of prizes.

Eileen won the foot race, and Agnes earned a cooking prize and another for the Irish jig contest. John even won the eating contest—he was small but could put so much away he was nicknamed "the kid with the hollow leg." And Catharine came in first in the beauty contest.

Mom won for having the most kids all living at home, and Dad took an award for the most innovative means of transportation!

The town big shot handed out the prizes, and after the beauty contest, Catharine had to again explain that she could not ride home with him because "she had to help with the little ones." He planted a kiss on her cheek, good-naturedly conceding defeat.

"STINKBUG" GOT THEM THERE

In 1932, my father, B.L. Casner, decided to go back East from California to see his folks and proudly show off us seven kids.

He had a 1924 Essex truck that he converted to a little house car we called "The Stinkbug."

It certainly was a strange sight back in those days (see the photos above). People always gaped when we stopped for a rest and the nine-member family got out of the car. We traveled like circus performers, but we made it!

DOROTHY GALLEY-SCHUCK • BANNING, CALIFORNIA

ALASKAN
ADVENTURES AWAIT

They made it to Alaska in an old Hudson, but it took a paintbrush to get them home!

DON LAMBO • PUTNAM VALLEY, NEW YORK

The adventure began in June 1947, when Air Force buddy Wally Laudenslager and I left Amsterdam, New York, for Alaska. "Slager" and I aimed to drive the 1,442 unpaved miles of the Alaska Highway in a beat-up 1939 Hudson Eight.

On the way to the highway, we stopped in a number of national parks in the United States and Canada and even got to take in the very famous Calgary Stampede.

When we reached the highway, the Mounties refused to raise the barrier until we satisfied the requirement of having spare parts and 20 extra gallons of gas in cans.

After we resolved that problem and got on the highway, we met only three or four cars a day. Everyone stopped to chat and check on the road conditions ahead. Eight days and many flats later, we passed through Canadian customs and into Alaska, about 90 miles from Fairbanks.

Fairbanks was a city of about 7,000 then, and Main Street was the only paved road. It was a frontier town in every respect, and we lingered there for a few days before heading on.

Bridge Washed Out

In Anchorage, we finally found a place to take a much-needed shower. After changing into clean clothes, we explored the town. It was raining heavily when we left Anchorage and headed for Valdez.

Soon after, we heard an ominous knocking in the old Hudson's engine, but we made it to that small town—even though our approach was hampered by flooded roads and a wooden bridge submerged in water. In fact, only its railings were visible! With the car in second gear and a very heavy foot on the accelerator, we made it across. The bridge washed away a short time later, so we were stuck in Valdez, which was waterlocked.

That didn't bother me because Valdez was beautiful and, being an artist, I painted for days. I placed my paintings in the window of a general store for anyone who was interested.

One night we met a sea captain who'd seen the paintings. Bill Lowman was piloting the *Vindicator*, a former Navy minesweeper turned cargo ship.

Seeing a possible way home, I complimented Bill on his great-looking ship and suggested that an insignia on the smokestack would make it unique.

After I spent a day or two on the design, Bill agreed to take us and the car back to Washington if I painted the insignia on both sides of the stack.

On the voyage back to the States, we stopped in Cordova for a few days, then headed for the inland passageway.

We made a cargo pickup at the Saginaw Bay cannery and another at Craig, with adventures all along the way. Finally, we arrived at Anacortes, Washington, where Bill lived.

His parents invited us over to their house and treated us to a musical evening with piano and song.

Then it was back across the country to New York with the knocking engine. It was touch and go the whole way, but we made it. The old Hudson, however, was done—two of the pistons were shot.

Surprised the Skipper

There's a postscript to this story. Some 46 years later, I dreamed about returning to Alaska aboard the *Vindicator* with my wife, Betty. Not having kept in touch with Bill for all those years, I had my doubts about whether that was still possible.

On the spur of the moment, I dialed information in Anacortes, got a number and called. Someone answered on the first ring. "Is this the skipper of the *Vindicator*?" I asked. It was!

"Do you remember the name a fellow named Don Lambo?" I continued. Without hesitation, he shouted, "The artist!"

We both reveled in the stories of our lives since that trip of long ago. I was saddened to hear that the *Vindicator* was lost at sea when she ran aground in fog after the instruments failed. Amazingly, Bill's mother was still alive at 102—God bless her!

In June of 1993, Betty and I flew to Seattle and rented a car for a side trip to Anacortes before meeting the cruise ship that would take us on our own adventure to Alaska.

Bill was expecting us, and we recognized each other immediately. At 77, he had a young, upbeat attitude. He was still fishing in his own boat.

After our reunion with Bill, my wife and I drove on to Vancouver and boarded the tour boat that would take us to Alaska. Even if our trip wasn't aboard the *Vindicator*, it did revive wonderful memories of my Alaska adventures nearly 50 years ago.

ALASKA ADVENTURERS. Don Lambo (on right in both photos) and skipper Bill Lowman met in 1947, and recently got back together. A watercolor painter and artist, Don once earned passage back to the Lower 48 aboard Bill's cargo ship by painting the insignia on the smokestack in the photo at left.

YOU NEVER FORGET
YOUR FIRST CAR

AN UPHILL BATTLE

I'll never forget my 60-horsepower 1937 Ford. It was long on looks and short on power.

After my sailor sweetheart and I were married in a lovely home ceremony, we bundled into the car and headed for our honeymoon cabin in the San Bernardino Mountains with a Just Married sign on the back and tin cans tied to the bumper.

It was a rough 100-mile trip, but we finally arrived at the approximate location of our cabin, only to find that no one in the vicinity knew its whereabouts. We gave up and pulled off the side of the road, spending our honeymoon night in the car.

At about 5 a.m., we were awakened by a troop of Boy Scouts who pounded on the car as they walked by during an early-morning hike. Waking up, we looked out the window and discovered our cabin directly across the road on top of a steep incline!

It was so steep that my frustrated husband couldn't coax our Ford up that hill, even though he gunned the engine again and again. He'd heard Model T's could sometimes be backed up steep hills, but that trick didn't work either.

By this time, people in the other cabins had been awakened by the roar of the motor and were out on their porches, watching. In desperation, we drove back up the road, turned the car around, came racing down, and swerved into the driveway.

The car just barely inched its way over the crest of the incline and coasted into the parking space of our cabin as the other guests applauded wildly.

My husband and I recently celebrated our 50th wedding anniversary, but I'll never forget my first car—and my first and only honeymoon!

BETTY TIERNEY
SANTA CRUZ, CALIFORNIA

RING-A-DING. Betty Tierney had this picture taken to show off her wedding ring, but her 1937 Ford showed up better.

SLICING THROUGH THE AIR

This White automobile (at right) was already an antique when it was given to my father in the 1920s on Long Island, New York. It was probably made by the White trucks people.

My mother is seated in the rear, and I'm looking out the window nearest the camera, which was the driver's side in this car. My father is holding my younger sister on the other side.

My older brothers and sisters referred to the car as "the old cheese cutter" because of the shape of the windshield, which was divided into a V.

I remember when Dad moved our family from East Marion, New York, to Winsted, Connecticut. The car was piled with our family of nine inside, our furnishings on top and our father's choice hens in crates that were strapped to the running boards.

DEBORAH BROWN • BATTLE GROUND, WASHINGTON

DATING DISASTER

I was 17 and working as a helper on an ice truck in a suburb of Washington, D.C., when I spotted a 1927 Oakland roadster in front of a customer's house. It had obviously been sitting there a long time, but the body was still good, so I bought it for $25.

I knew little about cars, but managed to pump up the tires and get it running. The next day, a friend and I stopped at a gas station. After putting in 3 gallons of fuel and checking the oil, the attendant chuckled and commented, "That's the first time I've even seen cobwebs on a dipstick."

Not long after, I decided to give a girl a ride to visit friends at a beach about 35 miles away. Halfway there we got a blowout. I didn't have a spare or even a patch, but luckily, a man who lived nearby lent me a good inner tube and were on our way again.

After a nice visit at the beach, we headed home late that night, only to have the same tire go flat. The girl had to be back to work early in the morning, so we decided to keep driving.

As long as the tire stayed on the rim, things weren't too bad. But then the rim wore off, and those big wooden spokes made for a really rough ride!

The spokes finally wore off as well. That wasn't too bad, either—once we got used to the car leaning way over on the driver's side. But when we got to a hill, we couldn't go any farther.

We sat there until a fellow in a Cadillac touring car came along and offered to push me up the remaining hills along our route. That worked pretty well. My Oakland had never gone that fast!

After the last hill, he left us and we were on our bumpy way again. The noise we made as we drove through Cottage City, Maryland, at 3 a.m. was something awful! When we stopped, I called the girl a taxi. It's not surprising that the lovely young lady never spoke to me again!

ROY HIGDEN • HYATTSVILLE, MARYLAND

FROM THE MOUTHS OF BABES

A 1936 Chandler was the one and only car my father ever had when I lived at home in Toronto in the '30s. That car was big and square and very roomy inside. My 5-year-old brother, Doug, and I had lots of space in the backseat with Mum and Dad up front.

When I was 9, we took a trip to Niagara Falls in that car. We brought our own food, beverages and games, and we had fun reading license plates and seeing who could get the best cribbage hand from the numbers.

But my most fond memory from that trip involves our drive home. It was dark and, already nervous about driving at night, Dad was bothered by some bright headlights behind us.

Doug was asleep, but I was trying hard to come up with some way to help Dad. I remembered when Dad brought the car home, he was so proud of the pull-down shade on the back window.

With those blinding beams streaming in, I leaned forward and told my parents I had an idea.

Strained as he was, Dad was a little short with me at first. But when I asked if I could pull down the shade, he realized right away it was a good idea. It was, indeed, a perfect solution, and Dad was more relaxed for the remainder of the drive.

I was a pretty proud peacock of a daughter after that, basking in the praise of my parents.

AUDREY ABRAMS • VENICE, FLORIDA

We Roamed West in a
FORD MODEL A

The open road held adventure for two girls in 1930. **LETHA SMITH** • HIGHLAND PARK, NEW JERSEY

When my friend Helen and I told everyone that we were "going West" in the summer of 1930, our families were worried and the neighbors were flat-out scandalized. The idea of two girls going off alone like that!

Helen was 18, and I was 24. I'd just put a down payment on a $600 Model A Ford, and we planned to drive to California to visit Helen's relatives.

On June 13—Friday and 13th—we drove out of Shinglehouse, Pennsylvania, loaded down with a gas stove, folding table, food boxes that were bolted to the running boards, a burlap bag filled with canned goods, and draw curtains for the windows.

What heady excitement we felt, alone on the open road, free to roam the West at will! We were thrilled to fly in the face of convention. We were pioneers! We'd show the folks back home we could take care of ourselves!

Economy was our watchword. All we really had to buy was milk, bread and fruit. Gas was just 8 cents a gallon, and Helen became adept at servicing the car while I fixed most of our meals.

Camping in the Car

We stopped at municipal campgrounds to use the kitchen and showers. When we were ready to sleep, the Ford's divided front seats converted into our "beds." We stashed the stove and provisions under the car, drew the curtains and locked the doors.

Our adventure was going pretty well until we reached Carroll, Iowa. There, a car shot out from a side street and smashed into the front door, shattering the glass and destroying a food box.

My heart sank. "So ends our adventure," I thought. "The folks back home were right."

"Not so," said Helen. "We'll get the car fixed and go on." We found a repairman named Tony who fixed the door and built a new food box—all for $30.

We lost our canned foods that day, too. We'd tied the bag to the rear bumper, and the bottom wore through. That night at our campground, we overheard a truck driver chuckling about something odd he'd seen—a trail of smashed canned goods strewn along the road. Helena and I had to laugh, and the next day our spirits soared even higher as we took to the road again.

Sleeping in Splendor

Yellowstone was the high point of our trip. Camping in a grove of trees on the shore of Yellowstone Lake, we slept under four blankets to keep warm. Nonetheless, we had to tear ourselves away from the idyllic spot, where friendly bears roamed and the fish measured up to 18 inches long.

We rolled south to Salt Lake City, Utah and into the desert. Here gas was priced at an exorbitant 12 cents a gallon, and we were forced to take cabins at $1.50 a night!

On to Lake Tahoe, Truckee Pass and Sacramento. We continued through the world's largest peach and apricot orchards, where we bough giant baskets of fruit for 10 cents.

At Yosemite, we spread our blankets over soft pine needles and slept beneath the giant sequoias and a blanket of stars.

Farther south, in California, Helen's relatives treated us to concerts, picnics, beach parties, museums and a lovely overnight trip to Catalina Island.

On July 30, we began the trip back home to Pennsylvania. It was a cool evening when we reached the Grand Canyon, which surely is the world's most sublime sight. Our second morning there, we were on a mule, heading into the canyon. We had pictures taken of us dangling our feet over the brink of a 1,100-foot drop to the river. "That'll shake up our folks," Helen said.

After the Grand Canyon, the rest of the trip was pretty tame. We just wanted to get home! On Aug. 17, we drove into Potter County, Pennsylvania. The daring wanderers of the West were welcomed home at last.

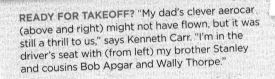

READY FOR TAKEOFF? "My dad's clever aerocar (above and right) might not have flown, but it was still a thrill to us," says Kenneth Carr. "I'm in the driver's seat with (from left) my brother Stanley and cousins Bob Apgar and Wally Thorpe."

MECHANICAL **MEMORIES**

INTERESTING AEROCAR

During World War I, my father worked for Curtiss Aeroplan and Motor Co. in Buffalo, New York. In his free time, he actually built a car in the cellar of our home. Of course the car couldn't fly, but my friends and I liked to pretend that it could. After it was completed, my father had to partially disassemble it and put it back together in the backyard.

The car had a Franklin air-cooled engine, airplane seats, and tires measuring 30 x 3½ inches. A hand pump on the driver's side kept air pressure in the gas tank. People who saw the unusual auto thought it was a race car.

In 1920, we packed up and moved to High Bridge, New Jersey. My mother and I traveled by train, while my father and one of his close friends took several days to drive the 300 miles in Dad's invention. With no roof or windshield, they were extremely grateful for good weather!

A few years later, Dad sold the car to a mechanic, who restored it to its original glory.

KENNETH CARR • ANNANDALE, NEW JERSEY

MELVIN'S GONE MISSING

As long as I live, I will never forget our family's move from Oklahoma to California.

My father bought a '33 Chevy, employed a driver we kids called "Mr. Roy" (my father did not drive, but thought he could if necessary), and attached a two-wheel trailer to the car to carry all of our household belongings.

With my parents, Mr. Roy, my three sisters and me squeezed into the car, and my five brothers nestled in between the furniture in the trailer (yes, they rode all the way in the trailer!), we set off for California.

It took four days, but what an interesting trip it was. As we neared Lordsburg, New Mexico, my father finally persuaded Mr. Roy to let him drive. That proved to be a big mistake—my father shifted the gears from low to reverse, thereby leaving the transmission in the middle of the road! We camped in a park, sleeping under the stars, for a couple of days waiting for repairs.

Another mishap occurred shortly after we left a filling station. We had traveled about 20 miles when one of my brothers began tapping on the rear window—our signal if anything was wrong in the trailer. My brother was yelling, "We lost Melvin!"

Unaware of where my brother Melvin might be, we hurried back to the filling station, but that search proved fruitless. Dad searched the trailer and found Melvin fast asleep inside Mother's big trunk! Looking back now, I feel that in many ways this trip was our own family's sequel to *The Grapes of Wrath*.

CARROLL FINK • JONESBOROUGH, TENNESSEE

NOT-SO-GENTLE REMINDER

My grandfather learned to drive in a Model A Ford, which had three pedals on the floor.

Around 1930, he bought an Essex with a rumble seat, but he could never get the hang of using its stick shift. Whenever he tried to shift into second gear, he'd accidentally shove the stick into reverse. After a while, he gave up on second gear entirely and went directly from low to high.

He also had problems stopping. Usually he'd just put his foot on the brake, causing the Essex to stall. Then he'd get out and walk away, forgetting to turn off the car or remove the keys. Often, when he came back, the battery was dead.

To prevent this, he put up a sign in the barn, right where he parked the car: "Remember the keys, sap!"

HOWARD MATTISON • CORAOPOLIS, PENNSYLVANIA

OUT OF FUEL...AND PATIENCE

My dad had a Chevrolet touring car back in the '30s, and he liked nothing more than to take the entire family on short rides around the lovely countryside in the evenings.

There was just one problem—we couldn't afford to keep much gas in the car. If anyone thought to ask about the gas before we set off, Dad would cheerfully say, "Well, there's enough to start out on, anyway."

As you'd expect, we ran out of fuel frequently. Since Dad didn't trust any of us to steer the car, he'd stay behind the wheel while my brothers, sisters and I—and even our mother—got out and pushed the car.

Puffing, sweating and groaning, we'd push that Chevrolet touring car to the top of a hill, then stand at the crest and watch it roll down the other side. Then we'd all trudge slowly down to the car so we could push it up the next hill. By the time we got home, everyone was completely exhausted—except Dad, of course!

I'll never forget one sweltering day when he came home from work just as Mom had finished doing the wash for the nine of us.

"You look tired and hot," Dad told her. "Let's go for a ride so you can get some fresh air."

"No, not tonight," Mom replied.

"Oh, come on," he urged. "I think it will be good for you."

"No, I can't go."

"Why not?"

"Oh, Pa," Mom sighed. "I'm just too tired to push that car again tonight!"

ANNA SANDA • WILLISTON, NORTH DAKOTA

Roam if You Want To

MOTORING PALS. "My mother, Sarah (rear fender), and father, William (running board, on left), and their close friends John and Helen Rhodes used to get together every Sunday afternoon at each other's houses and often went for a drive and a picnic," writes John Bitner from San Antonio, Texas. "The picture was taken around 1920 in Connellsville, Pennsylvania, where John and Helen lived. My parents lived in Smithfield. The two couples remained close friends all their lives."

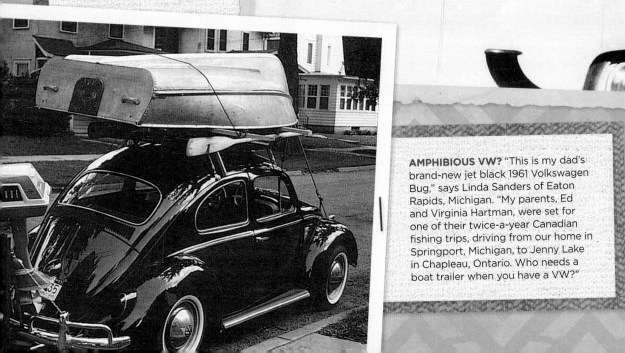

WAGON FULL OF MEMORIES. "Every year our parents packed us into our station wagon to visit our grandparents in Washington," says Kris Kasew, who lives in Kent, Washington. "This black-and-white photo is from 1953. We were in our new Chevy, just about to pull out of the driveway and head back home to Idaho."

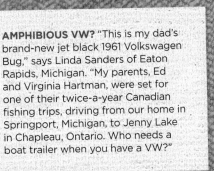

AMPHIBIOUS VW? "This is my dad's brand-new jet black 1961 Volkswagen Bug," says Linda Sanders of Eaton Rapids, Michigan. "My parents, Ed and Virginia Hartman, were set for one of their twice-a-year Canadian fishing trips, driving from our home in Springport, Michigan, to Jenny Lake in Chapleau, Ontario. Who needs a boat trailer when you have a VW?"

Fury Saw Many Miles

My parents, Kenneth and Vernetta Kapplinger of Farwell, Michigan, were thrilled to purchase a 1956 Plymouth Fury for $2,647.85 in 1957. It was the first family car I remember, and I loved playing with all of its push-buttons.

The Fury saw many miles in the next few years. That's my brother Karl, then 3, and me, 8, in front of mountain scenery on our trip to visit relatives in Jackson Hole, Wyoming, and Stockton, California.

DEBORAH KAPPLINGER • STEPHENSON, MICHIGAN

10082—OBSIDIAN CLIFF AND BEAVER LAKE, YELLOWSTONE NATIONAL PARK

HAYNES INC., YELLOWSTONE P

> ❝Those who dwell among the beauties and mysteries of the earth are never alone or weary of life.❞
> —Rachel Carson

CHAPTER 3

The Great
OUTDOORS

There is nothing quite as glorious as the unspoiled open space of the great outdoors. From the majestic Rocky Mountains to the heartland of the prairies, North America is home to an astonishing array of road trip-worthy wonders.

"In the summer of 1959, my parents, Jim and Gerry Ringelberg, moved our family from Dalton, New York, to Arizona," says Melissa Brady of Tyrone, New Mexico.

"We were headed for Wellton, Arizona, because Dad thought he might be able to get a farm there. He and Mom wanted to see the country on the way, so we were on the road for three weeks.

"On the morning of our departure, Dad's two sisters painted 'Westward Ho! The Ringelbergs!' and 'Arizona or Bust!' on the sides of our camper.

"We saw famous landmarks such as Mount Rushmore, the site of Custer's last stand (it's now known as the Little Bighorn Battlefield National Monument), Yellowstone and Grand Teton national parks, the Grand Canyon—and we visited some not-so-famous places, too. We camped in the Badlands and Black Hills of South Dakota."

Our great nation truly is America the beautiful, and with the awe-inspiring stories on the pages that follow, nature junkies can take a trip from sea to shining sea without even stepping outside the front door.

ON THE WESTERN SKYLINE. The Atchley family had many adventures while visiting the Centennial State. One of them was driving across the 955-foot Royal Gorge Bridge in Cañon City (above), which was the world's tallest suspension bridge in 1962. At right, the author's sister poses in front of the North Pole Village in Cascade, Colorado, at the base of Pikes Peak.

A Shift in **ALTITUDE**

A family with a yen for adventure barrels northwest to the great Rocky Mountains.

DANNY ATCHLEY • MINERAL WELLS, TEXAS

My dad used to sing a song called "When It's Springtime in the Rockies," and visiting that part of the country was something he had always wanted to do. So in July 1962 we packed up the family—my parents, my sister and me—and headed from our home in Dallas to Colorado.

Our first stop was Dodge City, a Kansas hot spot back in the era of the TV Western. We walked around the little town, which looked so much like the places we'd seen on the big and small screens. There was even a Long Branch Saloon, like the one the characters in *Gunsmoke* frequented! That night, even watching Marshal Dillon on TV in the motel room seemed special.

The next day we saw the Rockies. The very first glimpse of them after you've driven for hours across the Great Plains is absolutely amazing. Slowly, these glorious snow-topped peaks rise up in front of you over the sunlit horizon. That sight is something I'll never forget.

We stopped in Pueblo and then headed north to Colorado Springs and Pikes Peak. Dad was a little nervous about driving the steep mountain road up to the peak, and Mom wouldn't even hear of it. So we took tourist bus that took groups to the summit.

The next couple of days were filled with visits to such Colorado musts as Garden of the Gods, where we had a blast scrambling over rocks and taking lots of pictures of the gorgeous natural surroundings. Mom and Dad made sure Manitou Mineral Springs was on our itinerary, while my sister and I were eager to visit Cave of the Winds.

One of our most exciting adventures was seeing Seven Falls, a series of cascading waterfalls in South Cheyenne Creek. You have to climb many stairs to get to the top of the 181-foot falls, but it was worth it. To get to the breathtaking Royal Gorge, Dad drove the car across a suspension bridge perched more than 955 feet above the Arkansas River, scaring Mom half to death.

The Old West town of Buckskin Joe, a replica of an old mining community, gave us more great memories. We also went to the Cheyenne Mountain Zoo. Years later we learned that, at the time we were there, the U.S. Department of Defense was building a vast, secret system of bunkers nearby that would be used if case of a nuclear strike.

I was hoping we could visit Cripple Creek and the famous Broadmoor Hotel, but the high country did me in: I got an ear infection and we had to head home. Our vacation was cut short, but it was still one of the most exciting trips I've ever taken. I recently picked up a Colorado travel book and was pleased to see that all the places we visited are still there today. I hope to go back someday soon.

GRAND CANYON VIEW.
Travelers take in the stunning
view of the steep gorge carved
by the winding Colorado River.

GRAND ADVENTURE

BLOWIN' IN THE WIND

Whether we were heading to Grandma's or the
Grand Canyon, a family car trip was a real adventure
for us kids back in 1953. For Mom and Dad, it was
more like torture!

When we left our home in Austin, Texas, the six of
us packed into our old 1949 Chevy. My two younger
brothers, our older sister and I jammed together in
the backseat for hours—more than any siblings
should be forced to endure. Naturally, Mom was the
peacekeeper. She occupied us with silly games—
"Who can count the most cows on the left side of
the highway?" or an alphabetical version of "I spy"
with words we spotted on billboards.

But our favorite game, which we kids invented,
was "How long will the leaf last?" To play this, we
stuck a leaf to the hood or windshield of our car as
we left the house. Each of us predicted how long the
leaf would last before the wind or a quick stop shook
it off. Guesses such as "not more than 10 minutes,"
"until we get to Grandma's" or "more than 30
minutes but less than an hour" were all accepted.

The game could entertain us for hours as we
watched the helpless but defiant little leaf shaking in
the wind, holding on for dear life. Sometimes the leaf
would last the whole trip, especially if it got wet and
stuck to the car. Other times it would blow off just
down the street from our house. The winner usually

didn't get a prize, just the admiration of the rest of the family.

Soon after we started to play the game, we had to ban Dad from participating. After an early win, he got us kids to be perfectly quiet for 30 minutes, just as we'd promised to do if his time was the closest. We had laughed at his guess of "within 20 seconds," but then watched in dismay as he turned on the windshield wipers and brushed the leaf away. "Cheater! Cheater!" we cried. Mom told us to honor our promise, reminding us that we'd never made any rules preventing Dad's sneaky maneuver.

Once it was obvious that only a sudden blast from a passing truck would dislodge a steady leaf, we got bored and resumed our usual rowdiness. You know the drill: "Hey, he touched me! Mom, make him stop!" or "She looked at me funny and stuck out her tongue!" Mom tried her best to keep things in hand by threatening the worst offenders and forcing us to change places.

When we got really bad, we had to be wary of Dad's "vacation arm." With amazing accuracy, he could swat the offending kid with his free right arm. Of course, Mom would caution him that he needed both hands on the wheel. "You kids are going to get us all killed!" she shouted.

And then someone would notice that the leaf was gone. It had quietly blown away sometime during all the bickering, and no one could say exactly when it left.

KEN YOUNG • SEABROOK, TEXAS

FUNNY FIDDLER

Back in 1925, three friends and I took a trip into the Grand Canyon. We enjoyed the experience so much that we went back again the following year with a group of eight people.

The scenery was just as enjoyable the second time, but the real highlight of the trip came when we encountered a fiddler at the bottom of the canyon.

Since one of the men in our party happened to be a square dance caller, we ended up having a great time "do-si-doing" the evening away!

GRACE STANFORTH • FORT THOMAS, KENTUCKY

SMILE AND SAY "CACTUS"! Noreen Collier snapped this photo of her husband, George, and their children, Alfred, Gayle and George Jr., during a trip to Apache Junction, Arizona, in 1958. Noreen, of Jackson, Michigan, bought George a 35mm camera, but she became the family shutterbug. The only time he got to use the camera was when she handed it to him and said, "Here, you take one."

A TRIP TO REMEMBER

In the summer of 1918, my parents and I took a road trip from Southern California to Yosemite Valley. That doesn't seem far now, but getting there was a two-day adventure.

Highway 99 thorugh the San Joaquin Valley was a trip everyone dreaded, because it meant going over the steep Tehachapi Mountains. After slowly chugging up one side of the mountain, we came down the other side on a dangerous roller coaster of a road.

Far below we could see the road to Bakersfield, stretching arrow-straight across the flat, sizzling desert. In my 7-year-old imagination, I thought it was called "Baker's Field," because a person would surely bake in a long, hot field like that.

The road descending into Yosemite Valley was even worse than Highway 99. In fact, it was so steep, narrow and dangerous, only a few cars at a time were allowed down it.

Much Backseat Driving

My father's knuckles were white as he gripped the steering wheel. Down from the rugged Sierra Nevada we crept, as Mother clutched the side of the door, her eyes closed. She only opened them long enough to offer Father futile warnings about sharp curves and jagged rocks.

"Stop clucking, Netta!" growled my father, who always got irritated when Mother made her little *tsk-tsk* sounds. They both sighed in relief when we finally reached the valley floor safely.

At dusk we rolled through the gate of Camp Curry. A tent on a wooden platform awaited us, and everything inside was invitingly clean. The bedspreads and towels were whiter than white. Wash water waited in a big white pitcher with a matching bowl.

This was the closest thing to camping I'd ever experienced, and as I lay back on my iron cot, I thought I'd found my heaven on earth.

The next morning a chorus of birdsongs woke us early. Before we continued our trip, we drove all around the park on dirt roads, taking in stunning views of the mountains.

Waterfalls spilled down granite cliffs, making bits and pieces of rainbows dance in the sunlight. Mirror Lake lived up to its billing, because later, it was hard to tell when my father's snapshots of it were right side up.

A FAREWELL SIGN hangs at the edge of Camp Curry in Yosemite Valley to wish visitors well as they leave and start their journey home.

A Memorable Hike

Father and I went for a climb, even though Mother said it was too tough for a child. Our rugged trek to Vernal Falls took us more than 300 feet up. To me, the wide wall of falling water looked like a frothy blanket made for a giant.

Hiking another mile upstream, we made it to Nevada Falls. The steady roar from this spectacle drowned out all other sounds.

"I made it all the way!" I proudly proclaimed to everyone in the dining hall that night. In the evenings after dinner, everyone would sit around a big bonfire and the camp director would lead us in song. I still recall the smell of wood smoke sweetly mingled with the fragrance of the piney forest.

The nights ended with a "firefall." Aiming his megaphone at the towering cliffs, the camp director would yell, "Curry calling!"

Soon, an answering voice would echo down from another camp high up the mountainside. Then the

SHE WAS ONLY 7 YEARS OLD at the time, but Patricia Gooden has never forgotten the excitement of her family's automobile trip to the Yosemite Valley in the summer of 1918.

camp's burning fire log was sent rolling over the steep cliff.

For one brief spectacular moment, the shower of sparks resembled a waterfall of fire. It was a magnificent sight to behold.

In the years since then, I've made many pleasant trips to Yosemite. But the thrill has never been quite the same. There hasn't seemed to be as much water in the falls, as much sweet smoke in the air, or as much awe in the sheer, powerful granite walls.

It's likely because my memories have been magnified by the rose-colored glasses of childhood. Yet the sights and smells that so delighted my senses at age 7 will always live with me. It's a joy to know that I experienced the majesties of Yosemite in nearly pristine form, during a simpler time.

PATRICIA GOODEN • SEAL BEACH, CALIFORNIA

YOSEMITE'S FAMOUS "FIREFALL" glowed in this photograph taken at Glacier Point. The custom began in the 1870s, with a massive pile of glowing embers pushed gradually over a cliff to create the illusion of a waterfall of fire. This photo from Myrtle White of Gresham, Oregon, was taken around 1940. The attraction was discontinued in 1968.

Down in the Holler

Although it's been almost 50 years, my two younger brothers and I still chuckle over the trips we took to visit our grandparents Pa and Granny Baker in the mountains of eastern Kentucky.

Every three months or so, Mom and Dad would load us up in the Ford Ranch Wagon to begin our trip to Naphor Holler in Perry County. While an interstate took us from Louisville to Lexington, the route from there became increasingly winding and hard to navigate, especially at night.

It was usually around this point that the three of us would start pestering and aggravating each other in the backseat. Mom's orders to cut it out would work for only a little while. Then Dad would threaten to pull the car over, take off his belt and use it on our bottoms. Although we probably deserved it, he never followed through.

Dad usually drove at night in hopes that we would fall asleep. My smaller brothers usually got to lie in the rear section on top of pillows and blankets Mom brought, while I reclined on the bench seat.

I remember falling asleep while Mom and Dad talked quietly about things going on in our lives. Sometimes I woke to notice Mom napping and Dad holding the steering wheel firmly as we drove through the dark night. For some reason, this gave me a sense of security.

Once we got up into the mountains, the roads got twisty and steep, sometimes giving us boys motion sickness. The worst incident was on an Easter Sunday on our way back home after we'd gorged ourselves on Easter candy and were dressed, as my grandpa described it, "like Philadelphia lawyers." I remember Easter baskets being discarded on the side of the road as suit jackets and ties were placed in a far corner of the car.

Once we got to Naphor Holler, we had to cross a small river. If the water level was down, Dad would drive across with the windows down and we would hang out of them. If the water was too high, we had to cross a swinging bridge that looked to us like something out of a Tarzan movie. Planks were missing and the bridge looked very high as we crossed over what seemed to be the raging Amazon.

Finally, after a short walk down the only dirt road into the holler, we arrived at Granny and Pa's. No matter what time we showed up, we were welcomed with much excitement, and Granny immediately began cooking a country feast.

My brothers and I have talked about going back to Naphor Holler in the years since our last trip, but my uncle says it has disappeared because of coal mining in the area.

JAMES P. DILBECK • LOUISVILLE, KENTUCKY

WAYFARING MATES

I'm pushing 90 and just came across these vivid Dufaycolor transparencies taken in 1938. My buddies and I had a barrel of fun driving from Detroit, Michigan, to Great Smoky Mountains National Park in Tennessee. It took five days. We each spent $5 during the trip.

We camped along the way, cooking our own meals and roving all over the Smokies. One of the places we hiked was Mount LeConte near Gatlinburg.

One of the guys, Ralph Stewart, sprained his ankle when he stumbled into a hole in a farmer's yard while going to seek permission to set up a tent there. I also remember Al Meyers chasing me all over after he lost the heel of a boot and I said, "Al, you're no longer a heel."

I've lost contact with these buddies but will never forget our adventure.

GORDON PLAXTON • FARMINGTON HILLS, MICHIGAN

CAMPING WITHOUT
RESERVATIONS

During the first summer of our marriage, in 1969, Al and I decided to visit Wyoming's Yellowstone and Grand Teton national parks. We had very little money back then, so we fearlessly planned to camp out and take some of our own food along. We left our home in Nortonville, Kansas, with our car full of blankets and sofa cushions and our minds full of visions of high adventure.

The first day we gulped gallons of water as we motored through Nebraska's 104-degree heat. Our Dodge Coronet had no air conditioning, so we drove down the highway with open windows. The first night we stopped at a roadside park in Cheyenne, Wyoming, where we roasted hot dogs on the park grill. At bedtime we covered the car windows with road maps for some privacy. Al scrunched up in the backseat and I rested in the front.

We were awakened during the night by several teenagers talking and prowling around our car. They weren't touching the car or harassing us at all, so we just tried to ignore them and go back to sleep. Closer to the morning, a policeman arrived and directed a flashlight on our car. He left quickly, but we'd had enough for one night. We rose before the sun was up and left Cheyenne.

Deer and antelope appeared everywhere as we drove north through Wyoming. Sagebrush dotted the brown earth. But once we arrived at the Grand Teton park, we forgot about those barren landscapes and gazed upon the most beautiful sights. The view of Jenny Lake, with majestic mountains in the background, convinced us we were close to heaven.

Virtually next door was Yellowstone. We learned we had to stay in authorized campgrounds, which meant fees that subtracted a few dollars from our limited budget. We'd foolishly thought we could just set up camp anywhere we pleased. Oh, did we have a lot to learn about camping! But the excitement of seeing a black bear stroll down the road near our car made the unexpected fees seem trivial.

10082—OBSIDIAN CLIFF AND BEAVER LAKE, YELLOWSTONE NATIONAL PARK

HAYNES IN

©16253—LOWER FALLS FROM RED ROCK, YELLOWSTONE NATIONAL PARK

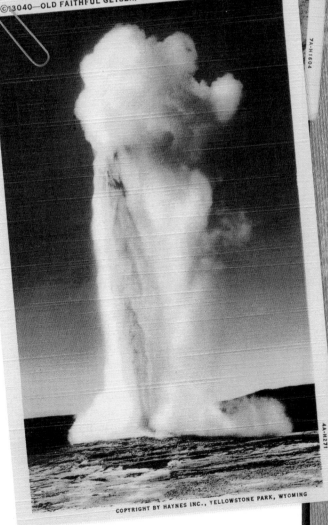

©13040—OLD FAITHFUL GEYSER, YELLOWSTONE NATIONAL PARK

COPYRIGHT BY HAYNES INC., YELLOWSTONE PARK, WYOMING

We found a campsite that had a vacancy and proceeded to pitch our improvised "tent," draping a blanket over a picnic table and putting cushions underneath for a bed. The next morning the blanket and car were covered with frost, and we ended up with head colds as souvenirs.

Yellowstone provided an unforgettable display of nature. Old Faithful erupted right on schedule; we didn't necessarily enjoy the sulfur odor, but the spray from the geyser was fascinating to watch. While hiking down to the splendid waterfalls, we saw a moose leisurely cross the Yellowstone River.

We were on our way home via the rocky roads of the South Dakota Badlands when we blew a tire. Al didn't want to risk driving the rest of the way without a spare, so we stopped at a service station. But the station owner wouldn't accept our credit card or personal check! Feeling hopeless, I escaped to the car and started to cry. An elderly gentleman saw what was happening and offered to help, which made the owner relent and accept our payment.

Shortly after we got home we learned that we had acquired another little souvenir: I was expecting our first child.

We occasionally took that child and the other three camping at a local farm pond when they were growing up, but now Al and I camp out at nice motels when we travel.

LINDA COLVIN FUNK • NORTONVILLE, KANSAS

The Bear
VACATION

A close encounter with a curious bear left them with a funny photo and a lifelong memory.

ANN GEORGE • VIRGINIA BEACH, VIRGINIA

My parents used to take my brother, Bobby, and me on vacation for a few weeks every summer. I remember when we were very little Mom would put the crib mattress in the backseat so Bobby and I could sleep while we drove through the night.

We argued, as all siblings do. One of us would complain to Mom that the other one had invaded his or her half of the backseat. At that point, Mom would announce that we would never be taking another vacation again!

But we had lots of fun, too. We played the usual car games, like spotting different license plates and counting the number of cows or road signs we saw.

As we got older, Dad let us help decide where we'd go and what we'd do. Mom's idea of a great vacation was to drive for most of the day, stop around 4 p.m. and get a nice motel room with a pool. Then she would stay in the air-conditioned room while the rest of us headed to the pool before dinner.

On one memorable trip, we followed Skyline Drive, which is part of the Blue Ridge Parkway in Shenandoah National Park in Virginia. We were driving along when we suddenly saw a bear! Dad quickly stopped the car and snapped pictures through the car window of the bear rolling around on the ground.

When the creature saw our car, it came right over to investigate. It got so close that Mom immediately rolled up the window.

Dad was fearless, however, and snapped a great shot of the bear through the window; you can just barely see Mom's reflection in the glass. She was cowering so close to my dad that the reflection made it look like the bear was wearing a dress! It was tense and exciting all at once, but after the bear scampered off and it was over, we were grateful no one was hurt.

Looking back, it was a good thing we only went on vacation once a year. That gave us plenty of time to forget our mishaps and just look forward to next year's trip.

BEARS RAIDED OUR TRUNK!

It was 1935 when my parents, brother, Uncle Hank and I decided to go to Yellowstone Park for vacation. We lived near Glasgow, Montana, at the time, and the round-trip was 815 miles.

We made the trip in a boxy car that I think was an Essex. It had a deep trunk where we stored our clothing, cooking utensils and food.

Actually, taking the food was almost our undoing. One day, a pair of bears decided to raid the trunk! The coffeepot, kettle and other items went flying as we all looked on, too terrified to move. When they'd finished their picnic, they just nonchalantly ambled off.

I remember that we had to make many stops going up the steep mountain roads, as we had to adjust to the thinner air at the high elevations.

My mother took some notes along the way, and at the end of our trip she penned a little poem: "I wish that I had tongue to tell, all I saw—and tell it well. Geysers, flowers, hill and vale, all could make a lovely tale. Mountains, rocks, sky and streams, formed to make a lovely scene. God made it all without a plan; so how coud I expain to man?"

It was 22 years before I had the opportunity to visit Yellowstone National Park again. We took our sons and found many things had changed. But more importantly, we found many things had not!

VIRGINIA LUGER • FORT YATES, NORTH DAKOTA

©17485—BEAR AT ATTENTION, YELLOWSTONE NATIONAL PARK

COPYRIGHT BY HAYNES INC., YELLOWSTONE PARK, WYOMING

Few Can Boast...
'I STOOD ON LINCOLN'S HEAD'

A 1940 trip to Mount Rushmore (then unfinished) gave a pair of newlyweds a privileged view of the famous monument.
ROY SIMPSON • FORT MYERS, FLORIDA

It was an experience I'll never forget. In 1940, I climbed to the top of Mount Rushmore and took pictures of the faces while standing on the heads of the presidents. This, of course, is strictly prohibited today.

It all started when I met Ruth Duncan in 1937. We both worked for the Bureau of Internal Revenue (later called the Internal Revenue Service) in Washington.

Ruth and I married in 1939. The following summer, we decided to drive our new Plymouth convertible to Ruth's hometown of Watertown, South Dakota, so I could meet her brother, who hadn't been able to attend our wedding in D.C.

BLACK HILLS BOARDWALK. Roy Simpson's wife, Ruth, climbed the wooden stairs that led to the top of Mount Rushmore. The monument was still under construction (photos above and opposite page) when the pair visited in 1940. Mount Rushmore was completed in 1941. The public is no longer allowed to climb it.

We drove much of the way on Highway 30. Through most of Ohio, the road was paved with red bricks! It made for a rather rough ride.

After visiting with Ruth's brother, we drove on to Rapid City. The temperature was 110 degrees, and without air conditioning, we roasted.

Ruth's brother, a traveling salesman, had told us he'd replaced the backseat of his car with a washtub in which he placed a block of ice, making for a cooler ride. So we bought a pail, filled it with chipped ice, closed the windows and opened the front vent. The air passing over the ice helped.

The welcome center at Mount Rushmore wasn't much more than a shack. Ruth and I walked around the area and saw a wooden stairway going up the mountain. There were no signs prohibiting us, so we started up the steps.

It was a long and arduous climb, but we eventually made it to the top, where we talked with several of the workmen. No one questioned our being there, so we just assumed the top was open to the public. We had a sensational view across the valley.

I don't know if any other readers can say they've stood on the heads of Washington, Jefferson, Roosevelt and Lincoln. If so, I'm sure they'll agree it was awe-inspiring.

MOUNTAIN VISTA. "This photograph reminds me of an automobile trip our family once took to Yosemite," says Betty Follas of Morgan Hill, California. "We stopped to photograph some begging bears on the side of a mountain road. While I adjusted the lens on my camera, a huge hungry bear poked his head right in the car window! Not only did he have bad breath, but I nearly fainted from our startling nose-to-nose encounter!"

Traversing Mountains

STUMP ANCHOR

In the summer of 1928, our family took a vacation trip to the Black Hills of South Dakota, where we saw the beginning of the work on the Mount Rushmore National Memorial.

My dad had built roads and bridges all his life, so he was deeply interested in the whole process. He struck up a conversation with the engineers, who took time to tell us all about their plans and even let us look through their transit at the workmen across the valley.

On the way back down the steep mountain road, our car's brakes started smoking and the clutch smelled hot. Dad stopped at a pile of stumps beside the road and hooked one to the car with his tow chain. That stump became an "anchor," safely slowing our descent.

I suspect Dad got that tip from the constructon crew; the workers must have piled those stumps there just for that purpose.

DON BURRILL • CASPER, WYOMING

BUCKLE UP

My boss and I were taking a trip through Canada in his Cadillac in 1956. He had seat belts installed in the car before we started.

Between Calgary and Edmonton, Alberta, we stopped at a little country service station for gas.

The owner of the service station was an elderly man. As he came out to wait on us, I was unhooking my seat belt.

He watched me, then said, "Oh, those are the safety belts I've heard about. That's so if you go over a cliff, you will take the car with you."

MARLIN SWANSON • BAKERSFIELD, CALIFORNIA

POWDER SAVED THE DAY

When I was a boy, we lived in northern Virginia. Once on a trip, we had to cross a mountain in Father's 1920 Chevrolet.

As we began climbing, Dad noticed that the clutch was slipping badly. He stopped at a garage to see what could be done, and the mechanic suggested we go to the five-and-dime store across the street and buy some talcum powder.

He then showed us how to lift the floorboard above the clutch so we could sprinkle powder on it. Sure enough, the trick worked! Although it took several applications, we made it over the mountain just fine.

CHESTER HARLEY • GREENVILLE, OHIO

IT BEAT PUSHING

When we drove the 20 miles to our uncle's farm in the '30s, we had to climb a very steep hill called Hog's Rest. About halfway up, the old Model T always slowed down considerably.

That's when Dad would say, "Everyone lean forward and help Lizzie get up the hill."

We children all did as he said, certain we were helping Lizzie chug her way to the top. We always made it.

ELEANOR STAMER
WHITEHALL, PENNSYLVANIA

ELEPHANT CROSSING

In 1936, we drove my Aunt Lucille from our home in Walsensburg, Colorado, to Grand Junction to live with her older sister.

We took Dad's 1929 Dodge. With its bright yellow body, black fenders and large spoked wheels, it was a car to be proud of—especially during the days of the Great Depression.

The trip was approximately 340 miles, and the route was mountainous, crossing the Rockies at elevations well above 10,000 feet. An unexpected event at Wolf Creek Pass will remain in my memory always.

Nearing the summit, we noticed cars slowing to a stop. When we got close enough, we saw the reason—a carnival was crossing over the mountain with the equipment and animals loaded onto trucks.

A large elephant had weighed down one of the trucks too much, and the animal had to be unloaded and walked over the 10,850-foot pass.

We had to wait while the elephant was led to the top of the mountain, but my 4-year-old sister and I didn't mind at all. Even though we'd never been to a carnival or circus, we could say we'd seen an elephant, and in the most unlikely of places—at the top of Wolf Creek Pass!

CHARLENE BEAGLE • ARVADA, COLORADO

1961

Follow that car! The Travelers umbrella follows you wherever you go. If you run into trouble on the road, you don't call home—just call the nearest Travelers representative. There are thousands of friendly, helpful Travelers Agents located throughout the United States and Canada ready to act promptly any time, anywhere you need help. And they offer *all kinds of insurance protection*—not only for your car, but for your home, your medical bills, your family's future. Call The Travelers man near you. You'll find him listed in the Yellow Pages. Start enjoying the convenience of one plan, *one man, one monthly check to pay under The Travelers umbrella of insurance protection.*

THE TRAVELERS Insurance Companies HARTFORD 15, CONN.

> 66 *May all your trails be crooked, winding, lonesome, dangerous, leading to the most amazing view.* 99
> —*Edward Abbey*

MAIDS OF THE MIST. Joan Dziedzic (on right) and her friend Gloria Biondo were all set to go under Niagara Falls when they had their picture taken in September 1958. Joan now lives in Brooklyn, New York. If she and Gloria had wanted to get even closer to the falls, they would have boarded the *Maid of the Mist* (above). This shot of that famed boat was sent to us by Gloria Mackley of Northbrook, Illinois.

NIAGARA FALLS
CANADA

"DEERLY" BELOVED. When Diane Arnold's family visited Mount Rainier in 1947, a black-tailed deer took a liking to her—or maybe it was the bread in her hand. Diane, who lives in Long Beach, California, says her grandchildren get a kick out of this photo.

DRIVE-THRU FOREST. "My grandma Dorothea Birkholz (on right) and Aunt Lanssa visited Underwood Park in Leggett, California, in March 1964," writes Sandy Berggren, Hopkins, Minnesota.

HEAVEN ON EARTH. "When we lived in Twin Falls, Idaho, our absolute favorite place to camp was Redfish Lake in the heart of the Sawtooth Mountain Range," says Alta Hardy of Flagstaff, Arizona. "This photograph was taken on a trip there in July 1953. Our son, Jim, is sitting at the table. I'm in the center and my Aunt Alice, who was visiting us from Las Vegas, is on the right. We couldn't have asked for a more perfect spot to camp."

REST STOP. Red buses loaded with tourists take a break at Logan Pass, the apex of the scenic Going-to-the-Sun Road, which cuts through Glacier National Park. It was a perfect place for sightseeing, taking pictures and stumping the driver with all sorts of questions. The author shared these photos of Glacier, where he worked in the 1940s.

'I Was a Jammer At Glacier'

If you visited Glacier National Park in the early '40s, I may have been your tour bus driver.

I first visited Glacier in 1939 as a delegate to the national Kappa Sigma convention. I was captivated with the natural beauty and returned the next two summers to work as a "gear jammer."

That's what they called the young men who drove the big red buses that carried the "dudes"—tourists—through Glacier and Waterton national parks.

I was living in Oklahoma City at the time. Four other fellows and I bought a '36 Ford for $125 and drove nonstop to Montana in May. We made $2 a day plus room and board.

The buses, which came from the White Motor Co. of Cleveland, seated 14 and had convertible canvas tops. Believe it or not, those 1930s models are still in use today. Park officials tried replacing them with new clear-domed models, but the dudes wouldn't hear of it. They loved those old red buses.

Like me, the other tour bus drivers in 1940-'41 were unmarried, college-aged young men. We had to be in good health to handle luggage and to lubricate, wash and polish the buses.

On our training drive around the park, we stopped at the Lake McDonald Lodge for lunch. Our waitress that day was a girl named Virginia Pyle. By the second summer, she and I were going steady, and we were married in '43.

Drivers saw lots of thrilling scenery and often had to identify the flowers, trees and mountains for the dudes. When we ran out of real names for the mountains, we'd sometimes use the last name of a fellow jammer.

The dudes could ask some unusual questions, like "How many trees are there in the park?" and "Which end of the lake is higher?"

Countless tourists have seen Glacier National Park from one of those great old red buses. If you visited in the early '40s, who knows? Maybe I was your friendly gear jammer!

HERMAN RUSCH • PLYMOUTH, MINNESOTA

NOW WHICH WAY? At the Hudson Bay Divide, gear jammers John Foster (left) and Herb McBride poured out a pail of water to see in which direction it would flow. The water reportedly disappeared into the dirt.

Camping Fun

FEW PEOPLE, ONE BEAR

Every year, my family camped in a national forest area of the Sierra Nevada called Soda Springs. My grandfather and great-grandfather had camped in the same spot going back to the 1920s.

We camped there in the '50s and '60s. It was about 10 miles down a logging road, far from the main road. Sometimes days would go by without us seeing other people.

The most exciting thing that happened was when a bear came into camp. They always seemed to go after the cookies, so Mom and I had to be very careful to not leave any out.

NANCY FULLMER • GUERNEVILLE, CALIFORNIA

DOG MET SKUNK, GOT BEAUTY TREATMENT

Our dog, Pepper, often came along on our family camping trips. One morning when she returned to camp from her morning stroll, it was obvious she had met a skunk.

One of the campers told my husband to give her a bath in tomato juice. When that didn't do the job, he tried Lestoil. After that bath, Pepper not only smelled better, her fur took on a beautiful glow.

DOROTHY TYC • ROCKFALL, CONNECTICUT

SKUNKED AGAIN

Our family became weekend campers during the summer of 1958. We drove to Johnson's Camp on the California side of the Colorado River, arrived about dusk, set up camp and had supper.

My husband, Orville, was an avid night fisherman, so he set off with his gear for the riverbank, where he'd stay until his stringer was full of catfish.

Our boys, Bruce and Doug, made their beds on the car seats and were about to open the sleeping bags for Orville and me in the tent. I was clearing up the camp after our supper.

It was then that a mama skunk and two babies came into view. I shoved the boys out of the tent, grabbed the two sleeping bags and yelled, "Run for the car!"

That's where Orville found us when he came back to the darkened camp—asleep in the car with the windows rolled up and all four doors locked.

RUBY ANN BROWN • HESPERIA, CALIFORNIA

YOSEMITE REUNIONS

My fondest vacation memories are of the late '40s, when our family would go camping in Yosemite National Park.

This was a big event for us. Dad packed the homemade trailer with camping supplies and we took off on the 10- to 12-hour drive from our home in Redwood City, California.

We always stayed at the same campsite. There were other families who came the same week every year, so Mom and Dad renewed old friendships.

Among the highlights for me were visiting the garbage pit where the bears came every night, and watching the "firefall," when burning embers were swept over the cliff at Glacier Point.

During one of those visits, I bought a turquoise ring from Chief Lehmi, who sold postcards and trinkets and performed for the campers. It's been more than 50 years, and I still have that ring, and I love telling the story of where it came from.

JACK BEVILOCKWAY • LIMA, OHIO

SIMPLE TENT STARTED MANY YEARS OF CAMPING

My most memorable birthday present was the blue canvas cabin tent (pictured bottom right) I got when I turned 10, in 1964. It was really a present for the whole family that I was happy to share because it meant we could go camping a lot now.

Only two months later, a new state-run camping and recreation area opened in Greenfield, just 25 miles from our home. It featured 252 heavily wooded, very private campsites, and it became a favorite spot for our family for many years.

Since then, we've gone from sleeping on the ground to air mattresses to Army cots. The tent was replaced by a pop-up camping trailer and finally a comfortable travel trailer that my wife, Terri, and I use at a seasonal campsite at Wells Beach, Maine.

Still, nothing tops the excitement I felt when we lugged that heavy canvas tent and all our gear and food to the old Chevy sedan and headed for a weekend at Greenfield State Park.

DEAN SHALHOUP • NASHUA, NEW HAMPSHIRE

ROUGHING IT. Above: Esther Davis (third from left) and family gather for a photo after setting up camp. Top right: Young Donna Wilson is ready for adventure, while Dean Shalhoup (right) has it made in the shade as he lounges next to his canvis cabin tent. Before the present-day trend of "glamping," campers were happy to leave the modern conveniences of home behind.

A '51 JUNKET brought friends together on Rainy Lake in Minnesota. Clockwise from upper left: Dave Olson; Bob Covert and Dave with the day's catch; Don Bowman; Bob and Don.

GONE FISHIN'
WITH MY BUDDIES

The fishing was especially good on Rainy Lake in northern Minnesota during a trip my buddies and I made back in the summer of 1951.

We lived in the Twin Cities area and traveled up to International Falls, where Don Bowman's brother owned a business flying people to remote lakes that were not accessible by road.

Once we got to Rainy Lake, near the Canadian border, we put our gear in a cabin that a buddy's brother owned and headed out to the lake.

Every boat deserves a name. So we decided to call the old lake cruiser of Don's *The Queen of Rainy Lake*. We used that vessel as a tugboat to haul two

other boats for miles and miles around Rainy Lake.

There were times when we'd fish from sunup to sundown. We had no problems getting our share of northern pike, sunfish and walleye, as this photo shows (above, center). Some of them quickly hit the frying pan for our dinners along the shore. We'd never be able to take that many fish with the limits that are in place today.

We were fairly serious fishermen, but we were also teens at the time—and mostly interested in girls.

But the fishing trip was a great memory for six guys who remained friends for decades.

BOB CRAWFORD • APPLE VALLEY, MINNESOTA

Lifting Their Spirits

In 1971, my grandparents Beverly and Walton road-tripped with friends to Great Smoky Mountains National Park. Here they are on the Skylift, taking in the spectacular view around Gatlinburg, Tennessee.

They loved taking their family on car trips, and by the mid-'80s, their travels included their kids' families, too. My grandparents were proud to show us many popular attractions in our home state, including Wisconsin Dells, Shawano and Eagle River.

RAEANN SUNDHOLM • WIND LAKE, WISCONSIN

CHAPTER 4

Roadside
WONDERS

Who didn't beg Mom and Dad to revise a family road trip to include a detour past some offbeat roadside spectacle—maybe the world's largest pistachio nut, or a life-size moose made of chocolate? Or perhaps it was a mom-and-pop truck stop, retro diner or abandoned ghost town that looked too cool to pass by.

"Many years ago, I was driving across Ohio on old U.S. Highway 20, headed back home to visit Mom and Dad in Illinois," says Clancy Strock of Gainesville, Florida. "Suddenly I noticed a sign that proclaimed: 'World's Only Living Two-Headed Calf, 10 Miles Ahead.'

"*What sort of swindle is this?* I wondered. *Probably another slick idea to bilk the tourists.*

"As I pondered the possibilities, the next sign popped up, announcing that the genetic marvel was only 5 miles away. But home was still many hours ahead, and I wanted to get there in time for supper. So I drove on.

"It's been almost 50 years since I saw those signs, and to this day I wish I had turned down that gravel road. Maybe I missed out on seeing one of Mother Nature's true marvels."

You probably remember a few similar weird and wacky tourist sights from your own highway adventures. Here are some of North America's most beloved and unusual attractions, including a few along the famed "Mother Road," Route 66. How many have you been lucky enough to see?

SIGNS OF THE TIMES. Classic Route 66 eateries include the neon-lit 66 Diner (right) in Albuquerque and The Big Texan Steak Ranch and Motel (above) in Amarillo, where dinner's free if you can put away 72 ounces of steak!

'The Mother Road'
STILL BECKONS

Route 66 takes you through a different America—the one that existed before interstate highways and chain hotels. **WITOLD SKRUPCZAK** • HOUSTON, TEXAS

When faced with a trip from Oklahoma City, Oklahoma, to Flagstaff, Arizona, I decided to shun the expressway in favor of a true slice of Americana—historic Route 66.

Sure, I could've taken I-40 and made the 864-mile journey in less than two days. Instead, I spent five days and drove quite a few extra miles exploring what's left of "The Mother Road." And instead of being a monotonous freeway trip, it's a journey I'll always remember.

Popularized in the famous 1946 song written by Bobby Troup and the 1960s television show of the same name, Route 66 is an American travel icon.

In its quirky stretches with glowing neon signs,

Art Deco-style buildings and kitschy attractions, you can still see the simpler roadside America that existed before the advent of freeways and faceless chain restaurants, motels and hotels.

Initially established to connect the central states to California, the 2,448-mile road stretched from Chicago to Los Angeles when it was completed in 1938. It quickly became America's most celebrated highway. Millions of folks traveled on it. Businesses sprang up all along the way to serve them.

But when the interstate system was completed, traffic on Route 66 dwindled. Countless highway businesses closed down, and entire towns faded away.

As I found out, though, America's love affair with

Route 66 is far from over. All along the route (more than 80 percent of it is still drivable), you can see colorful motel, restaurant and store signs that predate the proliferation of national chains. In fact, many of the old businesses have been renovated and returned to their former glory.

One such spot, the Wigwam Hotel in Holbrook, Arizona, reopened after being closed for 14 years. Each room is a separate structure shaped like a wigwam, but equipped with modern conveniences.

I discovered some of the best concentrations of historic businesses in Amarillo, Texas, and Tucumcari, New Mexico. In Tucumcari, for instance, you don't want to miss the Blue Swallow Motel, which is listed on the National Register of Historic Places.

Perhaps the best-preserved section of Route 66 is Central Avenue in Albuquerque, New Mexico, an 18-mile mix of classic old buildings and attractive new ones. Highlights include the recently renovated Nob Hill area, stretching for several blocks east on Girard Street, and the KiMo Theatre, which is said to be one of the world's best examples of Pueblo-Art Deco architecture.

Historic motels abound all along the route, too. Albuquerque's El Vado Motel on the Rio Grande, open for 63 years, still has its original furniture.

I loved visiting the El Rancho Hotel in Gallup, New Mexico, built by the brother of 1920s movie magnate D.W. Griffith. Many Hollywood stars visited when they filmed movies in the area. Some rooms are named after them, and the decor is rustic Old West.

The route is known for its many souvenir shops, but the Jack Rabbit Trading Post is the only one I know of with its own interstate exit—Exit 269 between Winslow and Holbrook, Arizona. You can't miss the legendary jackrabbit statue or the large sign that proclaims, "HERE IT IS." In years past, billboards used to sing the Jack Rabbit's praises for hundreds of miles.

I didn't go hungry during this trek, either. Many of Route 66's restaurants and cafes are throwbacks to the 1950s. In Oklahoma City, Ann's Chicken Fry House features a pink 1959 Cadillac parked outside next to a vintage gas pump. And Albuquerque's 66 Diner is known for serving green chili cheeseburgers and chocolate shakes on a gleaming chrome counter under deep-pink lights.

I also enjoyed poking around several museums along the way that are dedicated to Route 66's history. Perhaps the best known of these, the Route 66 Museum in Clinton, Oklahoma, displays a bright red Corvette—the same car that starred in the *Route 66* television series. It looks grand at night, gleaming in the well-lit windows as you slowly cruise past.

No doubt about it—you can still get your kicks on Route 66!

OUTDOOR ART. Chetwynd was named for a founding father, Ralph Chetwynd. The sculptures shown here, among dozens in town, were created by Terry McKinnan, Elmer Gunderson, Nyal Thomas and Ken Sheen.

A CUT ABOVE

Chain saw sculptures dot this charming town in British Columbia.

HANK AND GRETTIS BASHAM • PANAMA CITY, FLORIDA

While driving along the Alaska Highway in British Columbia on our way back home, we decided to take a different route—and that's how we discovered Chetwynd and its fabulous chain saw sculptures.

The town's welcome sign, which features three bear sculptures, immediately grabbed our attention. So we stopped at the nearby welcome center and learned that Chetwynd, a lovely town of about 3,100 or so friendly folks, is home to a total of some 50 chain saw sculptures.

Armed with a map that showed us the locations of all the sculptures, we headed out for a stroll. Talk about great photo opportunities—we saw creative sculptures depicting everything from eagles and prospectors to beaver and owls. It's unbelievable that anyone could take a chain saw and create artwork with so much detail.

The town's been adding sculptures ever since 1992, when residents decided to do something lasting as part of a celebration of the Alaska Highway's 50th birthday. Since then, almost a dozen artists have contributed sculptures.

All the carvings were so good that it's hard to say which were our favorites, although we really did enjoy the bears.

The town also boasts three windmills on one of the main streets that actually power lights strung from trees year-round. The town's also dressed up with five murals and tons of beautiful flowers—an absolutely charming place.

We learned the town celebrates its carving legacy by hosting the International Chainsaw Carving Championships every year in mid-June. It's just one more thing that puts this memorable town a cut above the rest!

Old Montana Mining Town Still Glitters

I was on a road trip out west when I came upon an amazing discovery. Just 90 miles from the western end of Yellowstone National Park is one of the Old West's most authentic ghost towns: Nevada City.

This lively mining town first sprang to life after gold was discovered there in 1863. The discovery created one of Montana's largest gold rushes; miners here found more than $100 million worth!

At their peak, Nevada City and Virginia City, a sister town about 1½ miles away, were home to more than 10,000 miners. The two towns served as the commercial centers for the many small encampments that popped up along the 14-mile Alder Gulch mining strike.

But by 1869, barely 100 people lived in Nevada City. And by 1876, it was practically a ghost town.

You'd never know it nowadays as you stroll down California Street, the heart of this pioneer town. You see, this isn't your typical ghost town.

The dirt streets here aren't lined with empty storefronts. Instead, you'll find rows of period buildings, including a school, jail and furnished homes. There are more than 90 buildings in all.

I was impressed with how real Nevada City looks. There is an authentic, fully stocked general store. Wagons parked on the street look as though they were just unhitched. Gold pans and picks lean on buildings as though the owners were inside, taking a nap. I saw laundry hanging on a porch and schoolbooks on classroom desks.

During my visit, I learned that the careful preservation and restoration of these buildings was the handiwork of Charles and Sue Bovey of Great Falls. In the mid-1940s, the two began buying up dilapidated buildings across Montana, effectively launching one of the first large-scale preservation projects in the Old West.

The Boveys saved scores of buildings from the wrecking ball. With dedicated hearts and hands, they embarked on the long process of relocating and rebuilding these historic gems.

After my impromptu visit, I can say without a doubt that Nevada City shines as brightly as the gold that sparked its birth 140 years ago.

CINDY MILLER HOPKINS
COLORADO SPRINGS, COLORADO

EUREKA! Old West aficionados can strike it rich in Nevada City. Visitors can take a 25-minute narrated stagecoach tour of the Alder Gulch gold strike area. During summer, they can travel to Virginia City, another ghost town just minutes away, on a gas-powered train when the steam locomotive isn't running, or have a seat and brush up on local history.

BEACON IN THE NIGHT. Mammoth gas station signs, like the one in the photo above, populated the landscape along America's highways and byways to bring a sweet sigh of relief to travelers when their gas gauge needles starting inching toward "E." "There was a flying red horse sign in Shakopee, Minnesota, back in the '40s," says Karen Hanninen of Minneapolis. "In the dead of night, you could see that Mobil Oil sign glowing miles down the road."

FUEL YOUR WANDERLUST

VISITING HER UNCLE WAS A GAS

Back in the 1940s and '50s, my uncle Kyle Woolman (pictured above) managed three gas stations on the Skokie Highway in Illinois, just south of the Wisconsin state line.

When our family took a ride to see him at one of the stations on the highway, now better known as Highway 41, we'd watch for the tall sign you can see in the photo (above right).

Called the Colossus Sign, it was known as the "largest, mightiest and most spectacular road sign in America." Standing 125 feet tall, it was visible from 5 or 6 miles away in either direction. Previously, the sign stood on South Park Avenue, near the Century of Progress Exposition grounds in Chicago.

My uncle had several old school buses parked behind the gas stations, and he rented them out to sailors and friends from the nearby Great Lakes Naval Training Center.

BERNICE TURNEY • GRAYSLAKE, ILLINOIS

DEALS ALONG THE WAY

We didn't have a whole lot of money in 1939, but my mother, Minnie, younger sister, Beverly, and I decided we could make the trip from our home in Barrington, Illinois, to California and back in my 1932 Pontiac sedan. I was 22 at the time.

A gas war was on along Route 66 in Oklahoma. Gas was just 7 cents a gallon, and the attendant gave me my change in silver dollars.

We stopped in Chandler, Oklahoma, after 6 p.m. and were directed to a boardinghouse for supper.

GETTING THEIR KICKS. Charles Terry and his sister Beverly on Route 66 in New Mexico.

Everyone else had eaten, but the landlady brought out an enormous variety of food and charged us 25 cents each for all the food we could eat.

I had to add a quart of oil to my car about every 40 miles, so I started buying it in 5-gallon containers. We got to Pasadena around Christmas but couldn't stay for the Rose Parade on New Year's Day because we were running out of money.

The trip home was uneventful, but I ended up using 25 gallons of oil. New piston rings solved the problem, until a month later a car hit me head-on and ruined the Pontiac, but the memories of that trip stayed with me forever.

CHARLES G. TERRY SR. • ELGIN, ILLINOIS

PUMP YOUR OWN

Years ago, you never knew what—or whom—you might encounter at a roadside gas station.

After completing my Navy duty, I decided to see some of America before returning home. I was crossing Montana when my car ran out of gas at the top of a hill. I was able to coast down to stop in front of an old house with a gas pump outside.

When I got out of my car, an old woman called down to me from a second-floor window, "Pump your own."

I did just that, and my total came to $3. Then a metal cup was lowered down the side of the house on a string.

"Put the money in the cup," the same woman commanded. I did, she pulled the cup up to the window, and I continued on my way.

ROBERT LEGEL • LIVONIA, MICHIGAN

GAS UP THE TANK

Driving through the South on our way from New York to Miami in the late '30s, we stopped for fuel at a rural gas station. It had the usual pumps with clear glass tops that enabled motorists to see the gas being fed into their cars.

In those days, there weren't many tourist rest stops. As was the custom, we carried our own food and a thermos of water in the car.

Along the way, we needed a refill, and Mother gave me the job. I asked the attendant where I might find water to fill the thermos.

Standing there in his bib overalls with one hand holding the gas nozzle, he gestured with the other and said, "There's a spigot 'round back."

For all my six years of life, water had always come out of a faucet affixed to a sink. So I figured a spigot must be something that looked like a faucet.

Going around the back, I found something that looked just like a faucet, but it was attached to a big drum. As I filled our thermos, I thought the water must have been in the barrel a long time because it smelled a little funny.

Back on the road again, we were about 10 miles from the nearest civilization when someone got thirsty. Mother opened the thermos, and a very strange odor permeated the car. That's when I learned an unforgettable truth—spigots can also dispense kerosene!

ALLAN LANDSMAN • YORBA LINDA, CALIFORNIA

FILL 'ER UP! Globe signs, like the one for Skelly atop the center gas pump, were once a familiar sight at roadside service stations.

Cruisin' Route 66 in Style

DAD WAS A DAPPER DUDE. "In the late 1930s, my father, Armend Grasse, saved the money he made at his first job, bought this car and took a trip west on Route 66 with a friend," says Darlene Thoresen of Brookfield, Wisconsin. "Dad was a farm boy from Waubeka, Wisconsin. But the way he's dressed, right down to the spats, is a far cry from what farm boys wore. I never saw him dressed like that. A few years after this trip, my dad married my mother, then he went into military service during World War II."

GO WEST, YOUNG WOMEN! "We drove from Oshkosh, Wisconsin, to California in 1952 when our friend Jane (second from right) married her Air Force fiance," says Lenore Dunlavy of Oshkosh (left). "Also on the trip were Joan (second from left); Marion (right), whose 1950 Chevy we used; and Delores, who took the photo. On the return trip, the four of us took Route 66—we still reminisce about it."

Off the Beaten Path

WANDERED WEST IN A WILLYS

Although we had seen much of the country through the windows of troop trains during our military service, my brother Tom, friend Al and I decided to take a more leisurely trip.

I had recently purchased a new 1947 Willys station wagon, and in July 1948, we drove from our homes in Philadelphia to Chicago so we could take the famous Route 66 west to California.

Our trip lasted four weeks and took us through 19 states. We often ate at the side of the road, using the tailgate of the Willys for cooking and dining.

We usually washed up in a stream or at gas stations. But every couple of days, we'd stop at a YMCA or a similar community center for a shower. We may have been vagabonds, but our military training taught us to be clean ones.

We motored through all the towns in the song "Route 66," passing through Kingman, Barstow and San Bernardino before arriving in Los Angeles.

We realized our boyhood dreams of seeing the Mississippi River, the Petrified Forest, Grand Canyon, the Mojave Desert and glamorous Hollywood.

We enjoyed every minute of the journey across the country and often took pictures at milestones (that's me in the photo at right, standing next to the California state line sign). It was an adventure that will be etched in my memory forever.

ROBERT MILLER • PHILADELPHIA, PENNSYLVANIA

HE THUMBED HIS WAY WEST

Many of my childhood days were spent alongside "The Mother Road." My family moved to Red Fork, Oklahoma, just outside Tulsa, in 1936, when I was 2.

My school bus stop was at a service station and tourist court on Route 66. When I got old enough, the owner let me pump gas and check oil for the customers who were headed west.

I used to sit for hours on the bench in front of the station and watch the cars and trucks go by. I remember seeing old cars with family belongings tied to the roof as they went west to try to find a better life.

Many celebrities traveled Route 66. Bob Hope came into the station one day. He had been playing golf nearby and wanted a soda pop.

I always wondered where the highway went.

> **All journeys have secret destinations of which the traveler is unaware.**
> —*Martin Buber*

When my dad said it went all the way to California, I became fascinated with the idea that one day I would travel the road. I got my chance in 1952, when I graduated from high school.

A friend and I hitchhiked to California on Route 66, sleeping on park benches, alongside railroad tracks—anywhere we could find.

I wouldn't try that these days. But I wouldn't trade a million dollars for the experiences I had on that incredible trip.

MONTE HANCOCK • TULSA, OKLAHOMA

DOWN IN THE BOONDOCKS. When the author stumbled upon this retro complex in South Dakota, he felt as if he'd been transported back to the 1950s. Boondocks includes a diner (above) and a vintage gas station (right).

ONE COOL **CROSSROADS**

Along western South Dakota's backroads between Deadwood and Mount Rushmore, I came across Boondocks, a real flashback to the 1950s located smack-dab in the middle of nowhere!

The diner here looks like a 1950s drive-in, with a few vintage automobiles scattered about to add to the atmosphere—a '49 Studebaker, '57 Thunderbird and '35 T-bucket caught my eye. Like the other customers, I parked across the lot to help preserve the period feel. Picnic tables placed strategically between the classic cars provide a great place to enjoy your meal.

Inside, I found a menu (lunch and dinner only) filled with not just classic cheeseburgers and milkshakes, but also such treats as a Fonz Burger and a Hawaiian Hot Rod, a chicken or beef sandwich with pineapple and cream cheese. I settled on a buffalo burger with a side of crispy homemade fries—and it was fantastic!

The atmosphere put me in the mood for some music, so I dropped coins into the Rock-Ola jukebox and played some Elvis tunes.

With all those old-fashioned automobiles, the 1950s-style gas station on the grounds is simply a natural. There are no modern brand names on the restored vintage pump—it simply says "Gas" and is topped with a glass display case.

The complex of buildings also includes a gift shop, designed to look like a small-town Studebaker dealership, with only a few cars inside. Plenty more were parked outside, along with a vintage boat. Inside, I found all kinds of '50s-themed collectibles and other souvenirs.

Between the gift shop and diner is a photo studio, situated in what looks like an old garage, offering sepia-toned portraits. Cabins and tent camping are also available.

The Boondocks is definitely the spot to be for travelers looking for a blast from the past. It feels like a little town stuck in the 1950s. If you find yourself road trippin' through this area of South Dakota, cruise on over—I think you'll dig what I'm sayin', daddy-o!

RICHARD WEISS • BLOOMFIELD, MICHIGAN

Fantastic
FOLK ART

Restored Totem Pole Park in Oklahoma keeps artist's tribute alive.

JUDY BLANKE-SEAMAN • CHELSEA, OKLAHOMA

Taking a road trip along Route 66? In Claremore, Oklahoma, you will find one of North America's most unique roadside attractions—the world's largest totem pole, built by nationally known folk artist Ed Galloway.

It took Ed more than a decade, from 1937 to 1948, to build the 90-foot totem pole, as a tribute to Native Americans.

He used 28 tons of cement, 6 tons of steel and 100 tons of sand and rock to construct the pole. It rises from the back of a turtle and features 200 carved pictures, including images of Native Americans and totem animals from the Pacific Northwest. It's quite a sight!

The totem pole is located in 10-acre Totem Pole Park, which took Ed many years to develop. It's now listed on the National Register of Historic Places.

Ed also made 300 fiddles, many with intricate inlaid pieces, out of various woods from around the world. In 1949, he finished the Fiddle House, an 11-sided building in the park where the fiddles are on display.

Much of Ed's unique style of monumental folk art can be traced to the years he spent in the Philippine Islands while serving in the U.S. Army during the Spanish-American War.

When he returned home, he began creating massive sculptures out of tree trunks, incorporating human figures with the fish and reptiles he observed during his stint in the Philippines.

If you visit this area, I'd recommend lunch at the Top Hat Dairy Bar in nearby Foyil. You can get a carryout meal there and take it with you for a picnic at the park.

I have fond memories of the park from when I was a child. I loved romping past the totem pole and other colorful totems on the property and admiring all the handmade violins. After a few years when the grounds fell into disrepair, it's great to see them vibrant once again.

FIDDLIN' AROUND. In addition to giant cement sculptures, Ed Galloway fashioned 300 fiddles, many of them now on display in the 11-sided Fiddle House (top), which he built by hand. His 90-foot totem pole (above right) and other large folk art pieces honor Native Americans.

ROUTE 66,
HIGHWAY OF SIDESHOWS

Giant jackrabbits, two-headed cows and more beckoned travelers during the 1950s.

DELORES JONES DENNIS • CHELSEA, OKLAHOMA

Today's highways bypass most towns and cities, and there's usually no stopping except for gas, emergencies or bathroom breaks. In our fast-paced world, that seems to be what most people want.

Not me, though! I miss those old roads that led you through every small town and offered plenty of places to stop and rest. Most of all, I miss the colorful roadside attractions.

When I was young, we traveled Route 66 from Standard, California, to Heavener, Oklahoma. We made that round-trip at least once a year.

Dad drove our old Ford as fast as he could so we'd have a little extra time to stop at the kitschy roadside places that offered so much fun.

Hopping Along

One of the best attractions was the Jack Rabbit Trading Post in Arizona. Near the store stood several large statues, and one was a huge jackrabbit. I have pictures of three generations of my family posing with that rabbit!

Trading posts beckoned all along Route 66, so there was keen competition for motorists' money.

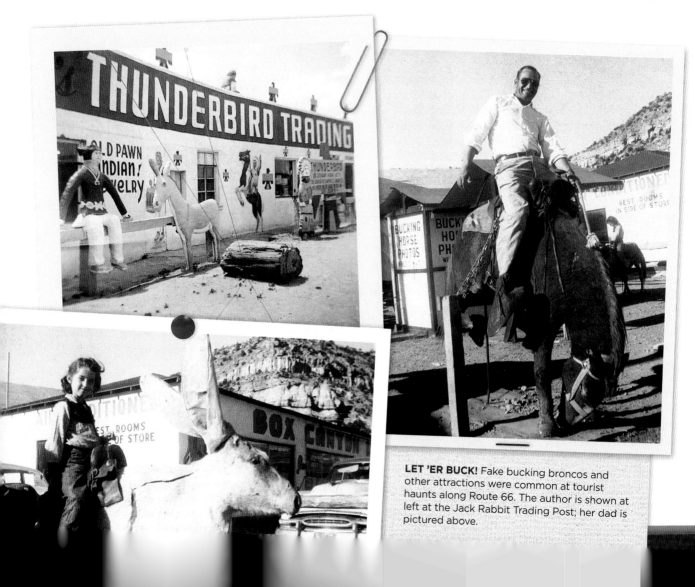

LET 'ER BUCK! Fake bucking broncos and other attractions were common at tourist haunts along Route 66. The author is shown at left at the Jack Rabbit Trading Post; her dad is pictured above.

What developed, therefore, was a highway lined with freak shows, playgrounds and miniature amusement parks.

Near the Painted Desert, you could buy colored sand in glass containers. At the Petrified Forest, you might purchase small chips of petrified wood. The Native American reservations offered handmade jewelry, mugs and other items.

Then there were the small places touting two-headed cows and other mistakes of nature. I recall one such enterprise that boasted a "rare" horned rattlesnake. Most travelers didn't know that all sidewinder rattlesnakes have horns.

My favorite roadside stops featured covered wagons, stagecoaches and statues of horses. You could sit in the wagons or on the horses and have your picture taken.

Another part of traveling Route 66 were the border-crossing stations at each state line. Officials would check for fruits, vegetables, plants and other contraband not allowed into a particular state.

One time, Dad wanted to transport some night crawlers and catfish he'd caught back home to northern California. He took two tin washtubs, put the fish in one and covered them with ice, then filled the other with dirt and night crawlers.

Mom told him he'd never get them home, but Dad just had to try. In the meantime, she took a small bucket and filled it with dirt and night crawlers.

Mom Baited Officials at the Border

We managed to pass through both Texas and New Mexico without being checked, but things changed at the Arizona-California line. Dad was told he couldn't carry the fish or the worms into California.

After arguing with the officer to no avail, he finally had to dump both the washtubs. Mom, however, got to keep her worms by placing some dirty diapers on top of the bucket.

Asked what was inside, she told the officer it was full of dirty diapers, and he was welcome to check if he wished. He thanked her but didn't bother.

Dad was so mad he wouldn't even talk the rest of the way home. I never knew whether it was because he didn't get to keep his fish and worms— or because Mom got to keep hers!

It was probably both, and for years afterward, Dad told us he was convinced the border guards gathered up those fish after we left for a big fish fry.

There will never be another road like Route 66. In some ways that's good, but in others it's a pity, because travel will never again be quite so much fun.

THEY FOUND THE JACKRABBIT.

My husband, Jerald, and I recently drove a 1961 Corvair from Michigan to California on as much of "The Mother Road" as we could. We found the Jack Rabbit Trading Post in Joseph City, Arizona, between Holbrook and Winslow. That's Jerald on the jackrabbit statue (above).

PAT FLINN · DEXTER, MINNESOTA

YOU CAN'T MISS IT

Back in the early 1960s, I was driving an 18-wheeler as a lease hauler for Lyon Van Lines in Los Angeles. I lived in Massachusetts, so on my first trip west, I decided to take Route 66 from Chicago and experience this famous road.

After many miles of driving, I saw a sign announcing the Jackrabbit was 100 miles ahead. As I continued driving west, more signs told me how much farther it was to this apparently noteworthy place. Those were boring miles, with no sign of habitation. Suddenly I saw another sign that read, "You have just passed Jackrabbit."

To this day, I get a chuckle out of it.

ROBERT SAUVE · SALEM, MASSACHUSETTS

Roadside Kitsch

CALL A PLUMBER! "While driving into Columbia, South Carolina, we naturally had to stop and photograph this eye-catcher called Busted Plug Plaza, billed as the world's largest fire hydrant," say John and Delores Theobald of Des Plaines, Illinois. "A local artist named Blue Sky created the broken fire hydrant sculpture, which is 39 feet high and weighs 9,800 pounds."

HIGH CHAIR. "This giant rocking chair stands at Doxey's Apple Shed Mercantile and Cafe in Penrose, Colorado," says Carol Dominguez of Penrose. "Built in 1990 out of hand-hewn Douglas fir logs, the chair is 21 feet high, 14 feet wide and weighs 9,100 pounds."

DAY OF THE DINOSAUR. "There wasn't a live reptile in sight when this photo was taken on our visit to the Reptile Gardens in the Black Hills of South Dakota," says Annie Rue of Everett, Washington. "My sons David (sitting) and Stephen and I were checking out this concrete monster when the photo was taken during the late 1950s."

LENDING A HAND. "During a family vacation to Prince Edward Island, my husband, David, couldn't resist joining *The Fishermen*, a concrete work of art created by Roger Langevin," writes Judy Hurlbert of Durham, Connecticut. "It stands in the community of L'Étang-du-Nord on Cap-aux-Meules, the most populated in a string of 12 islets that make up the remote Magdalen Islands."

HARMLESS FLIRTATION. "Back In 1950, my beautiful mother, Golden Davis, was visiting Last Frontier Village with family in Old Las Vegas, Nevada," says Kristen Spilman of Ventura, California. "My dad snapped this photo of Mom flirting with two cowboys."

GIVE HISTORY A SPIN. Vintage windmills like these at Mid-America Windmill Museum (above) in Kendallville, Indiana, are time-honored symbols of rural farming. The museum's largest windmill (at right) is modeled after the wooden Robertson Post windmill in Colonial Williamsburg, Virginia.

INHERIT THE **WIND**

A unique Indiana museum shows how windmills tamed the frontier.

CARL HARTUP • FORT WAYNE, INDIANA

Windmills have always fascinated me. So naturally, my wife, Mickey, and I had to take a road trip to the Mid-America Windmill Museum in Kendallville, about 30 miles north of Fort Wayne.

This 37-acre attraction boasts 49 operating windmills, and explains how these mechanical workhorses helped tame the frontier.

Our tour began in an 1880s barn made out of hand-hewn lumber. A video showed how both the westward-bound settlers and the railroads relied on windmills to pump water.

We learned that this area once boasted dozens of windmill manufacturers; one still makes water pumps in Kendallville. Other exhibits described the evolution of wind power from Colonial America through today's wind turbines.

Next, we took a winding path through the windmills themselves. You can't miss the largest one, the Robertson Post windmill, built here with blueprints from the Colonial Williamsburg Foundation.

Our visit coincided with the museum's annual windmill festival, which included an antique show, a craft sale and other festivities. Best of all, it all was set to the rhythmic squeaks and groans of the windmills overhead. How comforting to hear the song that has reassured countless farm families through the years. I recommend you come enjoy it for yourself. You won't be disappointed!

Iconic Kiss

This photo shows my husband, Tom, and me next to *Unconditional Surrender*, a 25-foot-tall statue in Sarasota, Florida, similar to the Alfred Eisenstadt V-J Day photo that ran in *Life* magazine in August 1945. Sculptor Seward Johnson created the statue, which is on the city's bayfront, north of Island Park Drive.

MARJORIE GILHOOLY • BRADENTON, FLORIDA

> **It's good to play, and you must keep in practice.**
> —Jerry Seinfeld

CHAPTER 5

Ticket to **FUN**

T he need for unabashed, high-flying fun knows no age limit. From old-time escapes like Coney Island to fanciful kingdoms such as Disneyland, these magical wonderlands enchant and inspire kids and adults alike.

"Each summer I counted down the days till my family's trip to Geauga Lake, an amusement park in Aurora, Ohio," says *Reminisce* Associate Editor Leah Wynalek. "On the anticipated morning, we loaded into the old minivan—sandwiches and juice boxes in the cooler—and headed to the park. Once through the gates, we split into groups to conquer our favorite rides.

"I got my thrills plunging down the log flume and lollygagging at the carnival booths, watching visitors try their luck at the ring toss. The day was a success if I left slightly exhausted and slightly sunburned, my fingers sticky from the fluffs of cotton candy that I had enjoyed before leaving the park.

"For a kid, a summer day at the amusement park is a joyride. Where else can you zoom upside down at high speeds or eat junk food with Mom's permission? Those hot summer days of winding through the queues and eating dripping ice cream cones are unforgettable."

We invite you to revisit the amusement parks, carnivals and other eye-opening destinations readers flocked to as kids. The admission is on us!

NEVER BORED ON THE BOARDWALK. Steeplechase Park was one of Coney Island's hot spots in the 1940s. Roni Borden never had to walk very far—her family's summer home was right on the Boardwalk (above right). At right, Roni and pal Arnie Smith were happy to pose to help draw customers to the photo stand.

Coney Island Boardwalk
WAS HOME TO US

With the world's greatest amusement park at her doorstep, this reader had super summer fun in the early '40s. RONI BORDEN • COLCHESTER, CONNECTICUT

A visit to Coney Island required some planning for most folks, but not for us. We just had to step out our front door!

When I was growing up during the '40s, our family rented a room at Coney Island for July and August. The rooming houses were right on the beach and the Boardwalk.

That residential part of Coney Island was not where the tourists flocked. There was a merry-go-round on 27th Street, just four blocks from our place on 31st. It wasn't fancy, but we could win a free ride if we caught the gold ring.

The merry-go-round cost a nickel, which Mother would give to me after supper, when my friends and I took the four-block walk.

"Be back by 9," she'd say. There was no worry about safety back then, but Mother thought it important for an 11-year-old to get her sleep.

Rides, Food, Fun

The merry-go-round was the only amusement in our section of Coney Island. But sometimes we walked down to 14th Street, where all the excitement was. In those days, Coney Island was a place where you could escape all the cares of life and just enjoy the rides, the sights and the sounds.

The flavors of Coney Island were unlike any to be found elsewhere. Who else could make a hot dog like Nathan's? Where else could you find the world-famous Shatzkin's knishes—pockets of dough filled with peppery potatoes or other good things.

Then there was the Bowery, a walkway several blocks long between the Boardwalk and Surf Avenue. All sorts of amusements were clustered there, including the Cyclone, Wonder Wheel, bumper cars and more food.

We could enjoy the Bowery and Boardwalk sights in an evening. But Steeplechase Park was altogether different—it took a lot more time to properly enjoy this wonderful place.

When I'd saved up 50 cents, I'd buy a ticket that I tied onto my clothing with a string. The ticket, good for one admission on each of the park's 50 rides, was punched each time I went on a ride. That took all day.

Photos for Fun

Coney Island also offered fun-seekers photographic souvenirs of their good times. There was a man with a cart and fake donkey on which several people could pose for a group photo.

Most chose to be photographed standing behind some hilarious drawings on cardboard with only their heads showing. The drawings depicted muscle men, fat ladies with short skirts, skinny ladies wearing bathing suits, or a child in a Buster Brown outfit.

A family friend owned one of these photo concessions. His son and I often posed behind the outrageous painted boards to help attract customers. I still have some of those photos.

As much fun as Coney Island was in the daytime, it was a magical world at night. If the bright and colorful lights weren't enough, there were fireworks every Tuesday night.

For half an hour, the sky would light up with cascading colors and brilliant whites. As each rocket burst forth its colors, a collective "aah!" went up from the crowd on the Boardwalk.

The amusement parks of today are fun, but don't seem to have the same magic as old Coney Island. Myabe it's because they don't have a Boardwalk.

As you walked that wide wooden promenade, surrounded by a festive crowd, your eye traveled from one bright light to the next. With the cool sea breeze washing over you, it seemed as if you could actually feel the magic.

SEE YOU AT THE FAIR! Delectable food, farm animals, thrilling rides and the chance to hang out with best friends or a sweetheart made local fairs the place to be in summer. Raymond Ehrle of Annapolis shared this August 1958 picture of the Montgomery County Fair in Maryland.

SPECIAL PASS
MOUNTAIN PARK
ROUTE 5, HOLYOKE, MASSACHUSETTS
(off Route 91 at Exit 17)
RIDE ALL DAY & NITE FOR $1.50 Per Person
Good Any Day, Any Time, When Park Is Open
See Schedule On Reverse Side
PRESENT THIS TICKET AT MAIN TICKET BOOTH
Excluding Sky Ride — No Refunds — No Rainchecks

TOP O' THE WORLD.
Visitors wait to board the Ferris wheel on a sunny day (left). Above: Millicent Barnard was happy to splurge on the $1.50 pass that bought her an unlimited number of rides at Mountain Park amusement park.

FAIRS AND CARNIVALS
MEANT SUMMER FUN

Carny Kids Collected Cash

My family spent summers at Lake Speculator in the Adirondacks in New York when I was a girl. A traveling carnival came to town each August.

The carinval had animals, and the children in town were given a nickel to walk them. I was given a pig named Daisy and walked her on a leash for exercise. I had so much fun and felt so important.

Under the big tent, before each show, there was a parade of the animals. When I saw Daisy in the parade, I felt a connection to "show biz." She was my pig!

My sister, who was 9 at the time, also earned some money while the carnival was in town. She worked out a deal with the local drugstore.

She got $10 worth of nickel candy from the store, then sold it for 10 cents a piece at the carnival. She later paid the store $10 and had a $10 profit for herself.

GLORIA KINN • ASHBURN, VIRGINIA

Deal for a Day

My pass (above) for the Mountain Park amusement park in Holyoke, Massachusetts, brings back lots of memories. I grew up in Agawam, Massachusetts, just a short ride away.

Several times every summer, our mother would pack deviled eggs, ham sandwiches, fruit, and some of her delcious baked treats, and off my sisters and I would go.

There were lots of rides we could go on for that $1.50, but the best of all was the merry-go-round. I didn't learn until much later that a lot of work and artistry went into painting those horses.

Years later, the park owner was offered $2 million for the merry-go-round, but he wanted it to stay in Holyoke. The townspeople raised $850,000 and brought the merry-go-round, which now sits in Holyoke Heritage Park.

MILLICENT BARNARD
FEEDING HILLS, MASSACHUSETTS

FERRIS WHEEL: A.M. WETTACH/RDAEB

A DAY AT THE
AMUSEMENT PARK

Money was tight in our family when I was growing up, so a trip to the amusement park was a rare and special occasion. When we did go, my parents took us to Fontaine Ferry Park in Louisville, Kentucky. A few times each summer, the park would offer Pepsi Wooden Nickel Day, and each ride cost a nickel.

The park had a legendary wooden roller coaster called The Comet. As you got to the top, you could look out over the Ohio River. It was the most fun and scary feeling of my young life.

Riding the Ferris wheel was another great memory. I remember being between my older brother and uncle as we sat in the benchlike seat with only a small bar to keep us from plunging to our death. When our seat was stopped at the top of the wheel to let someone off below, my brother would rock it back and forth. I begged him to stop and gripped the bar even harder. My uncle must have been a little scared, too, as he demanded that the rocking stop. As we sat atop the Ferris wheel, I waved at my sister on the pony ride far below.

Another memorable excursion was the Jungle Ride. This was a small building in which cars wonld back and forth on a thin railway. The outside was painted to look like a jungle, with snakes, gorillas and other wild creatures that promised great adventure to a 7-year-old.

Two people sat in each car, which entered the building 20 to 30 seconds apart. My friend Joey and his dad were a couple of cars ahead of us. It was pitch black inside the jungle. As the car moved through its route, a light would come on, illuminating a scary cannibal or witch doctor. At another point, you could feel dangling "snakes" or great gusts of wind while hearing screams and shouts from other riders in other cars.

When our car finally exited, I noticed the attendant using a white cloth handkerchief to assist a rider with a bloody nose. Joey later informed me that his dad yawned, stretched out his arms and accidentally hit another rider as the tracks brought the cars close together in the dark building.

Fontaine Ferry is long gone, but I still love going to amusement parks with my own two kids and hope to someday go with my grandkids. However, I am always extra careful to keep my arms and hands inside the car during the ride!

JAMES P. DILBECK • LOUISVILLE, KENTUCKY

Why We're All Goggle-Eyed

Of importance to everyone considering plastics

HERCULES
CELLULOSE ACETATE

HERCULES POWDER COMPANY • WILMINGTON, DELAWARE

> " I see nothing in space as promising as the view from a Ferris wheel. "
> —E.B. White

A Land of Imagination

DISNEY DEBUT. California's famous Disneyland had just opened—in fact, the photo at left was taken on opening day in 1955—when June Cunningham's family visited from their home in Turtle Creek, Pennsylvania. That's June's daughter, Joanie, and son, Bobby, being "taken into custody" by the policeman. Standing in front of Bobby is their cousin Debbie; another cousin, Jay, is shown at right.

AMUSING. "My wife, Marge (on the right), sister-in-law, Hazel O'Dell, and niece, Paula Freihage, enjoyed this ride in July 1965 at Doling Park in Springfield, Missouri," says Luke O'Dell of Siloam Springs. Doling Park opened in 1907. It was bought by the city in 1929; and the last of the amusement rides was removed in the '70s. During its heyday, the park boasted 19 rides, a penny arcade, a pavilion, a fun house, a lake and two bandstands.

SCOOTER-GO-ROUND. "I was stationed at Shaw Air Force Base in South Carolina in 1958 when we drove over to Columbia one weekend for the state fair," says Al Briggs of Austin, Texas. "Our daughter Pam was 6 when we took this picture of her on the carnival ride (left)."

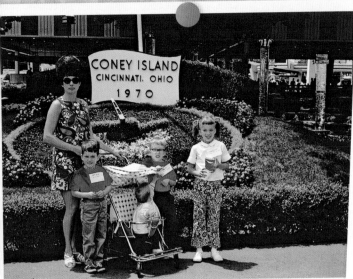

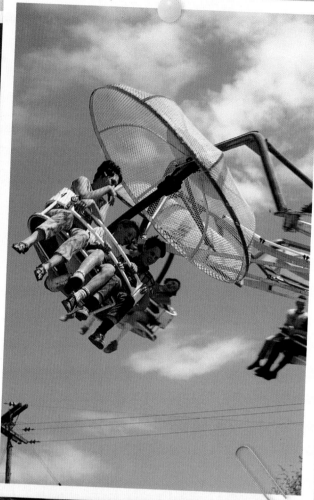

PARK ID'S. "Our family went to Coney Island in Cincinnati, Ohio, at least once a year," writes Marie Wood of Beech Grove, Indiana. She's pictured above with her children (from left) John, 6; Angela, 1; Brett, 4; and Cheryl, 9. "I put name tags on each one of our kids, except for the baby, just in case anyone ended up separated." Below John, Cheryl and Brett enjoy a wild and wacky water ride.

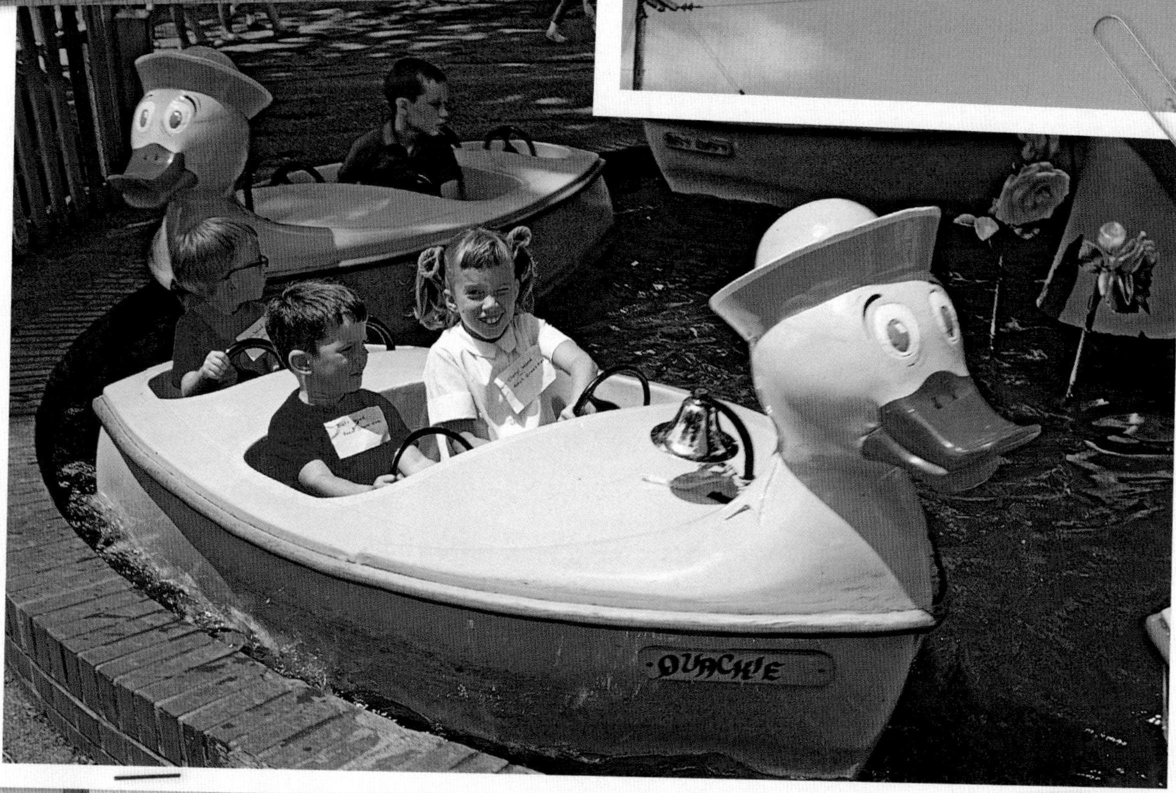

UP, UP AND AWAY. "How well I remember the rides at our summer carnivals—the Whirling Dervish, the Loop-O-Plane and the flying swings (top right)," says Maxine Foreman of Columbus, Nebraska.

FLYING SWINGS: EDITH JANE LANDFRIED

REACHING **FOR THE RING**

The carousel was her favorite part of the midway, and memories of riding with Dad still ring true.

CAROLYN LEWIS • LAKELAND, FLORIDA

Every summer when I was growing up, Mom and Dad took me on a trip to West Haven, Connecticut. It was there that I got to ride the wonderful carousel at Savin Rock amusement park.

Long before we arrived at the pavilion housing the magnificent machine, I would hear and feel the rhythm of the music. By the time I actually saw the carousel spinning, my knees were weak from excitement.

The three of us stood in the pavilion for a moment, listing to the music flowing from a huge band organ inside the golden marvel twirling in front of us.

Then, just when I thought my desire to climb on a horse was enough to make me burst, Dad bent down, smiled and asked me if I'd decided yet which horse I wanted to ride. He always reminded me to choose a horse on the outside row—we both knew why!

Mom never rode the carousel with us. Instead, she'd find a bench nearby so she could sit, watch and wave. It was always Dad who took me by the hand, saying, "Hurry, Carolyn!"

The two of us would dash through the crowd toward the carousel platform, dodging those just getting off. I rememer Dad lifting me high and placing me gently on the special horse I'd chosen.

MERRY-GO-ROUNDER. Carolyn Lewis (below) still has the brass ring from the days when her folks (below, left) took her for carousel rides at the amusement park. The old ring may be tarnished, but her memories aren't!

Time to Saddle Up

"Hold tight to the saddle horn with one hand," he instructed, "and to this pole with the other."

When I sat on my horse, I felt tall and proud. Dad secured the buckle around me, making sure my feet were firmly fixed in the stirrups. With his feet steadily planted on the platform, he'd smile at me and whisper, "Ready?"

I'd nod, then the skinny man sitting in a chair next to the band organ in the center section of the carousel pulled a big lever. The music rang out and the horse (and my stomach) moved up and down as the carousel began to whirl.

I giggled as the ticket man tried to keep his balance while weaving his way between the horses and chairs to collect tickets. Sometimes Dad gave me the ticket to hand to him—that always made me feel like a big girl.

While the carousel circled, we watched for my smiling mother. We saw her and waved as we passed by in a flash. She waved back, her face aglow.

Dad Ready for Action

As Dad stood beside me, I felt his delight and excitement in making this moment special for his little girl. His left arm rested on the back of my horse, and his right was poised to reach out over the edge of the spinning platform to seize a special treasure—the brass ring!

That ring was everyone's goal. If you could catch one from a hook that hung near the edge of the spinning platform, you got a free ride. Dad was very good at grabbing for the brass ring. The two of us got many free rides—and during the summer I was 6, he even gave me a brass ring as a souvenir.

Whenever I reminisce about those happy times, I pull out the brass ring. Though tarnished with age, it will always remain a gentle reminder of family togetherness—and a happy time when the most important thing in the world was our glorious grab for the brass ring.

MERRY RIDE...FOR SOME. "In this 1953 photograph, it's evident that my older daughter, Cheryl, is thrilled about riding a horse on the merry-go-round," says Bob Durling of Highland, Indiana. But Cheryl's sister, Linda, appears rather apprehensive.

> " *It's kind of fun to do the impossible.* "
> —*Walt Disney*

LET THE GOOD TIMES ROLL. There was no better way to enjoy a summer day than to escape to New York City's storied Rockaway Playland (above).

PLAYLAND **PARADISE**

AWAY TO ROCKAWAY

I was born and raised in New York City. Since our neighborhood was close to one of our favorite summer getaways, we didn't have to travel far to get there. The minute school let out, at the end of June, we packed our bags and set out for Rockaway Beach in Queens.

Dad commuted to work every day from the rooming house where we spent the summer—a no-frills rental, but one my folks saved all year to afford. My parents, my sister, Patricia, and I shared one large room with two double beds, one little bureau, a small table and a closet.

With fair skin, red hair and freckles, my sister and I couldn't avoid that dreaded first sunburn of the summer. We lay in that sandy bed at night, burned to a crisp, as hungry mosquitoes buzzed around us.

We had a community kitchen in the basement of the house. Each family was assigned a table with a little cupboard overhead to store food and snacks. Roomers cooked on three stoves, and there was always an assortment of delicious aromas in the air,

making you hope your mom was responsible for at least one of them.

Every meal was fun, because it was like dining with good friends for the summer. In the evening, a few of us gathered in the kitchen and listened to the owner play the violin. Kids who took dancing lessons all winter got a chance to do an Irish jig.

And there was a big bonus: Rockaway's Playland was not far from where we stayed. Mom and Dad took us to the amusement park twice each summer, as soon as we arrived and right before we left. The cotton candy alone was worth the trip.

My parents continued to go to Rockaway each summer long after their children married and moved away. They met up with old friends in the same rooming house and picked up right where they had left off, reminiscing about the fun we all had and the memories we shared.

Over the years I've had many vacations to wonderful places, but none compare to the lazy summer days I spent at Rockaway in the 1950s.

MAUREEN MURPHY REID • RED BANK, NEW JERSEY

WORLD FAIR WONDERS

Even though the Depression was on in 1933 and money was tight, our family decided to travel the 320 miles to Chicago to attend the World's Fair. Dad was an engineer on the Illinois Central Railroad, so Mom and I could ride for free.

To a wide-eyed 10-year-old from a small town, everything at the fair was marvelous. We saw Barney Oldfield set a speed record of 68 mph, and the Wonder Bread display was truly a wonder!

There was a complete bakery set up with glass walls. You could follow the dough through mixing, kneading, baking, slicing and wrapping. At the end, everyone got a sample. Having never had anything but homemade bread, I thought the soft white Wonder Bread was an amazing novelty.

All the fair's rides were set up on an island, and Mother said I couldn't go on them by myself. That's when my Uncle Harry stepped forward and offered to take me.

Oh, how I loved that man! I think we rode on every ride, including the huge double Ferris wheel, the "parachute drop" and even the "log chute."

Later, reunited with the rest of my family, we had our pictures taken and put on the back of a pocket mirror. Then we lunched in the Black Forest of Germany, where we watched an ice skating show. Imagine! An outdoor ice rink in August in Chicago!

It was a trip I'll never forget.

MARY LAZZARI • MOUNT VERNON, WASHINGTON

FAMILY SUPPORT. Grandfather Earnest Moore visited the author during his stay at the TB sanatorium in 1952.

AMUSEMENT PARK SURPRISE

It was a summer day in 1951, and I was 4. I was a on a drive with my parents and maternal grandfather and not paying much attention to where we were going. Then I spotted a large amusement park ahead. It was Revere Beach in Revere, Massachusetts.

I was surprised when we stopped and got out. The air was filled with the aroma of cotton candy, popcorn and roasted peanuts. There was a magical commotion of music, bells and vendors beckoning passers-by to try their luck. How wonderful!

I went on every ride. My grandfather rode on the gigantic roller coaster with me. I'll never forget the look on his face as we descended those slopes!

I couldn't believe how lucky I was to be the only kid of six in our family to get to go to this place. But even as I was having such a terrific time, something was not quite right. Every once in a while, I detected a sadness in the eyes of Grandfather and my parents.

I found out why after we left. We weren't going home. I was being taken to a hospital, called a TB sanatorium, where I was told I would have to stay for six months. My stay actually lasted a year and a half until I got well. I hadn't even known I was sick!

When I look back on that summer, I can't help but think of how brave my folks and grandfather were—how their hearts must have been breaking, even as they smiled. Their selfless gift was the nicest thing anyone has ever done for me.

PHILIP HUTCHINSON JR. • TROY, MAINE

FUN IN THE SUN. Sporting identical swimsuits, Maureen (on left) and her sister, Patricia, enjoyed the beach, rides and attractions at Rockaway's Playland in Queens, New York.

WILD RIDES. Vistors brace themselves as they take the plunge on a wooden coaster (above) at New Jersey's Palisades Amusement Park in 1955. At right: The American Eagle, a double-track roller coaster at Marriott's Great America in Gurnee Mills, Illinois, awaits its first passengers in 1980.

Riding a **FLYING COMET**

"No more Kiddy Land, Ma. I'm 8 years old now."

It was the summer of 1950, and we were headed for the amusement rides and other joys of Lincoln Park in North Dartmouth, Massachusetts.

As we topped the hill at Route 6 and Reed Road, Ma laughed and said, "OK, no more Kiddy Land."

My excitement was building. I could see the round windows of the ballroom, and all of a sudden, there it was—the biggest Ferris wheel in the world!

After we parked, Dad gave us money for tickets, and my sister and her friend went their own way. He then headed for the pavilion for some clam cakes and beer while Ma and I took off for the rides.

I hoped to go on the train ride first, one of my favorites. But instead she led me straight for—oh, no, it couldn't be—The Comet, which was the biggest roller coaster. I protested that I was only 8, but Ma said, "Don't worry. You can handle it."

Then I saw the sign, with a cutout body of a boy, that read "You must be this tall to ride." I thought I was safe then, but arms from behind picked me up so my feet weren't touching the ground and my head moved above the sign.

Before I could protest again, Ma had pushed me into the car, pulled down the bar to hold me in, and told me to hold on. I thought, *Of all the moms in the world, I have to get one who likes roller coasters!*

When we came to the sign at the crest of the first downhill run, all it said was "Last chance." Before Ma could grab me, I slid down between the seat and the front of the car, closing my eyes as tight as I could.

It was like falling off the edge of a cliff staight down. With the noise, the speed and the car shaking so much, I hoped I would never be this scared again. Compared to the first drop, the rest of the ride was much less terrifying.

When the ride came to a stop and I tried to get out of the car, Ma pulled me back down and said that unitl I could sit up straight and look over the first drop, we were going to stay on the coaster.

It took me five more trips before I could do that. We rode a total of seven times, the last time because I wanted to! I was no longer afraid of the big coaster.

My sister and father couldn't believe I had gone on The Comet. And when I found out that I was the only kid in my class who had ever been on Lincoln Park's biggest coaster, I decided I wasn't mad at Ma anymore. I felt proud.

Ma is gone now, and so are the Lincoln Park amusements, but I'll always remember my first ride on a high-speed Comet.

GENE BARBERO • HAMPTON, VIRGINIA

King of Coasters

My first ride on a fast, wild roller coaster like the one above was at Coney Island amusement park in Cincinnati, Ohio. In the split second just before the long, terrifying plunge, I prayed, "Please let me make it, and I promise to never ride a coaster again." Like many promises, it was soon broken!

FRANK FLORENCE • BUTLER, KENTUCKY

Lincoln Road and Washington Avenue Business Section, Miami Beach, Fla.

TEXAS

Connecticut

Fresh Buttered POP CORN

HOT ROASTED PEANUTS

CHAPTER 6

Life's a BEACH

What better way to escape life's hectic pace than with a shoreside getaway, where all you need is a bathing suit, a beach towel and a patch of sugar-white sand?

"Every weekend, my father took our family to the New Jersey shore," writes Margaret Peters Mortimer of Philadelphia, Pennsylvania. "Father went deep-sea fishing in the Atlantic Ocean while we girls would spend the day bathing in the ocean, sitting on the beach and having fun on the boardwalk.

"One time as Mother and I said goodbye to him, my sister dove off the dock and quickly came running back as the water was too choppy to swim.

"The fishermen usually came back around 4 p.m., but as we waited past that time, we grew anxious.

"They finally arrived, looking very haggard, and told us all about a violent nor'easter that had come up and almost capsized the boat!

"Wives and husbands who had been on the boat were weeping and embracing. One man knelt and prayed. Father then added that while all this was going on, he was on his hands and knees, too—looking for his teeth!

"This was a beach trip to remember—the day our ever-cheerful dad washed away our fears and gave us a good laugh."

We're happy to say the beachy-keen stories on the pages that follow will provide smooth sailing into the past without jarring out any teeth. Share in all the fun when the ocean lovers of yesteryear flocked to sun-soaked sandy beaches.

POINT PLEASANT PORCH-SITTERS. Author (in front) and her friends rented a cottage in New Jersey in 1935. They enjoyed the quiet of the shore and the sounds of the Big Bands at the pavilion.

Beach Cottage Vacation
SIGNALED FREEDOM

A trip with seven friends to the Jersey shore in the '30s promised excitement.

AMELIA WILLIAMS • FEASTERVILLE, PENNSYLVANIA

The Great Depression was winding down when I was a high school senior, but we still couldn't spend money frivolously.

As a result, seven friends and I organized monthly moneymaking activities throughout our senior year and saved diligently, planning a vacation together after we graduated.

When school ended in our hometown of West Orange, New Jersey, we pooled our money and were thrilled to discover we had enough to rent a cottage for two weeks at the Jersey shore!

Our dream cottage in Point Pleasant was on a narrow walkway that ran all the way to the end of the boardwalk.

In those days, we would never have been allowed to go without a chaperone. Luckily, the parents of one of our group employed a widow with a 6-year-old son. She agreed to go if she could take him.

When one girlfriend and I arrived at our little cottage, everyone else was there, and our chaperone had purchased our groceries. Our chattering and giggling reached a crescendo before we changed into bathing suits and headed for the beach.

Basking in Carefree Days

After securing a place on the sand with our beach blankets, I realized how tired I was. I flopped down and let the hot sun lull me into drowsiness. I was relaxed, yet I had a pervasive feeling of uncertainty—I realized I had never been this unsupervised.

On most nights, we all went dancing at Jenkinson's Pavilion. We loved the music of Big Bands with the tenor sax sound that was so popular then.

At midnight, we returned to the cottage and went to bed. When the talk of boys finally subsided, it got very quiet. While drifting off to sleep, I listened to the sound of the ocean slapping the shore as the tide came in. I still love that sound.

One morning, I woke up very early and tiptoed out onto our wooden porch. I could see the ocean and the boardwalk and a few people walking and riding bikes.

I put on a bathing suit and coverall and walked down to the beach. The sand was cool under my feet as it squeezed up between my toes. It was hard to walk in the sand. I went to the water's edge and walked a long way before I stopped to drink in the stillness. The quiet was broken only by the cawing of seagulls and the sound of the ocean waves.

A Wave of Realization

The water sparkled in the early morning sunlight. It was very beautiful and peaceful. Somewhere on that beachfront, I left the giddy high school girl behind and became an adult. As I slowly walked back to the cottage, I knew I would have to come back here again.

We did return for two more vacations before marriage, careers and families broke apart our little group. When we closed the cottage door for the last time, I was saddened by the sense of finality and the ending of such a fun and exciting phase of my life.

Last summer, I visited Point Pleasant for the first time in 60 years. I was thrilled when I saw many of the same boardwalk attractions were still there, seemingly unchanged. Jenkinson's Pavilion looked the same as ever, and I longed to hear the swing and sway of a Big Band.

I walked to the end of the boardwalk and looked to my left, and there it was—the same little cottage where I had spent so many carefree days!

I felt a keen excitement when I looked at it. I just wish I had withstood the ravages of time as well as that seemingly fragile little house.

UMBRELLAS GALORE
During my teen years, we would go to the beach at Galveston, Texas. We could always count on lots of colorful umbrellas and much laughter with good buddies. My, how we loved the sights and sounds of a special day at the beach!

VERNICE GARRETT · TEXAS CITY, TEXAS

Long Island Kids Loved
HOT TIMES ON THE SAND

Summers on Long Island in the '30s were scorchers. There were no backyard pools or air-conditioned homes in our neighborhood, so we kids found relief by spraying each other with the garden hose—or by playing on the sympathies of our parents and pleading for a trip to Jones Beach.

A drive to the ocean was relatively inexpensive, especially when families were willing to share cars. Excitement would mount as we crossed the Great South Bay and caught the first glimpse of the ocean beyond the barrier beach. What conditions lay ahead at the shore? Would we find a rough surf or gentle swells?

Don't Forget the Tide

Usually, we arrived early to stake out a good spot. Being too close to the surf could lead to soaked belongings if you forgot about an incoming tide.

The beach was always a medley of sights, sounds and smells. But for me, the sounds remain the most memorable. There was the roar of the surf, shouting swimmers and a constant babble of voices. The new portable radios kept "sleeping" fathers abreast of doings at Ebbets Field or the Polo Grounds—or the actions of the Yankees!

Often, above the din of surf and voices, a piston-banging biplane passed overhead, towing a banner touting "Johnson's All-White for All-White Shoes." Or a skywriter, engine droning, scrolled a smoky "J-e-l-l-o" or "P-e-p-s-i" for the audience below.

The beach seemed to produced big appetites—Mother said it was the clean salt air. Before long, sandwiches and thermoses were unpacked.

Sometimes, a special treat was in order. That meant a quick trot over the hot sand to the pavilion, where a vendor was ready to tempt our sea-air appetites. Five cents brought a juicy hot dog; for another nickel, we could add Mello-Roll ice cream.

The sand near the pavilion was cool and felt great on our bare feet. But soon we'd have to prance back across the scorching sand to the umbrella's shade.

We were always ready for another swim, but unfortunately, some "health expert" had convinced all mothers that no child should swim for at least an hour after eating. So we suffered, counting off the minutes until we were released!

As the afternoon waned, we layered Unguentine or Noxzema on our salt- and sun-saturated skin. Before long, the crowd began to stir, indicating that departure time was approaching.

Time to Pack Up

Adults shook out the beach blankets, picked up toy pails and shovels, and took down the umbrellas. They brushed sand off kids who, reluctant to leave, watched the last of their sand castles wash out with the incoming tide.

Teenagers took a final plunge, while the shell collectors packed up their treasures.

With kids in tow, the parents funneled into the dank tunnel leading to the parking lot. Then it was off across the causeway for the roasting, traffic-tossed ride home.

Now, as I look back on those days, Jones Beach seems the perfect symbol of an age of innocence. Its carefree, relaxing atmosphere allowed people to put aside Depression worries and forget the overseas war talk then beginning to proliferate.

The rest of the world could seek its own destiny on those sunny summer afternoons in the '30s. For us, they were a time to play and enjoy our dreams.

GEORGE SMITH • AVON, NEW YORK

BEACH BUDDIES. George Smith, second from left, and three of his little friends took in the sun and surf at Jones Beach back in July of 1935. A wonderful way to beat summer's heat, the beach was a hit with kids of all ages!

BEACH WAS THE BEST

As soon as school was out in the '50s, we started planning for our glorious annual one-week stay at Windy Hill Beach, South Carolina.

The beach was only 30 miles from our home in Tabor City, North Carolina. But to my two younger sisters and me, it was a world away.

We took along almost everything we needed in the Hudson. Our mother thought groceries were more expensive at the beach, so we loaded the car down with food. A truck tire inner tube that we used for floating in the ocean was tied to the roof of the car.

Mother was not a traveler and would only go as far as the beach or to visit her family in Branchville. I was in eighth grade before we went to the mountains of North Carolina.

At Windy Hill Beach, we stayed in a cottage an uncle had built. It had a huge screen porch where we ate, slept and spent many fun hours reading or playing the card game Authors.

It was a quiet and safe place in the '50s. We were allowed to go to the beach by ourselves, and Mother gave each of us a quarter for a foot-long hot dog and a bottle of pop at Moony's.

To give you an idea of Moony's atmosphere, the owner had a picture of himself framed in a toilet seat! But Moony's hot dogs were the best. I consider myself a hot dog lover, and none has ever compared. Moony made his hot dogs "all the way." That means the wiener, probably a cheap one, was covered with ketchup, mustard, onions, chili and some slaw.

Another reason we loved the beach was that we were allowed to break many of the usual rules. Our parents were strict, but the week se spent at the beach was an exception.

At Windy Hill, we could stay up as late as we wanted. I was a born night owl, so staying up late and reading was my thing.

Several years ago, my youngest sister told me what she loved most about those carefree weeks at the beach was being able to drink all the Cokes she wanted.

We were even allowed to ride on the running boards of the Hudson, a definite no-no at home.

We took full advantage of the relaxation of the rules. (In later years, our parents denied they ever let us get away with such behavior.)

I've traveled a great deal since those days, but

PICTURE PERFECT. Sisters Gayle (above, from left), Kitty and Sue Kelly posed for Dad in 1947 at Windy Hill Beach. In 1954, Hurricane Hazel destroyed the pier behind them, but Gayle still has the camera (center photo) Dad used to take the picture.

no vacation has ever compared to those with my parents and sisters at Windy Hill Beach.

My parents and youngest sister have passed away. In 1954, Hurricane Hazel destroyed the pier at Windy Hill Beach. My uncle's cottage is still there, although it looks smaller.

But those summers of long ago are forever in my mind—and I can still taste the hot dogs at Moony's.
GAYLE KELLY GARRISON • PLEASANT HILL, CALIFORNIA

WHAT A **SAND BLAST!**

Three race fans motored to Daytona for the final "500" on the beach.

LYNN CASTLE • BOONE, NORTH CAROLINA

On a Friday afternoon in February of '58, I headed to Florida with my younger brother, Steve, and our friend Bob Greer to see the last Daytona 500 auto race run on the beach.

In my new Chevrolet Impala convertible, it was a long trek from our home, high in the Blue Ridge Mountains of Boone, North Carolina, to Florida by way of two-lane roads. For two 19-year-olds and a 16-year-old, this was high adventure.

It was well after midnight when we arrived in Daytona. All the hotel and motel rooms for miles around were full, so we joined a crowd of people camping on the beach. Rolled-up quilts on the sand served as our sleeping bags.

We mountain boys had never seen the Atlantic Ocean and knew nothing about the tides. A few hours later, we woke up when the rising water started splashing our feet.

It wasn't until the sun came up that we saw as many as 200 people camping around us. From looking at the assortment of people and the lack of actual camping equipment, it must have been impromptu. Most were young male racing fans who found it easy to rough it for a few hours.

In those days, before fast-food joints were common, we packed our own supplies—homemade pimiento cheese, deviled eggs, a 5-gallon milk can of water, and cans of Vienna sausage and Beanee Weenee.

We also brought eggs and bacon, but the wind kept whipping up the flame on our Coleman stove, eventually igniting the bacon grease. This caused Steve to dump both the food and the skillet into the sand.

We made do with a makeshift breakfast from a nearby gas station's offerings. Even now, we laugh at our race-weekend breakfast of Fig Newtons and orange juice, a combination sure to lock your jaws with every bite.

On Saturday, Daytona was teeming with fast cars and excited race fans. Spontaneous drag races broke out at nearly every stoplight.

At night, a few daredevil drivers raced up the wide, flat beach, seeing only as far as their headlights would illuminate. Others simply cruised through town, showing off their vehicles.

We had left harsh winter weather in Boone, so I was determined to take down the top and show off my convertible. It was a little chilly even in Daytona, so we rode around with the top down and the heater running.

On Sunday, after paying $2 for a ticket and 75 cents for a program, spectators created an infield by parking by the sea oats and palmetto bushes that separated the highway from the beach. We all sat on the hoods of our cars, happily watching the race.

As is still true today, the Blue Angels did a flyover before the race started. Like many people there, we boys had never seen a jet up close, much less hear one, so the scream of the Blue Angels zooming low over the ocean was a shock. Many of the spectators hit the sand and covered their heads, but after the shock of the first pass, we were fascinated. I used more than half the exposures on my Brownie 110 box camera just trying to get a snapshot of the planes.

Soon the stock cars were racing over the spots where we'd been sleeping just a few hours earlier. Each 4.1-mile lap of the race ran south for 2 miles on a closed stretch of Highway A1A and a couple of miles along the beach, connected by turns of banked sand pushed up by a bulldozer.

There was no public-address system, so all the spectators knew about the position of the racecars was what they could see. A few fans ran back and forth across the dunes between the sand and the highway to watch the cars coming and going.

As soon as Paul Goldsmith took the checkered flag that afternoon, the thousands of race fans lining the beach got into their cars and loosely organized into eight to 10 parallel lanes, driving up the beach to connect with A1A.

We drove all night, finishing the 600-mile, 14-hour trip to Boone just in time for Bob and me to return to our Monday morning jobs and Steve to return to his classes at Cove Creek High School.

We didn't think about the historical significance of seeing that last race on the sand. We've seen a few 500 events at the Daytona Speedway and watched the rest on TV, but they can't compare to the thrill and adventure of seeing beach-racing stock cars on a magical weekend in 1958.

BEACHCOMBERS. Before the stock cars' tires dug into the sand (opposite page), Lynn Castle captured the Blue Angels (center and bottom photos above) on film. Castle's new '58 Chevy (top photo) had just 300 miles on it when the boys left home. Their plan was to find Daytona, then turn left to find the beach and the race.

Bathing Beauties

NOT TAKEN FOR GRANITE. "At the end of the school year in 1940, the big event was a picnic at the old swimming hole," writes Avis Grant (above, second from right) of Farmington, Maine. "We felt the quarry in North Jay, Maine, was special because the granite for Grant's Tomb had been cut there." Right: Joan Wilson of Huntington Beach, California, visited nearby Laguna Beach with daughter Stephanie, 9 months, in 1948. "It was our vacation place for years, as we loved the ocean," Joan says. "In years to come, another daughter and a son also enjoyed this spot."

BEACHSIDE FOOD TRUCK. "The vendor in this photo reminds me of a local character we called 'the peanut man,' who would station his pushcart on our main street many years ago," says Mary Ryan of Cyclone, Pennsylvania. "The tantalizing aroma of those hot roasting peanuts, which were only a nickel a bag, was almost impossible to resist."

LOUNGING BY THE POOL. "This group lounging by the pool brings back memories of our trips to the shore to swim," says Lyla St. Louis of Freeport, Maine. "A group of us neighborhood kids always went together. One day someone's dog accompanied us, and while we were all out in the water, we looked up to see that dog striking off across the sand, dragging a string of hot dogs that was supposed to have been our lunch! You can be sure that old dog never went with us again."

SWIMSUIT ISSUE. The newspaper in Hobbs, New Mexico, ran this photo of sunbathers at the country club in 1949, says Betsy McDaniel Young (left), now of San Diego, California. The others are Velma Wise, Barbara Wise and Jo Ann Roush.

HOME AWAY FROM HOME for Dorothy (at right) was the Goodbar Guest House, where she waited to meet up with friends Betty (above) and Betty's husband, Cedric (not pictured).

MINNESOTA TO MIAMI

Did I dare to stay here alone? A week ago, I'd left the frigid cold of Minnesota to meet my dear friend Betty in Miami Beach. But now I was here in Florida and she wasn't.

"You can do it," I said to myself. "You've dreamed for years of seeing Miami Beach—now you're going to do just that!"

Betty and her husband, Cedric, a Navy airman, were moving to Miami, where Ced's squadron was being transferred. She'd invited me to visit, but I'd had to leave Minnesota earlier than planned, and Betty and Ced were still in transit. I had no way of telling her about my change in plans.

Making the best of it, I got on the bus and headed south, calling home every chance I got to check with Mother and to see if Betty had called. I was 20 years old and had never traveled far from Minnesota.

A Leisurely Drive into Spring

I found plenty of chances to call. Buses had to obey the lower wartime speed limits and stopped often. We made stops in Milwaukee, Chicago, Indianapolis, Cincinnati and Chattanooga.

As the bus rolled along, I saw spring developing. There were leaves on the trees, and fragrant lilacs were in bloom.

A variety of interesting people rode the bus back in 1944 (there was an unwritten rule that trains were reserved for servicemen). But as we drove farther south, most of the passengers were servicemen going on furlough or returning to their bases.

By the time we made it to Chattanooga, it was hot and I was tired. I called Mother, but there was still no word from Betty. Mother reminded me Betty's aunt and uncle, Helen and Clyde, lived in Chattanooga and encouraged me to call them. I did. They treated me like a princess for four days.

I stayed in their daughter's bedroom (she was at college). We toured the city, shopped, dined out, rode a steamboat and took a tram ride to the top of Lookout Mountain. Clyde and Helen's generosity and hospitality greatly enriched my trip.

That goodwill continued when I left Chattanooga. Clyde was part owner of a bus line, and he treated me to a ride from Chattanooga to Jacksonville on a new bus that featured a lavatory, a vending machine and a steward who gave us information about the countryside as we rode along.

It was dark when we reached Jacksonville. I bid goodbye to my luxury bus and boarded a much less lavishly appointed model that was headed for Miami.

I slept, awakening as we neared Daytona Beach, where the road followed the coastline. I stared wide-eyed at the palm trees, the wide white sand beaches and the gorgeous flowers that lined the highway.

I arrived in Miami Beach alone, but I was determined to make the best of it. Thanks to Helen and Clyde, I still had most of my money. I took a room at the Breakers Hotel on 24th Street for $5 a day.

The room was huge, with wicker furniture, bamboo blinds and open windows that let in the salty breeze. The door opened onto a boardwalk that led to a private beach.

It was all wonderful, but I couldn't shake the sad feeling that I had no one with whom to share this paradise. Then I decided there was no use moping. I changed into my swimsuit, headed to the ocean and jumped into the breakers. There's no thrill quite like that first swim in the Atlantic Ocean!

As I was relaxing in the sun after my swim, I heard a phone ring. On the beach? The phone was mounted on a pole, I learned—and the call was for me! It was Mother!

"Betty is in Miami!" she said. I dashed right to my room to call Betty at the number that Mother had given me.

Within an hour, Betty was at my hotel, where we both shrieked with joy, then hugged and cried with relief at finally finding one another.

An Enjoyable Reunion

I then went to Miami, where Betty and Ced had rented a room at the Goodbar Guest House, a block from Biscayne Bay Park.

Ced was on the base most of the time, so Betty and I shopped for souvenirs and enjoyed excellent food at restaurants where the Office of Price Administration had frozen the prices. (A complete dinner with beverages cost around $1!)

We went to the movies, took an excursion to see homes of the wealthy, and talked and laughed until we were exhausted. One night around midnight, overcome with hunger, we pulled on clothing over our pajamas and ran a block to the hamburger stand.

I'd arrived on Monday and had to leave by Saturday. But the memories of my short stay in Miami are so engraved in my mind that there were few surprises when I recently reread my old diary from the trip.

There was suspense, surprise, laughter and dazzling scenery, all while making friends and gaining pen pals. God must have sent a flock of guardian angels to keep me safe during all my adventures. I will always be thankful.

DOROTHY FOSS • ST. PAUL, MINNESOTA

D. C. 62—Lincoln Road and Washington Avenue Business Section, Miami Beach, Fla.

POSTCARDS FROM THE PAST. The colorful cards Dorothy Foss brought back from Florida remind her of the fun she had on the beaches there.

> ❝ She walked on, comforted by the surf, by the one perpetual moment of beach-time, the now-and-always of it. ❞
>
> —William Gibson

SUN BUDDIES. Author Virginia Chamberlin (right) frolics in the surf with Barbara in 1936. Right: "This is me with my parents, Adele and George Behsman, on the Asbury Park beach in 1928 New Jersey," says Selene von Bartheld of River Edge. "What I recall most is being hot and sweaty and the itchy wool suit inching up little by little. Of course, the rubber bathing slippers just completed the outfit."

MISHAPS AND MORE
LED TO FUN IN THE SUN

UNSUITABLE ATTIRE

My neighbors, the Flaggs, were like second parents to me, taking me on vacations as a companion to their daughter Barbara.

In 1939, they rented a cottage on the Connecticut shore. This was the year clothing manufacturers began experimenting with bathing suits actually made of rubber.

A pretty girl came strolling down the beach and waded into the water. Soon she started yelling for help. It seemed her rubber bathing suit had split right down the middle.

Mr. Flagg ran for a towel and brought the girl back to shore.

I'll bet that pretty girl never bought another suit like that one.

VIRGINIA CHAMBERLIN • CORONA, CALIFORNIA

WHAT A CLIFF-HANGER!

My friends Wally, Frank and I graduated from high school in Campbell, California, in 1917. Before starting classes at Stanford University, we thought it would be fun to spend a few days on the beach at Santa Cruz, 30 miles away through the mountains.

Wally's dad agreed to let us use his 1916 Overland for the trip. We started at about 8 a.m. and had soon made the 5 miles to Los Gatos. From there, the highway was just a crooked, narrow gravel road climbing up to the summit and down the other side.

After we'd fixed the second of two flats, the car stopped. The problem turned out to be a leaking float in the vacuum tank, which fed gas to the engine. We closed the hole with chewing gum, which held for a few miles and then had to be replaced.

About 10 miles from Santa Cruz, we skidded on some loose gravel and the car wound up hanging on the side of a cliff!

Eventually, we found a man with a truck who said he knew just what to do. He cut down a tree about 20 feet high and trimmed off the branches. Then he opened both rear doors of the car, ran the tree through and chained both sides of the car frame to the tree.

The three of us hung on the long end of the tree, which protruded out over the road. Our weight was enough to keep the car from rolling down into the ravine as the man expertly pulled it up onto the road with his truck.

He then towed us into Santa Cruz to a garage, where we had the leaky float soldered. Afterward, we were able to enjoy our stay at the beach—even though it had taken us an entire day to travel 30 miles.

ED VANDERGON • BUFFALO, MINNESOTA

BREAKING DOWN IN PARADISE

One of my favorite memories happened on the way to Monterey, California, from our home in Burbank for a two-week vacation. We were in our first new car, a 1956 Chevrolet station wagon.

Dad took a wrong turn, and we wound up in the little town of Cambria Pines. To make matters worse, a clogged oil line led to a broken crankshaft. We were stuck until new parts arrived by bus from Pasadena. As it turned out, though, my brother, my friend Tom and I had more fun in that little town than we had on most of our other vacations. We climbed the rocks by the ocean, explored the tidal pools, swam, built sand castles and hiked along the stream near our motel.

We've been back several times. But we'll never forget that summer of 1956, the wrong turn and the broken crankshaft that ended up giving us such a great vacation.

FRED BRENDEL • TUJUNGA, CALIFORNIA

BATHING CAPS

Whenever we went to the beach, if the boys wanted to swim in the ocean, they had to wear their sailor caps so I could quickly and easily see where they were among the other swimmers. In this photo, taken in June of 1957, are (from left) Mike, 8; Pat, 6; and Joe, 3.

GRACE MICHAEL • ELLICOTT CITY, MARYLAND

OFF-ROAD ADVENTURE. Although they didn't plan to go off-roading on their 1917 drive to the beach, Ed Vandergon and his pals managed a short "side trip." See Ed's memory at left.

Memories of a
MAGICAL PLACE

Pleasant summer weekends at a creekside bungalow still swim in her head.

MARILYN HUMMEL RACK • SINKING SPRING, PENNSYLVANIA

There were many Friday afternoons in the summers of the 1940s when I waited very impatiently for Uncle Benny to come home from his job as a trolley car conductor.

Those were the weekends I would spend with him and Aunt Ruth at their bungalow along Maiden Creek, near Reading, Pennsylvania, a magic place from my childhood.

Off we would go in their old Dodge, with me comfortably seated between them. We always stopped before we got to the bungalow for Uncle Benny to buy a 25-cent block of ice for the icebox.

Then up the pike we'd go until we turned onto a gravel road and up a hill. Soon we'd pass under a concrete arch that proudly proclaimed "Maiden Creek Estates" and a row of tidy bungalows would come into view. Ours was the third on the left.

The bungalow had three rooms. There was a tiny kitchen with a kerosene stove, a cupboard and the icebox. The front room held a big table where we had our meals and the adults played pinochle in the evenings. A large bedroom had studio couches that could be turned into beds, and an old Victorian dresser that held a gramophone. Many throw pillows covered with gaily printed feed-sack fabric adorned the couches.

Before too long, neighbors began a promenade along the walkways in front of the bungalows. We'd join in the greetings and listen to the latest gossip until it was suppertime.

Supper was often communal. It was always more like a picnic, thankfully, with no pot roast, peas or that dreaded liver!

Afterward, a contented mood took over as kerosene lamps were lit and the fireflies winked in the darkening sky.

The bungalow was near the creek, so the nights were cool and our sleep was sound.

There was always a great breakfast, usually with pancakes. Sometimes, an early-rising fisherman would share his catch of "sunnies," which Aunt Ruth would roll in cornmeal and fry to a delicious crisp.

We kids liked to swim in the "crick" and row our boat. But this required adult supervision, and we wanted more crick time than the adults were willing to give us.

I couldn't understand why Aunt Ruth would rather listen to Rudy Vallee on the gramophone than swim with us kids, or why Uncle Benny preferred listening to the Phillies on his portable radio to rowing our ancient boat down the stream.

Unfortunately, Uncle Benny died young and the bungalow was sold. Half a lifetime later, I went back for a visit. The bungalow looked the same as I remembered. But it seemed much smaller. The magic was gone but the memories live on!

Perfect Day at the Beach

One of the best things about growing up in Southern California was being close the beach. It was an hour's drive from our home in Rosemead.

Besides playing in the gentle surf, we had sand castles to build, shells to collect and sand crabs to dig for.

The dark-haired boy in the picture below is Billy. The tall girl and blond boy are his cousins, Shirley and Bobby. I'm the little girl on the left.

We're all shivering in the photo, having just come form the water. It appears Billy is yelling at me, an ordinary occurrence since he bossed me around constantly. You see, it was my mission to tag along after these bigger and older kids, trying desperately to fit in. I remember having a good time the day we made this trip to Belmont Shores, near Long Beach.

Billy's mom, "Aunt" Marian, was my mother's landlady and dear friend. Marian had an ironclad rule that kids couldn't go back in the water until an entire hour after eating.

SCAVENGERS. The author (left)—"Patsy or Patty Ann, depending if the other kids really wanted to get my goat"—is with friends Bobby, Billy and Shirley.

On this very afternoon, we decided to spend our downtime in pursuit of empty pop bottles, as each brought a 2-cent refund. We scattered out and scoured the beach for discards while seagulls dipped and circled overhead.

We worked our way toward the little store down the beach and soon had more bottles than we could carry. I was sent back to where the grown-ups were to fetch one of the old blankets we used at the beach.

It seemed like it took forever as my short legs churned over the hot sand. Mixed with far-off calls of other kids playing on the beach, I could hear both Billy and Shirley yelling, "Hurry, Patsy. Run!"

Grabbing the blanket and starting back, I felt the moment crystallize—the sun, the sparkling sea, the faintly tarry-salty aroma in the air. The surf rolled in with a muffled roar, churning toward the beach in a series of small waves that stretched out past the end of the pier.

Doesn't Get Much Better

Then came a realization—the big kids needed me. I belonged!

Using the blanket as a sling, with each kid holding a corner, we carried the bottles.

Before long, the sand's action, aided by the weighty cargo, wore a hole in the blanket and bottles began to work their way out.

At the store, we turned to discover what was left of the blanket and a trail of empty bottles stretching back as far as the eye could see. It took quite a while to retrieve them all.

Then we discovered the store owner wouldn't accept the sandy bottles. He directed us to the house outside, and Bobby handed Billy each bottle to rinse and fill.

Shirley took each one and emptied it, then gave it to me to place in one of the wooden crates lined up against the building. There must have been over 100 bottles.

Flushed with our victory, we returned to the grown-ups with the money we'd earned. They were impressed, but we did have to endure some scolding over the ravaged blanket.

On the way home, we stopped at Curry's ice cream store and I traded my share of the money for their famous mile-high strawberry cone.

It was a perfect end to a great day at the beach.

PATRICIA DOOLITTLE • APTOS, CALIFORNIA

Trip to 'the Shore'
WAS A DELIGHT!

When this family headed for the beach, it was time to get out the rubber shoes.

JUNI DUNKLIN • SANDERSVILLE, GEORGIA

Long before the Great Depression, my family's annual summer trip from Baltimore to the shore at Atlantic City was a magnificent outing that kept us children excited for days beforehand.

My sister, Edwina, and I (at right with our governess, Florie) made separate piles of things we were going to take. We each had inflatable rubber swimming rings—mine was an alligator; Edwina's was a camel. Our black cotton swimsuits had to be examined for holes, which were promptly sewn.

Daddy had a white web belt that he wore over his one-piece suit. I recall this belt was bleached in the sun for days before the trip.

Mother's rubber parasol had to be wiped and aired. It was black to match her two-piece swimsuit, which had long sleeves and ruffles around the neck and pantaloon legs with frills at the cuff. Even her swim cap had frills.

Caps Were "Snappy"

Edwina and I also had snug-fitting caps to protect our ears. I can still hear the loud *snap!* as Mother fitted them over our heads. We all wore swim shoes, too. Mother's matched her black stockings, Daddy's were large and looked like rubbers, and ours were rubber and canvas, and filled with water when we tried to swim.

Another exciting part of the adventure was riding to the beach in Daddy's big Hupmobile. We sat in the back with a dustcover over our laps, having fun with our beloved Florie.

Daddy wore his driving cap, enormous goggles, and a long scarf over his driving coat. Mother had a generous veil over the wide brim of her hat, a long coat like Daddy's and a dustcover on her lap. These covers were to protect us from the dirt and bugs that flew about us as we tooled along at a thrilling 30 mph.

On the way, we played a game to see who could smell the salt air first. When the wonderful tangy aroma reached our waiting nostrils, my sister and I would squeal in excitement. We used to wonder if the people who lived at the ocean all year ever got enough of that intriguing smell.

When we finally arrived at the beach, we kids would leap out and race across the sand to be the first to put a toe in the water. Mother and Daddy would look on indulgently as we splashed in delight, then call us back to help unpack the car and move into our rented cottage.

Splashes and a Scare

One year we arrived at the beach a few weeks earlier than normal. As usual, Edwina and I quickly plunged into the waves, but all at once, my sister was gone!

Standing in ankle-deep water, I looked everywhere but couldn't see her. Florie came running toward me, calling out, "Where's Edwina? Where's Edwina?"

Just then, Edwina's head popped up several feet away and she began calling for help. Florie ran in and pulled both of us out of the water. "My poor babies, swimming in cold water!" she kept saying over and over.

Later, when we were bundled in towels and Mother had almost kissed us to pieces, Daddy explained that the cold water had probably given Edwina a cramp and then she'd gotten the breath knocked out of her when she'd doubled over in the waves.

Whatever actually happened, we were all grateful that things had turned out all right.

Our days on the beach were usually a lot more relaxing than that. I shall always treasure the memory of my family lolling on the warm sand— Mother with a book and Daddy with his cigar.

But that fond memory often comes with a wistful feeling—a wish that we could once again enjoy tooling along a narrow highway at a snail's pace or get so much pleasure out of a simple trip to the beach.

DOWN THE SHORE. New Jersey's crown jewel is its 130 miles of white sand beaches hugging the Atlantic coastline. This photo, taken sometime in the early 1900s, shows folks enjoying sand and surf on the famous Jersey Shore in Atlantic City.

◀ 1950

Two Ways to Play it Smart in the Sun!

Cool-Ray SUN GLASSES

American Optical COMPANY

> 66 *The seashore is a sort of neutral ground, a most advantageous point from which to contemplate this world.* 99
>
> —Henry David Thoreau

WEEKEND **AWAY**

Recently, my wife and I were taking advantage of the preseason rates at a motel in Ogunquit, Maine. As usual, I woke early, while Terry enjoyed sleeping in.

On this day, my early wanderings took me to Moody Beach. As I sipped coffee, my mind drifted back to our first visit to this beach in the early 1970s.

It was a month after our wedding. Our budget was paper-thin, and we were still trying to furnish our small one-bedroom apartment. The car we drove used more oil than gas, had four bald tires and was missing a spare.

But youth knows no fear. With $30 in our pockets, we bought four quarts of oil, gassed up and headed for Maine. Along with minimal clothing, we brought along a large pot, a rack from the oven, an old metal coffeepot, a jug of water, two cups and a few kitchen utensils.

Since Ogunquit charged a parking fee, we went straight to Moody Beach, which had free parking in a dirt lot. We walked the beach all day, ate nothing and lived on—love, of course.

In the late afternoon, we splurged and bought a small live lobster for Terry, a steak for me, two potatoes and a small jar of instant coffee. We gathered firewood, and as the sun set, we scooped a hole in the sand, put a few stones around the circle and started our fire. By the time the flames had produced coals, the moon was out.

With the potatoes in the coals, I boiled a pot of seawater for Terry's lobster. When the lobster started turning red, I put my steak on the rack. Wrapped in a blanket against the cool night air, we cuddled next to the fire and listened to the steak sizzle as sparks flew off to the sea.

After our meal, I pushed the soft sand into a hollow just big enough for two bodies wrapped in a blanket. With the stars above and the sound of the waves, we enjoyed the night.

The next morning, Terry, never really an outdoors person, asked, "Where's the bathroom?" When I pointed to the dunes, she said, "Oh, no—I can't!" In the end, nature overcame shyness.

Later, we walked 2 miles on the sand to Ogunquit and paid a dime each to shower in the bathhouse, then enjoyed our day.

Leaving the beach, I realized I had lost our little pouch, which held just enough cash for the tolls home. We spent an hour retracing our steps, but we found it!

When we got home, our humble place seemed like the Ritz.

JIM ORCUTT • SOUTH EASTON, MASSACHUSETTS

SUN, SAND AND SURF. Newlyweds Terry and Jim Orcutt spent a memorable vacation in Maine for just $30.

Strolls on the Beach

This photo of three friends happily skipping along the beach reminds me of walks I used to take with my boyfriend after a Sunday afternoon date. We didn't actually go swimming, but our clothes always got wet anyway from wading in the surf. When I was a teen, I thought the beach was the most romantic place in the world.

SYLVIA ROBERTS • ESCONDIDO, CALIFORNIA

"Life is either a daring adventure or nothing."
—Helen Keller

CHAPTER 7

Back**trackin'**

Motorists by the millions set out every year to see what awaits them on the open road. But if the view from behind the wheel is making you a little weary, there are other means of transport that offer as much adventure and excitement.

"When I was a boy, I was lucky enough to have parents who took me and my sister on many overnight train trips," says Allen Johnson of Chelsea, Alabama. "Dad was a Coca-Cola bottler, so most of our trips were from Birmingham, Alabama, to New York City or the east coast of Florida.

"It was a different world than the one viewed from an automobile. I'd see the backyard of a rural shack with a woman stirring an iron pot full of laundry—or, as the train slowed down pulling into a city, I might find myself looking through the window of a small flat at a family eating dinner.

"Lonely scenes of farmhouses huddled in the moonlight, or empty main streets in small country towns, made me feel all the more snug as I drifted off to sleep to the rhythmic swaying and *clackety-clack* of the wheels.

"There was excitement within the train, too. Excursions to the dining car involved pushing open heavy doors, then crossing shifting steel plates where a wave of noise made talking impossible."

Automobiles aren't the only way folks saw the sights. Here, read heartwarming stories from those who traveled the country on trains, buses, bicycles and canoes, as well as blimps and even roller skates!

RIDIN' THE INTERURBAN. J. Russell Calvert used many modes of transportation to get back home to Los Angeles, including an electric interurban train like the one pictured above. These trains were a popular means of commuter travel between cities in the United States and Canada from approximately 1900 to 1925. They were a hybrid of urban streetcars and traditional railroad trains.

'I Traveled 500 Miles in
18 HOURS ON $1.25'

As a boy of 15, he learned how compassionate some people can be.
J. RUSSELL CALVERT • TUSTIN, CALIFORNIA

In the summer of 1927, I was working at a remote boys' camp on the upper end of Echo Lake in the High Sierra of California. One evening in June, a forest ranger came across our lake in a motorboat. This was an unusual event, for we seldom saw visitors.

The ranger had come to deliver a note to me. It read, "Come at once. Your mother is failing fast. Aunt Nora."

I was devastated. Mother, a widow, had been ill for some time and was being cared for by her sister in Long Beach. That was more than 500 miles away. Somehow I had to get there—as quickly as possible!

The Journey Begins

The head of the camp looked at the handwritten scrap of paper and quickly said, "Get some things together. I'll take you down to the end of the lake."

We jumped in his speedboat and raced 3 miles to the other end of the lake. After docking, he drove me another 2 miles out to Highway 50 in his Studebaker convertible.

There he wished me good luck. "You'll need some money," he said, and handed me $75. That was quite a bundle back then!

I stood by the road with my thumb out, and a vegetable truck slowed to a stop. When I showed the driver my note, he said, "Hop in. I can take you as far as Placerville." That was 50 miles down the mountain. I was on my way!

It was 9 p.m. when I arrived at the Placerville bus depot. I was told there would be no more buses departing until morning.

I left the depot, determined to hitchhike farther.

Then I heard the sound of a train. Lugging my little valise, I wandered out back to find a steam engine and 10 freight cars, ready to go.

I found the train's engineer and showed him my note. Carrying passengers on a freight was strictly forbidden—but he motioned me aboard!

That train pulled into the Sacramento freight yard about 1 a.m. I thanked the engineer and made my way to the passenger station. The ticket agent told me the next train to Los Angeles was at 8:30 a.m.

I was too anxious to wait around. When I showed him my note, he suggested I try the airport. I hailed a cab and paid the driver 75 cents to take me there.

Stuck in Sacramento?

Unfortunately, there were no flights south until dawn. Frustrated, I sat down in the dark and tried to figure out what to do next. Then I heard the sound of an airplane engine warming up.

Walking to a hangar, I found a man checking over a two-seat biplane. Once again, I pulled out my note.

The pilot shook his head and explained that he was going only as far as Bakersfield, about 120 miles shy of my destination. Besides, he said, he wasn't licensed to carry passengers.

In desperation, I offered to pay him to take me to Bakersfield. He refused to take any money, but shrugged and said, "Aw, what the heck—I'll take a chance if you will." I climbed into the plane and off we flew!

Dawn was breaking as we touched down in Bakersfield. The pilot made some phone calls and found a friend who was driving to Los Angeles in a few hours.

I hung around the airfield until the friend arrived to pick me up—in a Cadillac! He drove me all the way to the train terminal in downtown Los Angeles. There I bought a 50-cent ticket for the electric interurban train that would take me to Long Beach.

Just in Time

I arrived in time to spend some precious final hours with my mother. Two days later, she died in my arms.

That trip to Los Angeles is an experience I shall always treasure. Not only did I get to hold my dear mother one last time, I had quite an adventure getting there.

In 18 hours, I had ridden in a speedboat, a Studebaker, a vegetable truck, a steam-powered train, a taxi, an open-cockpit biplane, a Cadillac and an electric train, all for only $1.25.

Without the help of six compassionate people, I could never have covered those 500 miles in time to see my mother again. To them I will always be grateful. It was a lifelong lesson in how good some people— even total strangers—can be in times of need.

GRANDPA CONDUCTED
TRIP OF A LIFETIME

When I was born in October 1934, it was to be a grand occasion, as I would be the first child of an only daughter, Ida Peterson Haynes. Sadly, though, one day after I was born, my mother died, leaving Grandma and Grandpa Peterson to raise me.

Grandpa Charles was a tall man, 6-foot-4, and went by the name of Long Pete. He was soft-spoken and always willing to take care of me. We often went to the park, where Grandpa played checkers with friends, and we went to the movies to see Roy Rogers, Hopalong Cassidy or the weekly serial.

Grandpa taught me to play pinochle, and I listened with wonder to the stories he told of coming west to Utah not long after the pioneers.

He was retired from the Southern Pacific Railroad and had a lifetime pass to travel on the railway whenever he wanted.

One day, Grandpa asked, "Michael, how would you like to go to New York City and see the Empire State Building and the Bronx Zoo?" *Wow!* The thought of a trip across America on a train was very exciting to a boy of 6.

Finally, the day arrived. I remember the smell of the steam locomotive and the size of the big train cars. Grandpa always had his railroad watch in his vest pocket, so we knew the departure was on time. The train started to move. The sound of the rails and the rocking of the cars are still vivid in my memory.

It took four days to travel from Ogden, Utah, to New York City. This meant that we would have to sleep on the train in a Pullman car. What an experience, lying in the upper berth of the sleeper! All that kept you from other passengers was a canvas curtain that had a zipper to keep it closed. All night long, I could feel the swaying of the car and hear the clickety-clack of the wheels as the train sped through the darkness. Once in a while, the train would cross a switch and make a loud noise.

Eating in the dining car was special. Each day at breakfast, lunch and dinner, a porter would come through to announce the opening of the dining car. He carried a chime that made a musical sound to announce meals. Even better was when the porter came by selling cheese sandwiches for 25 cents. I really enjoyed this treat.

We finally arrived in New York City, and I will never forget the massive Grand Central Station. This was the largest building I had ever seen. The hollow, echoing sounds inside were unique and special as announcements of train departures were sounded.

Grandpa and I went to the top of the Empire State Building and visited the Bronx Zoo. I still remember the smells of New York City, all the traffic and the throngs of people. After two days, we started the journey home.

I feel so blessed to have had a grandpa like Long Pete. His railroad watch has a special place in my heart. I will always be grateful that I could take the trip of a lifetime with him.

MICHAEL HAYNES • MEDFORD, OREGON

185:—DOWNTOWN SKYSCRAPERS, NEW YORK.

MAGNIFICENT MANHATTAN. The author had the trip of a lifetime exploring the skyscrapers and other sights in New York City with his grandpa, known as Long Pete (below).

NICE AND BRIGHT. Eileen Volk's graduation dress (at right) was spotless before her first train trip.

CALAMITY **ON A TRAIN**

CAUGHT IN THE ACT

I had two train adventures as a child, and I'm proud to say I survived both.

When I was 13, in 1929, I accompanied my grandmother on a trip to California.

After some time I got tired of sitting and looking out the window. So I decided to explore the train and ended up outside on a small deck at the end of the train.

All was well until I saw a porter. Thinking he'd make me get inside, I hid. I was soon surprised to discover that he'd locked the door and was even more surprised—and a little scared—when the train entered a tunnel.

After passing through the tunnel, the porter unlocked the door and I went straight to Grandmother. She was flabergasted, but after several handkerchiefs and "spit baths," I survived.

Five years before that, there was a train wreck two blocks south of my home. My mother, who was about to go shopping, told me in no uncertain terms to stay away from the wreck.

While she was in town that day, she bought two pictures of the wreck from a local photographer.

When she got home, she asked me who the little boy pictured on top of the boxcar was.

It was me!

GEORGE ELLIOTT • TECUMSEH, MICHIGAN

MEMORABLE FIRST RIDE

I took my first train ride in 1937 as a high school graduation present from my father (above). We lived in New Jersey, and he had to go to New York City for business.

One the day of the trip, I proudly donned my street-length white graduation dress, white hat and gloves—after all, I was going to the city, where ladies always wore hats and gloves.

Hearing the whistle as the train neared the station gave me chills; I had never been this close to a train before.

Father found room in the first car and gave me a seat facing forward so I wouldn't miss anything, and I enjoyed every minute.

Unfortunately, the weather that day sent the smoke from the coal-fired engine blowing directly at us. When we arrived in New York City, my dress was black and white, and my face looked like a coal miner's. I wanted to cry.

We took a cab to Dad's office, and the women helped clean me up and took me to lunch.

I enjoyed the day, but was happy to return to my hometown that night.

I can't remember if my mother had my dress dry-cleaned or washed, but I do know I threw my hat in the wastebasket.

EILEEN VOLK • STEWARTSVILLE, NEW JERSEY

HAPPY TRAILS. Frank and Edna Baur (at right in '47) took many trips along Route 66, including their very first Greyhound ride as a married couple.

Rollin', Rollin', Rollin'

BUSED TO THEIR HONEYMOON

Edna and I (above right) were married at 6:30 p.m. Sept. 11, 1947. I was 18 and in the U.S. Navy, and she was 16.

We crossed the Eads Bridge from East St. Louis, Illinois, to St. Louis, Missouri, to catch a Greyhound and travel Route 66 to Kingman, Arizona, for our honeymoon.

The toll collector on the bridge laughed at us. When we got to the bus station, we found a sign my younger brother had made on the back of our car. "Just married," it said. "Our moms said we could."

The bus driver, whose last name was Day, saw that we were newlyweds and let us on first to get any seats we wanted. We chose the first seat on the right-hand side.

Then five men got on the bus and took the first three rows behind the driver. They'd taken a three-week vacation and were headed home to California.

The first night, the men told every newlywed joke they could think of. We were embarrassed, but the other passengers enjoyed it.

We had breakfast in Tulsa, Oklahoma, and then got a new driver named Knight. The men continually asked Mr. Knight why he drove in the day and Mr. Day drove at night.

As a wedding present, I'd bought Edna a battery radio with a clamp so she could connect it to the window for better reception. The men would sing songs and I'd try to get them on the radio. When I did, they immediately started singing another song.

By the time we got to Kingman, the passengers were one big happy family. It was sad to leave our new friends, and we still think of them often.

FRANK BAUR • FLORISSANT, MISSOURI

BUS LINE GO-BETWEEN

When I was a college student, in the late 1930s and early '40s, I often rode the bus from Jefferson City, Tennessee, to my home in Etowah.

The Jefferson City bus station was in the Tallent drugstore owned by Jepp Tallent. The Etowah bus station was in the Tallent drugstore owned by Jepp's younger brother, Bruce.

Each brother gave me verbal messages to take to the other, such as "When are you going to pay me what you owe me?" or "I'm writing a check on your account. I hope you have enough money to cover it."

As beautiful as the scenery was on the trip, I most looked forward to the free Cokes I received from the brothers when I delivered the messages.

HELEN TULLOCK • DELANO, TENNESSEE

DAD TRADED TRAIN FOR A BUS

In 1946, my father, Ernest Denman, had just finished building a summer cottage on Lake Couchchiching, about 100 miles north of Toronto, Ontario.

Dad was eager for my mother, Adelaide, to see it, and I opted to go along. Since Dad was a railroad man, we met him at the train station after he worked half a day one Saturday. It was a very hot day, and everybody wanted to get out of the city.

Mom and I were able to get seats together, but Dad ended up in another coach. The train was old and had been pressed into service when the war was on. There was no air conditioning, and we stopped at every little town along the way.

When we got to Washago, our destination, we looked for Dad to help with the luggage, but he didn't appear. I did my best to carry all of our bags while Mom kept her eyes peeled for Dad.

Mom began to worry and asked the trainman where her husband was, not realizing that the man wouldn't know who her husband was.

After I explained the situation, they held the train to conduct a search. However, Dad definitely was not on board.

As the train pulled away, we wondered what to do next when we heard a shout and were astonished to see Dad running across a field toward us.

He had not had lunch and got off at an earlier stop to grab a bite, but the train left without him.

Dad got to a bus station and, luckily, a bus was getting ready to leave for the north, so he hopped on, arrving about the same time the train did.

GRACE DENMAN • PENDER ISLAND, BRITISH COLUMBIA

LET HIM BE!

Our family was part of the migration west during World War II. In the spring of 1945, Dad got a job in the Navy yard in Bremerton, Washington, and left our upstate New York home. We were to follow on the bus after he found housing.

It was late at night when my mother, three siblings and I boarded the bus. I was 8 years old at the time. As people started to sleep, I began to run up and down the aisle.

Soon, the driver began to lose his patience and asked me to go stretch out on the big long seat in the back.

The next thing I knew, a lady was poking my feet and I heard the driver say, "Lady, if you wake that kid up, you're going to walk!"

RICHARD SMITH • LYNNWOOD, WASHINGTON

TICKET TO RIDE. "In March of '62, my father, Arnold Leavitt (center), traveled by bus across the United States," says Virginia Wilson of Port Orange, Florida. "He'd bought the longest ticket the Trailways bus company had ever sold. The 23 sections made a strip 6 feet long! The manager, Mr. Moody (far right), and the driver (left) stood with him for a photo."

THE HONEYMOON
EXPRESS

Newlyweds' trip in a World War I Jenny was the adventure they never forgot.
HERTHA HILDEBRAND • DAVENPORT, IOWA

Thanks to a handsome boyfriend who flew his own World War I Jenny, 1924 (when I was sweet 16) was a memorable year! Ernie and I met in a gymnastics class and dated for two years. Even though Ernie gave me a diamond engagement ring, Father was reluctant to let us go out on a date. Ernie was a factory worker, and Father thought his girl "deserved better."

One Sunday Ernie came over in his family's Model T. Father wouldn't let us go for a ride together, so we glumly sat in the car talking.

"Let's elope!" I ventured. "Mother goes to her club Friday, so you can fly us to Chicago and we'll get married there." Ernie agreed and said he'd ask his boss for some time off.

That Friday, right after Mother left, I dashed about, packing some clothes in a cardboard case. (It had to be lightweight for "old Jenny"!)

I dressed in flying togs, but Ernie showed up in his best suit and tie. His boss had advised him to get married first, then fly off: "That way, if they catch ya, you're already married!"

Fearing Mother's return, we quickly went to Ernie's house. He'd confided in his mom that morning, so Mother Vogel helped me change into suitable wedding wear.

We drove across the Mississippi to Rock Island, Illinois, and were married at the Church of Peace. Our marriage license cost $2, and we gave the reverend $5.

Then we drove back to the Iowa side and Wallace Flying Field, where Jenny was waiting. Into the blue we flew as a honeymoon couple!

Since Jenny couldn't hold much fuel, we made a lot of landings along the way. It seemed like a fuel truck was always nearby when we touched down. (The drivers knew we needed gas.)

It took us two days to get to Chicago. We intended to land at a certain airfield, but when we flew over that city, we couldn't seem to find the airport.

Fuel was getting low when Ernie finally spotted a small open space near a cornfield. He took a chance, landing in some mud. A friendly farmer emerged from the corn, asking, "What's your trouble? Engine?"

"No," Ernie admitted sheepishly. "We can't find the airfield!"

The farmer knew a private field close by and notified them. Soon a four-engine plane flew low overheard and the pilot motioned for us to follow—but we were stuck in the mud!

Luckily the farmer had some long planks. Ernie lifted the plane as I pushed the planks under the wheels. We used the rest of the lumber for a makeshift runway and took off with our fingers crossed.

After reaching the airfield, we asked about a taxi. A friendly reporter overheard and offered to drive us into town to find a hotel.

On the way, I pointed out a brilliant sign advertising a hotel. "Are you sure?" the reporter asked. "That's the Edgewater Beach—and it's very expensive."

Ernie and I looked at one another and smiled. We were on our honeymoon, after all. "Why not?" we said.

When we drove up, the doorman stepped to the car and frowned at our oil-spattered faces.

> "**The world is a book, and those who do not travel only read one page.**"
> —St. Augustine

AIRBORNE HONEYMOON. Hertha and Ernie took a daring honeymoon flight to Chicago. They arrived home safely, as the paint job on Ernie's plane attests.

E. F. VOGEL.
HONEYMOON EXPRESS
1924

"You'll have to excuse this couple," our new friend explained. "They've just arrived in their own plane." We were escorted into that beautiful hotel just as a party of guests came down dressed for dinner. We wanted to hide!

After a shower and change of clothes, we found a quiet coffee shop. Both of us wondered what the folks back home thought about us running off.

All I'd left behind was a note asking the first one in our family to see the iceman to please ask him to save some ice for our box, too.

What Would Father Do?

Of course, Father was furious. He had my sister's husband drive him up to Clinton, Iowa, where he checked all the hotels. looking for us!

Meanwhile, Ernie and I enjoyed an exciting time in Chicago. We started for home on Monday afternoon and arrived at Wallace Field the next

day. Ernie's brother, Clifford, met us there and painted Honeymoon Express 1924 on the side of the airplane (above).

I was so relieved when my parents greeted us with open arms—they were just happy that we were safe.

Eventually Father learned to like Ernie, who was always willing to help with a project. After Father passed away in 1934, my aunt told me that he'd once remarked, "The one son-in-law I thought I wouldn't like turned out to be the best of all!"

Ernie and I had three children and shared 18 wonderful years together before he died. I'll be 90 soon and still live in the home we built in Davenport.

Today I'm blessed with my children, 14 grandchildren and 12 great-grandchildren, and the priceless memory of a romantic flying adventure that never fails to lift my spirits.

AIR SAILOR. George Broome (right) helped pilot a blimp like this one on a cross-country trip in 1955. Everything went well until the mountains loomed—and three men had to be left behind for the ship to make it.

'LOW AND SLOW'
WAS THE WAY TO GO

A blimp trip across America in 1955 gave this sailor a view of the country most folks never see.
GEORGE BROOME • TOMS RIVER, NEW JERSEY

When I enlisted in Naval Aviation in 1939, I chose lighter-than-air training as a way of honoring my late father. I was only 3 when he lost his life as a member of the crew of the ill-fated Navy dirigible *U.S.S. Shenandoah* in 1925.

During World War II, I piloted blimps doing anti-submarine duty with convoys leaving New York and in various stations in Brazil.

I have many fond memories of my 42 years of service as a Navy pilot. But one stands out—the blimp ride I took in 1955 from Lakehurst, New Jersey, to the naval station in Santa Ana, California.

A K-type Navy blimp was being transferred, and I was one of four pilots in a crew of 10, including two mechanics. Ground crews were also sent ahead with

a portable mast that anchored the blimp when we couldn't land at a naval lighter-than-air station.

Smooth Sailing

That type of blimp cruised at 50 to 60 mph, though headwinds or tailwinds could affect our speed greatly. The trip was scheduled to last for two weeks and would be part of our annual training in the Navy Reserves.

The K ship we flew was not rigid and had no internal framework. It was filled with helium, which is not flammable, like the hydrogen that ignited and destroyed the *Hindenburg*.

The first leg of our trip, from Lakehurst to North Carolina, was uneventful. Then it was on to Glynco, Georgia. From there we flew over the Okefenokee

Swamp. What an awesome sight that was from the air! Flying 200 feet up at about 300 mph, we were able to view what few people ever see on a commercial flight.

When we got to New Orleans, we had a little "engine trouble." As a result, we were grounded for some time. That gave us some free time to take in the sights along Bourbon Street.

The news of our mission must have preceded us, because after we landed in Dallas, all four pilots were asked to appear on the local TV news. If that was not exciting enough, the beautiful movie actress Yvonne De Carlo was on the same program!

Miles of Texas

The leg from Dallas to El Paso took us over a lot of Texas. There were huge cattle ranches and miles and miles of farmland. Just as we landed at El Paso, a thunderstorm blew in and rained mud balls as big as oranges!

The next leg of the trip was to take us over the Rocky Mountains. Blimps are not designed to fly at high altitudes because the helium expands as the ship rises. If it expands too much, the gas has to be valved, either automatically or manually, to keep the blimp from bursting.

But valving so much gas means a blimp will lose lifting power. To make sure we could get over the mountains, we left all our unneeded equipment in El Paso, including the cookstove and bunks, as well as three of the enlisted crew.

Once we were over the mountains, we followed the beautiful valleys of California all the way down to our destination near the coast.

A cross-country trip in an airplane would never have provided the leisurely thrills and magnificent sights we experienced in that low and slow blimp.

I know—because they flew us home in a military DC-3—and that wasn't nearly as much fun as being in the blimp!

PRICELESS VIEW. George Broome and the crew who flew in the K-type Navy blimp witnessed gorgeous views of mountains and valleys, like the landscape pictured below.

Transportation Nation

SOLO TO CHICAGO. "I was 16 in 1938 and decided to ride my bike from our neighborhood in Milwaukee to downtown Chicago and back," says Leonard Schultz of West Allis, Wisconsin. "Fearful no one would believe I had made it, I decided to call home once I got there and reverse the charges. My mother accepted the call but was clearly not as thrilled as I was that I had biked to Chicago. The ride home took longer, and I must have looked as weary as I felt, as twice I was offered rides by truckers. But I kept on. Accepting a ride would have been defeat."

PRECIOUS CARGO. This young boy was secure in his seat on a luggage cart as his family waited for a train in 1963. This image from Joe Stabile of Sioux City, Iowa, also shows several schedules for the Milwaukee Road, which was the first railway to use electric lights in its passenger trains. The Milwaukee Road merged into the Soo Line in 1986.

SYLVIA TAKES TO THE SKY. When Sylvia Wege was about to board this plane sometime in the '50s, her husband, Maynard, couldn't resist taking this going-away shot. Maynard, who lives in Seattle, thinks the plane she's climbing into was a Convair 340.

ALL ABOARD. "I have suitcases packed and I'm out catching the train with my daughters Carolyn and Barbara in Fort Worth, Texas, for a visit with my parents in El Reno, Oklahoma," says Janet Clark. "The photograph was taken in 1955, when Barbara was 2 and Carolyn was 3."

STILL PADDLING. Jon King (on left above) with longtime friend Jim Farver along Oregon's Rogue River. At right, he's shown with buddy Rich Selden (on left) before setting off on their journey on the Rock River.

ROCK RIVER ROVING

In the summer of 1956, my friend Rich Selden and I set off on our great river adventure.

We'd grown up in Sterling, Illinois, a small city on the Rock River, and were about to be high school seniors. My dad always had a canoe lying about or hanging in the garage, and we enjoyed many family outings on the river, as well as on lakes in Wisconsin and Minnesota.

In pleasant weather, I would frequently paddle upstream with Rich for an overnight camping trip. In those halcyon days, one could pitch a tent almost anywhere along the river without trespassing on anyone's property. So it was only natural that we took to the river for our summertime adventure.

Rich was far more organized than I was and procured some county maps that gave us a clear picture of the river's course. He also determined that the town of Jefferson, Wisconsin, would be the best jumping-off point.

We piled our camping gear into my '46 Ford and secured Dad's canoe onto the top. We had a friend drive us to Jefferson, a trip of about 140 miles in those days before interstates. When we arrived, we packed all our gear into the canoe, said goodbye to our friend and pushed off into the great unknown.

Our first major obstacle was Lake Koshkonong, a sizable body of water that was running a rather heavy sea because of a brisk wind. Undeterred by

the sight of spray-covered powerboats seeking refuge in the river, we intrepidly set forth on our journey.

If you've ever been in the middle of a large body of water while paddling a canoe into the wind and waves, you know that you seem not to be advancing at all. This was true for us, so we decided to hole up on the beach until the wind abated.

All was well until the final couple of yards before beaching, when we capsized, drenching all our gear. We managed to rescue everything and spread it all out on the beach to dry.

It was midnight before the wind finally subsided enough for us to brave the lake again. We had only a flashlight to signal another boat in the unlikely event that we saw one in the moonless night. It was quite a relief to reach the lake's outlet, where we dragged the canoe up, turned it over and used it for shelter until dawn.

The rest of the canoe trip was much less threatening. We set up camp whenever and wherever we felt tired or decided we'd done enough for the day. Our meals, for the most part, consisted of hamburgers, hot dogs and peanut butter.

We had to portage around eight dams and did a lot of paddling, but any time we worked up too much of a sweat, we just slipped out of the canoe for a refreshing swim.

It took us six idyllic days to make it home to Sterling, tanned, tired and just a little hungry for some home cooking.

It was some years later, at the start of the environmental movement, that *Time* magazine showed a picture of foam at the base of the dam in Oregon, Illinois, citing the Rock River as one of the most polluted in the country. It's probably a good thing that we didn't swallow much of it during our many years of river recreation!

JON KING • STANWOOD, WASHINGTON

We Followed That Dream

These newlyweds took a trip across America in 1921—on roller skates!

BLANCHE CARSON DAVIS • WASHINGTON, D.C.

Jack and I were newlyweds in the spring of 1921. He was a professional skater whose dream was to skate across America, setting a long-distance record.

I'd never skated in my life, but I agreed to join him. On May 21, after a few months of lessons, we started off from Philadelphia's City Hall with a bang—I fell flat on my face when I stepped off the curb.

I quickly righted myself and we skated west on Market Street to Lancaster Avenue, and from there on to the cross-country Lincoln Highway.

Our skates, weighing 4½ pounds apiece, were riveted to our shoes. Since much of the Lincoln Highway was unpaved then, we had to do a lot of walking in those skates. The only time we took them off was when we slept.

Whoa...No Brakes!

Our first major obstacle was Pennsylvania's Tuscarora Mountain. At that time, I hadn't yet learned to stop, and as we crested the huge hill,

RUT ROLLERS. Blanche and Jack Carson faced rutted roads and rainwater, as this photo taken near Belle Plaine, Iowa, shows. "When we'd stop, Jack would dig the mud off the rollers to show people that we really were wearing skates," Blanche says.

I knew I was going to have trouble braking on the downgrade.

Jack found a big branch in the woods and tied a rope to it. By dragging the branch with the rope, I had the brake I needed to keep myself from going too fast.

A man driving up the mountain stopped and took our picture. Later, we had copies made into postcards and sold them along the way to help cover expenses.

We had no mileage goal for each day. Instead, we looked for rinks, fairs and parks where we could put on skating exhibitions to earn living expenses.

Some small-town newspapers along the way wrote about our trip. We also got publicity from national publications such as *Variety* and *Billboard*. When motorists offered us rides, we always refused—and we asked them to write a testimonial in our notebook to verify that we hadn't accepted.

Near Springfield, Ohio, we ran into a very persistent motorist who insisted that no one would know if we rode. He said, "Just sit on the running board and let your skates roll along the road. That'll be skating."

"No," we replied. "That'll be cheating."

Feat Wasn't Phony

Finally the man told us who he was. "I'm the editor of the *Columbus Dispatch*," he said. "I just chewed out one of my reporters for writing a story about you. I was sure you were frauds."

He then apologized and wrote a very kind story about us in the next day's paper.

Thanks to such stories, our reputation preceded us.

People showed us kindness and hospitality along the way. A young woman near Belle Plaine, Iowa, was waiting for us at the end of a hot day with a welcome glass of lemonade and an offer of supper. Many others opened their hearts and homes, allowing us to spend the night with their families.

A little more than two years after we started, our trip ended at City Hall in Portland, Oregon. I'm unsure of the date because I didn't quite finish the trip—exhaustion overcame me just short of Portland, and I was hospitalized briefly.

Jack did finish, however. I don't know whether he set a record for long-distance skating, but as far as I know, we were the first to skate across the United States. It's something nobody can take away from us, and the satisfaction and sense of achievement are with me to this day.

> "Put me on a moving train if I'm sick, and I'll get well. It's good for mind and body to get out and see the world."
>
> —Maria D. Brown

LET'S PEDADDLE. Author Carlton Brown and Roger Luther (above) biked 700 miles from Illinois to Minnesota in 1945—but came back on the bus. Right: "This is my dad, Jacob Mansberger, 28, on the bike he rode from Mount Wolf, Pennsylvania, to Tampa, Florida, in 1927," says Norma Jean Mansberger of York, Pennsylvania. "He's leaning on the shack he built for himself while working for a contractor in Tampa."

BICYCLE ODYSSEYS

GO NORTH, YOUNG MEN

When classmate Roger Luther and I set off on our bicycle trip from Zion, Illinois, to northern Minnesota in June 1945, we were well prepared.

We packed our single-speed, balloon-tired bikes with camping gear, spare brake parts and inner tubes. We'd already made a 45-mile "shakedown" pedal to Milwaukee, Wisconsin, the year before, so we felt Minnesota was within reach.

We pedaled a total of 11 days to reach our destination—Crane Lake, Minnesota—but the trip actually took more than three weeks.

We stopped for a week in Viroqua, Wisconsin, to visit Roger's uncle, and spent another week in Maiden Rock, Wisconsin, on my cousin's farm. On our best day, we biked 90 miles.

At Crane Lake, where we helped out at a resort, we fished and canoed for the first time. One day we canoed 18 miles to a cabin Roger's grandfather had near the Canadian border.

We didn't ride the 700 miles back home. We shipped our Schwinns and took the Greyhound bus.

CARLTON BROWN • ROCKFORD, ILLINOIS

L.A. TO SAN FRANCISCO

It was a sunny June morning, in 1939, when I left my home in the southeast Los Angeles suburb of South Gate and headed out on my Ranger bicycle.

My destination: San Francisco and a world's fair. During my ride, I wore a pith helmet, breeches and high boots. People passing me on Highway 101 said I looked like Frank Buck, a famous wild-animal hunter. I made it all the way to San Francisco, but hitchhiked back home. It was the greatest adventure of my young life and an unforgettable milestone of 1939.

BART OXLEY • BELMONT, CALIFORNIA

Enjoy the Ride

The pretty lady smiling for the camera is my aunt Henrietta, whom I called Aunt Etta, back in the 1940s, ready to depart on one of her trips.

She would leave from her home in Detroit and head south to see her mother in Tennessee, or her sister in Cincinnati, or her brother in Indiana.

Aunt Etta liked to travel by train as well as by bus when she was younger. Later in life, she would sometimes take an airplane. "You don't see as much,'" she would say, "but it is faster." Aunt Etta was right. You don't see as much if you're in a hurry. That's why I like to take my time and enjoy the ride.

RUTH MEDLEY • CANTON, MICHIGAN

CHAPTER 8

Big-City
ADVENTURES

Not all road trips point to a natural attraction. The big cities dotting our vast landscape offer camera-toting crowds a wealth of architecture, history and culture.

"In 1944, I was a 19-year-old Army sergeant about to head overseas," recalls Raymond Daum of Carmel, California. "I'd always wanted to see New York, and with three days left on my furlough, *this* was my chance.

"As the plane approached the city, I glued myself to the window to await my first glimpse of the Manhattan skyline. Feeling sorry for a GI with no place to stay, the airline arranged to put me up at the Plaza Hotel. My room overlooked Central Park!

"The next day, I enjoyed a spectacular view from the observation deck of the Empire State Building. I also walked up and down Fifth and Park avenues and took a buggy ride through Central Park.

"The highlight of the trip was when I saw my favorite singer, Hildegarde, perform. Toward the end of the show, she announced, 'Now I want to sing one of my favorites for a special guest—a young Army sergeant seeing New York for the first time before he goes overseas.' I was thrilled to my boots as she sang 'I'll Be Seeing You.'

"My last stop was Times Square. Wide-eyed, I took it all in—the neon lights and all the people in 'the city that never sleeps.'"

Big cities mesmerize us with their giant skyscrapers and teeming streets. Turn the page to see how these great metropolises sparkled for awestruck road trippers.

WASHINGTON MONUMENT
WASHINGTON
DISTRICT of COLUMBIA

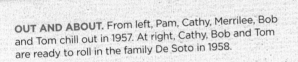

OUT AND ABOUT. From left, Pam, Cathy, Merrilee, Bob and Tom chill out in 1957. At right, Cathy, Bob and Tom are ready to roll in the family De Soto in 1958.

Beyond the **BACKYARD**

With duties and discoveries, this mom made sure the kids were never stuck in idle.

CATHERINE FITZPATRICK • MEQUON, WISCONSIN

Summer can be a torment to St. Louisans when the sun is scorching and the humidity turns the air to chowder. By mid-June, the city slips into a sort of perpetual lassitude that, before air conditioning became commonplace, was purely a matter of survival.

I was a child of St. Louis in this era and the second of six kids born to Merrilee Meier Underhill, a woman who thrived on summer and regarded lethargy in youngsters as evidence of the fraying of their moral fiber.

From the moment school let out for summer vacation until it reopened, Mom filled our mornings with chores disguised as wholesome activity. We inched across the patio, a virtual hot skillet, yanking out tufts of grass growing between the bricks. We Spic-and-Span'd the De Soto until the chrome fins gleamed and the whitewalls dazzled. We poured Ivory Soap Flakes into a tub and washed the dog, a docile Airedale that emerged with a coat as soft as a baby's bottom.

"Yoo-hoo!" Mom would call up the stairs to us. "Girls, the silver needs polishing! Boys, the garage needs sweeping!"

Afternoons were no less busy, but a lot more fun! Mom was a master at ferreting out public tours she felt would improve our general health, broaden our world view or implant a deeper appreciation of anything she felt was worth appreciating.

"Hurry, girls," she'd say, piling us into the De Soto, a two-toned oven in the searing heat. "Bob, Tom, c'mon. They may start without us." And off we'd go to the streets of St. Louis.

We patted the velvet noses of Clydesdale horses

and marveled at their platter-sized feet. We skipped through Forest Park's glassy Jewel Box greenhouse and recognized the gorgeousness of orchids. We tiptoed into the art museum and trailed nervous fingers along the sarcophagus of a mummy, afraid a hoary pharaoh might rise up at any second.

At the Cathedral Basilica, we craned our necks to make out the biblical scenes depicted in colorful mosaics. At the Museum of Transport, we crawled like ants across retired steam- and diesel-powered trains and tried their dusty levers.

If we weren't spending the day in the city, Mom drove us to Treecourt, a cluster of swimming pools in a mosquito-infested valley. The baby pool was shallow with rounded edges and a decidedly yellow cast. The main pool, chlorinated and crowded, featured diving boards of varying heights and lines of floating rope at each change in depth.

Mom preferred the third pool, the one constantly refreshed by an underground mineral spring that poured out of a huge steel pipe girdled with rivets. The water was so cold and sulfurous that most people avoided it, but minutes after we arrived Mom would buckle the chin strap of her bathing cap, dive in and swim 15 laps, smooth as a seal. "Come in!" she'd call. "You might like it!"

By late July, Mom would run out of healthful jaunts and educational junkets, a dilemma she solved by ferrying us to the public library. One blistering afternoon she selected three thick books from the shelves and dropped them in my arms: *The Nun's Story*, about a Belgian woman who overcame a crisis of faith; *Annapurna*, about courage on a Himalayan expedition; and *Gone With the Wind*, the classic Civil War romance. I was 13, and that August flew by in a flash of turned pages.

By packing our summers with activity, adventure and discovery, Mom introduced us to a world beyond the backyard, saved us from the curse of idleness and held fast the threads of our moral fiber.

CAPITOL IDEA. At Missouri's state Capitol in Jefferson City, the author says, "We discovered that the lady on the dome was the goddess of agriculture." Pictured with their mother, Merrilee, around 1963 are (from left) James, Tom, Ken and Bob.

Big Apple Tour
COST A NICKEL

I was born in New York City in 1911 and grew up in the Big Apple.

During the Great Depression, I moved to Newark, New Jersey, where I found a job in a small factory. One day, a co-worker asked if I'd show him around the big city. That was just fine with me, for I truly enjoyed any excuse to come back home to Father Knickerbocker's great village.

But our whirlwind tour had to be an economical one, since we were earning only 45 cents an hour. I had to plan carefully.

On a Saturday morning in June of 1934, we each deposited a nickel in the turnstile at the Park Row terminal. I planned the trip so that we would ride trains operated by two companies that had elevated subway lines—Brooklyn-Manhattan Transit and Interborough Rapid Transit.

At 9:05, a Fulton Street local train left Park Row, taking us across the East River via the Brooklyn Bridge. We were treated to a sweeping view of New York Bay, Governors Island and the Statue of Liberty standing tall on Ellis Island. Ahead of us lay the tremendous view of Brooklyn's skyline.

We transferred to another local that went over the Williamsburg Bridge and then underground to the Canal Street Station in Manhattan.

> ❝We travel for romance, we travel for architecture, and we travel to be lost.❞
>
> —*Ray Bradbury*

Next Stop, Coney Island!

A West End express took us over the Manhattan Bridge, from which we looked out on the Navy Yard and the Wallabout Market. Soon we crossed Coney Island Creek and were at the "World's Playground." Before us lay the sparkling Atlantic Ocean.

From there, a Brighton local took us on a long trip through three boroughs. It ran aboveground for about 3 miles and then dipped down, down, down into a tunnel beneath the East River to Manhattan.

The train continued beneath midtown, dove under the river again and finally emerged at Queens Plaza. We were underground for an entire hour, with no scenery to enjoy, but it was still a fascinating experience for my friend.

By then it was lunchtime, but there was no place to eat in the station. We decided to press on. We boarded an Astoria el local and rode to the next stop, where I knew a way to transfer to the IRT Second Avenue local without paying another fare.

This train took us back to Queens Plaza and across the Queensborough Bridge, from which we could see Roosevelt Island in the East River. Upon reaching Manhattan, we headed downtown through the financial district, ending up at Whitehall Station.

Giants at Polo Grounds

The next leg of our trip was on the Ninth Avenue el through Manhattan's west side, eventually passing the Polo Grounds, where the New York Giants baseball team played. The train then crossed the Harlem River into the Bronx, letting us off at 167th Street and Jerome Avenue.

We made three short transfers to connect with the City Hall local. It crossed the Harlem River back into Manhattan, passing through German Yorkville (where I now live) and finally to a familiar terminal.

We were back where we had started six hours and 45 minutes earlier. During that time, we had been on 11 trains and covered more than 79 miles with only a half-mile of duplication.

You can still make more or less the same trip today, but it won't be nearly as scenic as ours. Most of the trip is now underground.

I've heard of many bargains in my life, but nothing has ever come close to that memorable daylong tour we took for a total cost of 5 cents apiece!

HARRY COTTERELL • NEW YORK, NEW YORK

Glass

New York World's Fair 1939

Chicago Visit Was
FILLED WITH WONDER

Back before World War II, most Americans lived in small towns or, like my family, out on the farm.

We didn't often stray far from home because automobiles were undependable, tires seemed to blow out every 75 miles, and the lousy roads were filled with potholes or mired in mud.

Even the legendary Lincoln Highway—the country's "main street" between the East and West coasts—was nothing more than a narrow two-lane strip that twisted and turned as it followed along old wagon train routes.

So, for most of us who grew up in the country, a trip to the nearest big city was a huge event. For some, this happened but once each generation.

For those of us living in tiny Sterling, Illinois, the nearest big city was Chicago—a place of mythical proportions sitting beside a lake so big you couldn't see across it (or so they claimed).

Chicago supposedly had buildings even taller than a silo. According to our local newspaper, it was run by a man named Al Capone.

Our pigs and cows became pork chops and T-bones at the Chicago stockyards, and somehow the prices for our corn and oats were decided upon in a mysterious place that was called the Chicago Board of Trade.

Memorable Drive

In 1933, when I was 10, we made our first car trip to Chicago, 110 miles away.

Mom packed sandwiches in a picnic basket, and Dad squeezed lemons so we'd have lemonade in our big thermos bottle. Somewhere around De Kalb or Sycamore, we pulled off the road and had lunch, sitting on a blanket under a big elm tree.

We stayed with Aunt Florence, who lived in an apartment house in Chicago. I soon discovered that apartment houses were places that smelled of cabbage and had no lawns to mow. It seemed like a bizarre way for people to live.

I spent a sleepless night on the living room sofa, listening to car horns, streetcars, sirens and people talking on the sidewalk down below. Didn't anyone in this town ever sleep?

I vividly remember our visit the next morning to the top of the Tribune Tower. The elevator was considerably faster than the one in the Central National Bank building back home, yet the ride seemed to last forever. When the doors opened, we stepped outside onto the observation deck.

Wow! We could see all of North America! But even from this eagle's perch, we really couldn't see all the way across Lake Michigan.

FROM UP ABOVE. Chicago skyscrapers bask in sunlight in this glorious aerial view of the city.

Windy City Sights

Back down on the street, we hopped aboard one of the double-decker tourist buses that traversed the streets of Chicago. We climbed the little spiral staircase to the top deck and rode up Michigan Avenue until we reached the Lincoln Park Zoo, the first zoo I'd ever seen.

Nothing in my textbooks at school had prepared me for the sight of a genuine, living and breathing giraffe or elephant. I decided the zookeeper had the best job in the world.

Next we went to the Merchandise Mart. That was when when the National Broadcasting Company had both a Red and Blue network, and—if my memory is correct—both networks had studios in the Mart.

As we peered through glass windows, the guide pointed out celebrities we'd known only as famous voices coming out of our Silvertone radio.

There was a soap opera broadcast in progress, and we watched, fascinated, as the actors stood at microphones reading from their scripts. Nearby, the sound effects man busily rang bells, banged doors and made cloppety-clop footsteps with wooden blocks. Radio would never seem quite the same to us again.

Remember the Barn Dance?

Chicago was also home to the WLS *National Barn Dance*, which in those days was a radio showcase for country talent. I was eager to see the musical and comedic acts. But, alas, we couldn't get tickets.

After dark, before returning to spend another night with Aunt Florence, we walked over to view the splendor of the fountain in Grant Park.

We sat on a bench, marveling at the colored lights and the changing water patterns. It was probably the grandest thing I had ever seen.

The following morning, we visited Marshall Field's department store. Of course, we couldn't afford to buy anything, but just seeing the most famous store in Chicago was an adventure.

Many Fascinating Floors

The first floor alone covered more area than all the retail stores in Sterling put together—and there were five or six more floors to explore. "Who in the world buys all this stuff?" Dad wondered aloud.

Later, we walked around the Loop, terrified by the overhead thunder of the el train. I couldn't imagine ever risking my life on that speeding, clanking monstrosity.

That evening we headed for home, pausing briefly so I could see the Vatican of baseball—the home of the Cubs, Wrigley Field.

My Cubbies were out of town that week, but at

TODDLIN' TOWN. This Chicago street photo shows where the current Hilton Chicago is located, at 720 S. Michigan Ave. In the 1940s, it was the Stevens Hotel.

least I got to see where they battled the fearsome Pittsburgh Pirates and the hated St. Louis Cardinals.

Mom had come down with a case of pinkeye, and tears streamed down her cheeks as we drove into the setting sun. The blinding glare also caused Dad to miss a stoplight, and he was flagged down by a policeman.

The cop leaned down to look inside the window and he sized things up at a glance: Here was an angry-looking man and a red-eyed woman with tears flowing down her face—obviously a domestic quarrel had been taking place.

The officer patted Dad on the shoulder and said something about how he should keep his eye on the traffic and do his quarreling at home.

That may have been the only time in history that a case of pinkeye ever helped a driver beat a traffic ticket.

We got back to the farm late that night, having suffered just one flat tire on the way home. The dogs came bounding out to greet us. Dad and I changed clothes and went to the barn to do the milking.

The big city was a lot of fun, but it sure felt great to be back home.

CLANCY STROCK • GAINESVILLE, FLORIDA

Savvy in the City

JEEP JAUNT. "Our group from Red Wing, Minnesota, took the train to Chicago around 1943 to visit a friend stationed there as a WAVE," says Mary Lynn Johnson Blondell of Rochester. "We were outside the Stevens Hotel—now the Hilton Chicago—when we spotted the empty jeep at the curb and took an impromptu photo. From left are Betty Hall; Marge Kohn; Lorraine 'Danny' Danielson; a WAVE friend of Betty's; Shirley Hanson; and me at the wheel."

LINCOLN LADIES. These well-dressed young women in their fashionable cloche hats were lined up outside Washington's Lincoln Memorial for this 1922 photograph. Graduates of the High School of Commerce in Worcester, Massachusetts, they were on a class trip, says Claire Rogers of Sodus, New York. Claire in the seventh girl from the left, wearing the dark coat.

VIEW OF THE BAY. "My wife, Jeanette, posed with our daughters, Donna (left) and Deborah, at Point Loma National Cemetery, near the entrance to San Diego Bay," says Arnold McLain of Smithfield, North Carolina. "A fuel pier is at left, and the North Island Naval Air Station is at right. This was in 1956, years before the Coronado Bay Bridge was built."

THE CORE OF THE BIG APPLE. Times Square was bustling in this 1940 photo.

DESTINATION: D.C.

EGG ROLL DIDN'T LIVE UP TO BILLING

During spring break in 1969, we took a trip from our home in the Midwest to Washington, D.C. We had read that the White House Easter Egg Roll was an event not to be missed.

With our children—Craig, 11; Dickie Jay, 10; Susan, 7; and David, 5—we took in the national monuments, museums, cherry blossoms and other sights. We also visited with friends.

On the day of the egg roll, we dressed in our finest Sunday clothes and arrived early—very, very early. Even so, we found ourselves in a line that stretched all along the White House fence and around the corner.

The sky was cloudy, and our children's moods matched the weather as the waiting went on and on.

When we finally got inside the gate, the kids' dispositions didn't improve. There was not much to see—no eggs (were we supposed to bring our own?) and no president (I think he was out of town).

People just milled around, and a bagpipe band played. It was not a pleasant day.

It wasn't until three decades later that the event took on a new significance. A picture of our children from that day was hung on a wall in a White House office and remained there for several years.

The office was that of our son Richard Tubb, personal physician to President George W. Bush. (He doesn't go by "Dickie Jay" anymore.)

And at the 2003 egg roll, Richard's daughter, Katie, served as one of the egg staffers (below).

JUNE TUBB • VIROQUA, WISCONSIN

"THIS IS BORING!" That's what the Tubb family seemed to be saying at the White House in 1969. From left (starting from right of pole) are Dickie Jay, David, Craig, Susan and dad Richard Sr.

LAND OF THE FREE. Arlington National Cemetery (above) and the Lincoln Memorial (above right) are among the many D.C. monuments and museums that celebrate our nation's rich history and heritage.

CABBIE TOOK THEM FOR A RIDE

Years ago, an associate and I were in Washington, D.C., on business. I wanted her to see some of the sights, but we were short on time, so we decided to just take a taxi around the Mall.

The driver obliged and drove slowly, pointing out the memorials and the Smithsonian. He was especially proud of President Lincoln for freeing his ancestors from slavery. The well-informed cabbie told us many stories and kept driving around.

After a while, I checked my watch and found we had been touring for 3 hours! Worried about the cost, I asked to return to our hotel.

The driver said he had a few other things to show us and took us out to Arlington National Cemetery, Washington Cathedral and Embassy Row.

Finally back at the hotel, I asked anxiously (and hoping it didn't show), "How much?"

He said we'd been with him a long time, and the cabs didn't come cheap in Washington. He fumbled for a pencil and paper, jotted something down and handed it to me. The note read, "In appreciation for your willingness to allow me to share my city, your fare is free."

We were dumbstruck and insisted on paying, but the driver resisted. We learned that he had been off duty when we hailed him and had worked on his own time—but we did manage to give him a big tip.

CAROL SUE BRODBECK • YPSILANTI, MICHIGAN

STARSTRUCK NEWLYWEDS

When we married in 1956, we took a week's vacation and motored to Washington, D.C., staying at the Hotel Hamilton.

One evening we visited a nightclub, knowing Pat Boone was scheduled to appear. During the performance, a photographer visited our table and asked if we'd like our picture taken with Pat after the show. We agreed, and after the show, she took us backstage for a photo (below; Pat is on the left).

What a surprise and thrill to chat with this congenial man and have our picture taken—I think we paid $10. He also autographed the inside of the folder holding the picture.

CHUCK AND BETTY ZEICHERT
SHEBOYGAN, WISCONSIN

BIG PAYOFF IN THE **BIG APPLE**

Time to get up. *Clap! Clap! Clap!* By smacking his bedroom slippers together, my father followed his morning routine to wake up my mother and me.

Having spent his childhood in a rural area, my father loved big cities, so for several summers, we took a week-long trip to New York. That's where we were headed on that late August day in 1953.

We lived in Lynchburg, Virginia, where my father, Dr. H. Conrad Blackwell, was the pastor of Centenary Methodist Church.

We stayed at a hotel in Times Square and walked to Radio City Music Hall as well as radio and TV studios. We took our meals at a Childs restaurant and at a Horn & Hardart automat to save time and money.

One day, my father obtained tickets to *The Big Payoff*, a popular television show starring Randy Merriman. Bess Myerson, Miss America of 1945, was his partner but happened to be on vacation during our visit.

The show's standard format featured a male contestant who was asked four questions in his area of expertise. The correct answers won prizes for himself and a female relative, usually his wife.

My father, a shy man by nature, hesitated to fill out a contestant application, but my mother talked him into it. We were chosen to be on the show two days hence.

To give the show a twist, I was allowed to sit on the raised "throne" while my mother waited backstage for the results.

I can't recall the first two questions. But the third question had to do with some fairly obscure treaty, and my father knew the answer instantly.

The final question asked for the author of *The Power and the Glory*. My father came through again with the correct answer: Graham Greene.

At that point, my mother appeared amid applause and the announcement that we had won the "big payoff"—an exciting moment.

Among the prizes were clothes for my mother and me. But the two biggest prizes were a full-length mink coat for my mother and a two-week trip to Paris for my parents in November. It was their first trip to Europe.

Of course, I fell heir to the fur coat. It was in good condition for many years, although it is now beginning to dry out. Even if I can no longer wear it, I will always keep the coat as a reminder of a happy adventure with my parents in the Big Apple.

HARRIET BLACKWELL HOOK
GEORGETOWN, DELAWARE

ALASKANS WED
ON TV IN NEW YORK

I came to Ketchikan, Alaska, to visit relatives in early 1951. This small island town, accessible only by steamship or aircraft, had so few young ladies in the workforce that someone actually approached me on the street about a job.

So I began working for the Army Signal Corps' Alaska Communication System, which provided the area's telephone and telegraph service.

The young Army fellows introduced me to Joe, one of their fishing buddies, and we began dating.

We were both in our 20s and liked being independent. Each of us had said we'd probably never marry. But by the spring of '52, we'd met each other's families and knew we were in love.

Our friends said we should try to get on CBS' *Bride and Groom* TV show. We never dreamed we had a chance, but we wrote to the show anyway. We couldn't believe it when we got selected!

Trek Was Harrowing

On Dec. 19, 1952, we started out for New York in my new car, with Joe's mother as chaperone. We nearly wore out a pair of tire chains just getting through Nevada.

Before crossing into Utah, we almost lost Joe's mom at a service station on old Highway 30. We filled up, and Joe bounced into the driver's seat and took off. I asked, "What about your mother?"

Joe slammed on the brakes and looked into the backseat, astonished his mom wasn't there. We went back and called for her at the door of the station's outhouse. She was stuck—the door lock wouldn't budge! The attendant finally had to get a screwdriver and take the door off at the hinges.

We passed through Iowa on Christmas Day. Very few places were open, but we finally found a small diner where we could get a bite of lunch— and not much more. The owner had scaled back supplies for the holiday lull. Our ham sandwiches were made with just one slice of bread.

Arriving in New York City, we were astonished by the bright twinkling lights. We stayed at a private home in New Jersey and went back and forth to the *Bride and Groom* set in New York to "practice." Two marriages took place during each half-hour show, before an audience of about 35.

Our ceremony took place on New Year's Eve. A young fellow from my Alaska office was home in Pennsylvania on leave, so he was Joe's best man.

THE HAPPY COUPLE. Barbara and Joe Hassell were selected from about 75,000 couples to be married on CBS' *Bride and Groom* show in 1952.

My mother-in-law gave me an old lace veil, a new blue garter and a borrowed diamond pin, so I had something old, new, borrowed and blue.

The show provided my beautiful wedding gown. Joe's tuxedo never arrived, so he was married in his blue suit. We'd bought our own rings, but the show provided a set, too. Joe's was a gold band, and mine was set with three Keepsake diamonds.

Honeymoon Was Paid For

After the wedding, Joe and I left on a five-day, all-expenses-paid honeymoon to Virginia Beach.

From there, we drove on through Florida, along the Gulf Coast, west to California, and then up to Washington and Alaska. It was the trip of a lifetime. We kept a daily diary and still love to read it every few years.

Bride and Groom provided a wonderful send-off for a young couple just getting started.

BARBARA HASSELL • KETCHIKAN, ALASKA

FAREWELL
TO THE FARM

I grew up on a 160-acre Minnesota farm during World War II. Gas was rationed and new cars were nonexistent, as all metal went to the war effort. A family road trip was a memorable occasion.

Our vacations were usually the result of rain, as Dad could not work in the fields on those days. One stormy Friday morning, he walked into the house and unexpectedly declared that we should make that trip to Iowa that we had been putting off. Mom looked incredulous at this sudden announcement. The loaves of bread rising on the stove had yet to be baked and the dishes needed to be washed. Sighing, she switched gears into travel mode.

Our destination was Fort Dodge, Iowa, where our relatives resided. To us kids, this was the "big city."

The Minnesota countryside was boring to travel through, and we made a big fuss about breathing Iowa air as we crossed the state line, which was delineated by a huge sandstone sign. It seemed to take forever to travel those few hundred miles. I am sure Dad never hit 50 mph, which may have been the maximum speed for the old 1937 Ford.

My sister and I always traveled standing up, hanging over the front seats because we could not see out the back windows. They were safety windows, with a layer of cellulose acetate between the layers of glass. Unfortunately, this material had deteriorated and turned green, making the countryside look like an underwater scene.

One fun way to pass the time was to read the gaudy advertising billboards that thrived along the highway. These signs proclaimed exciting things to see and do in the city. Mom read the Burma-Shave signs, and we all laughed at the clever rhymes.

We arrived after dark and were enchanted by the bright neon lights on the downtown buildings. We pointed and exclaimed in excitement as we saw the names of the big department stores, restaurants and drugstores. As we passed a huge department store, we were impressed to learn that Mom had worked there when she was young.

When we got our relatives' home, my aunt, uncle and cousins greeted us with a buzz of welcome

READY TO ROLL. In this 1941 photo, the author (front row, left) poses alongside her twin sister, Jane Johnson Crowe. Behind her are older brother Robert Johnson and older sister Wilma Johnson Pestorious.

chatter. They were a big family and lived in a large house. It felt like we'd landed on a different planet— they had electricity, running water and an indoor bathroom. Those things alone made their house a fabulous destination!

We'd had a long day and settled in for sleep. Each of us kids was paired with the cousin closest to us in age to share a bed on the screen porch. What fun! I awoke the next morning to the clip-clop of horse's hooves as the milkman made his deliveries.

After breakfast, our cousin Nancy took all the kids for a ride on the city bus. After a few blocks, she pulled a cord over a window to alert the driver we wanted to get off at the next stop, which happened to be right near a corner candy store. We bought wax lips, tiny wax pop bottles and boxes of candy cigarettes. We strolled back to Nancy's house wearing our huge wax lips and acting silly. Walking in the city without our parents was a bit scary, but mostly exciting!

Sunday marked the end of our fabulous road trip to Fort Dodge. The miles dragged by as we made our way home. When we finally arrived, we were happy to be free of the confines of the Ford. It was quiet and peaceful in the farmyard. There was no neon sign in sight, only the moon beaming brightly over our shoulders as we trudged up the path to the house. My sister and I thought that was a pretty fabulous destination, too.

JEANIE COLLINS • EDEN PRAIRIE, MINNESOTA

Happy Day

This slide is from August 1957, on the day I proposed marriage to the beautiful girl pictured, Mary Jane Eversole, whom I met at the University of Illinois. The Michigan Avenue buildings in the background look over Grant Park in Chicago, where we both worked.

CHUCK HIPPLER • MONTICELLO, ILLINOIS

WELCOME TO
HAMBONE
TENT & TRAILER PARK

OFFICE

Paige © '04

"To travel hopefully is a better thing than to arrive."

—Robert Louis Stevenson

CHAPTER 9

Miles of
SMILES

Two-lane highway adventures are a treat for anyone looking for a welcome change of scenery. Mile after mile, there are so many pleasures and treasures to soak up.

"For kids in the Brooklyn tenements during the '50s, a trip to the country in the summer was a reprieve to the highest heaven," says Joel Hamm of Bluemont, Virginia. "The 'country' in this case was New York's Catskill Mountain region.

"The Catskills were just 100 miles from Manhattan, but for us, that was an all-day trek. We'd leave Brooklyn passing through the Brooklyn-Battery Tunnel. Emerging at the tip of Manhattan, we crawled through the city streets until we reached the West Side Elevated Highway. After crossing the George Washington Bridge, we knew we were getting close when brick buildings were replaced by whitewashed wooden houses.

"With the sun dropping toward the horizon, we kids drifted off into a kind of highway hypnosis until jolted awake by the crunch of tires on a gravel driveway. Here birds chirped, insects buzzed and warm breezes wafted over uncut grass. While Mom and Dad hauled our luggage from the car to the cabin, we kids romped off into the sunlight—freed at last for another delightful summer far from tenement shadows."

Readers reminisce about their favorite hideaways, money-saving tactics and the kindness of strangers in this cheery chapter that's sure to bring a smile.

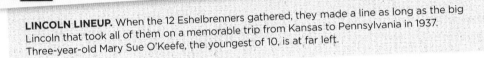

LINCOLN LINEUP. When the 12 Eshelbrenners gathered, they made a line as long as the big Lincoln that took all of them on a memorable trip from Kansas to Pennsylvania in 1937. Three-year-old Mary Sue O'Keefe, the youngest of 10, is at far left.

One Car...12 People...
1,200 MILES

There were no minivans in 1937, but this family had no problem getting everyone into their big Lincoln. **MARY SUE O'KEEFE** • BRONAUGH, MISSOURI

In 1937, a one-way trip of almost 1,200 miles was an adventure in itself. What made this one even more unusual was that besides my mama and papa, Sophia and Carl Eshelbrenner, there were 10 little Eshelbrenners, ranging in age from 3 to 19. I was the youngest and known as "the caboose."

The trip was from our home in Fort Scott, Kansas, to Lancaster, Pennsylvania, where our parents were raised. Our mother had left in 1915 and Daddy in 1917, the year they were married.

Eventually the family settled in Fort Scott, where my father and grandfather William Leitz founded the Fort Scott Sausage Co., later renamed the Fort Scott Packing Co.

Our big Lincoln sedan, with three rows of seats, could accommodate all 12 of us, but there was no room for luggage.

We filled a trunk with clothes and fastened it to the back of the car. Additional bags were stuffed under the seats and tied to the running boards.

Squeezing all 12 of us into the car was nothing new. We went for a drive every Sunday afternoon. We called these our "root beer drives" because Dad always stopped and bought root beer for all of us. Sometimes, though, my brothers and sisters wanted ice cream cones.

Since I was the youngest and the apple of my father's eye, they would nudge me and say, "Ask Daddy." They knew if I asked, Dad usually would let us have ice cream.

The trip took two days. When we stopped for the night, we could afford only one room. The drivers got the bed, while Mother and the rest of us slept on the floor or in the car.

Having a dozen people show up created lodging problems for our relatives in Pennsylvania, too. No one family had room for all of us, so we were farmed out to different relatives during our stay.

But the trip and the stay were delightful. It was such fun seeing all of our relatives and the beautiful countryside where our parents had grown up.

One memorable event on the way home demonstrated my mother's demeanor and careful planning. One of my aunts had given her some straw hats. To transport them home, she tied them to the driver's side of the car. Somewhere along the way, someone tossed a burning cigarette out of his car. It landed on the hats and set them on fire.

When we realized what had happened, the driver stopped the car and all 12 of us scampered out the passenger side. The fire was extinguished with a thermos of lemonade that Mother had prepared for the trip.

It was great being a part of a large family, even though at first we had very little and lived in a three-bedroom house where we slept crossways on the beds.

We have fond memories of growing up, and the eight of us who are still around often get together and talk about those good old days.

IN A VACATION RUT? SO WHAT!

Every summer for as long as I can remember, our family rented a little cabin on Tea Lake in Lewiston, Michigan, for a week. But in the summer of 1952, Mom and Dad decided that instead of going to the lake, we'd go out to the "Wild West" and see the Badlands, the Black Hills and Mount Rushmore in South Dakota.

We started out early, as usual, on a Saturday morning. This time we drove right past Lewiston and on to the Straits of Mackinac to take the ferry over to the Upper Peninsula. This was before the bridge was built.

I remember my heart stopped a little as we passed the exit for Lewiston. We'd made a lot of friends there during our vacations over the years. My parents, though, seemed proud of themselves to be heading off on a new adventure.

We drove on for hours through the Upper Peninsula, seeing nothing but trees, farmland and a few towns. Every 100 miles, my sister, Janice, and I traded places—first one of us got the floor with the pillows, then we'd trade and one would get the backseat.

I missed Lewiston. I figured I was entitled to one week in the summer of swimming, walking in the woods, fishing, sitting by the campfire, and playing until late at night with a bunch of other kids.

I had a feeling Mom and Dad missed Lewiston as much as I did. They, too, had made a lot of friends at the lake and enjoyed taking part in the cookouts, playing cards, and driving out at sunset to look for deer.

By the end of the second day, we hadn't even reached the Badlands yet. The only thing my folks had seen was me and Janice arguing in the backseat.

All of a sudden, Dad stopped the car and said, "Let's go back to Lewiston and see our friends!"

We all yelled, "Yes!" and headed back to our familiar place for the rest of our vacation. Although we didn't get the same little cabin we always had, we were able to get another at the same resort on Tea Lake.

Looking back, as bad as those three days in the car seemed, I think there was a bonding between us we wouldn't have had otherwise.

We laughed and sang songs, and our parents told stories from their past. And we ended up back in Lewiston. I'll never forget that vacation.

DIANE RICHARD • PARMA, MICHIGAN

U-TURN WAS THE RIGHT TURN. In 1952, Diane Richard (center, with her dad and older sister, Janice) hoped for the family's usual great vacation. But that year it took a little longer to get there.

QUAINT LODINGS. Marlene Meimann sits on a bungalow porch (left) in Winchester, Virginia, while on her honeymoon with her husband, Kenneth. They also stopped at Drake's Spanish Court in Coatesville, Pennsylvania (above).

ROAD TRIP ON A DIME

CHEAP HONEYMOON BANKED A WEALTH OF MEMORIES

My husband and I have been married for more than 50 years. I had to chuckle recently when I went over the cost of our honeymoon.

I took notes from our 10-day trip in 1952, driving from Long Island, New York, onto the Blue Ridge Parkway to the Carolinas and back. The total cost was $170.54, including $61.50 for our overnight accommodations and $16.75 for gas. Our most expensive supper was $3.52 for the two of us.

The biggest luxury was staying at the bridal suite of the Garden City Hotel on Long Island on the first night—$16!

Other nights on the trip were more down to earth, including a $4 motel room in Dansbury, Pennsylvania, and a $5 cabin at the Lee Jackson Tourist Court in Winchester, Virginia—"a darling little place with a private bath," I'd noted.

We turned down a beautiful $7 room at Elkin's Motor Lodge because of the expense and settled for the $5 room, which for us was sheer luxury anyway. It had maple boards for the walls, draperies made of real fabric (plastic curtains were common then), a radio, a modern square bathtub and two beds.

I was 18 and Ken was 20 at the time. We must have looked too young to be newlyweds, as Ken had to show our wedding certificate to one motel owner before he would rent us a room!

MARLENE MEIMANN • QUEENSBURG, NEW YORK

SEE THE USA

In 1940, three other young teachers and I decided to spend our summer vacation touring the country. I contacted Conoco Oil's Travel Bureau and got a wonderful response—a large map of the U.S. with information about our stops, including Texas, California, the Pacific Northwest, Salt Lake City, the Badlands and our hometown of Pittsburgh. That's me pictured below at Crater Lake in Oregon.

I was the bookkeeper for our trip. Our 36-day trip covered 9,373 miles and the total car expense was $468.27 for 650 gallons of gas, 51 quarts of oil and a tire. My share was $156.09.

We weren't big eaters, so after eating a hearty breakfast, we settled for snacks, then enjoyed full evening dinners at good restuarants. The cost ranged from 60 cents to 85 cents each.

Thanks to motor courts, rooms were in the $1-$2 range for two double beds with a bathroom. For miscellaneous expenses, including a dentist's filling for one of my teeth, I spent $25.58.

The grand total for me was $241.20. You can understand why my friends today laugh and have trouble believing I spent so little money on such an amazing trip.

FRANCES NUERNBERG • PITTSBURGH, PENNSYLVANIA

THEY WON THE GAS WAR

When I was discharged from the Army at Fort Hood, Texas, in June 1955, my friend Vernie from our hometown in Indiana took the train south so we could drive back home together.

The plan was to drive from Fort Hood to Galveston, then along the Gulf Coast to New Orleans, before heading north to Indiana.

At the time, gasoline was selling from 20 cents to 23 cents a gallon. But we ran into some "price wars" along the way, and one time I was able to fill up for 12 cents a gallon.

But this was nothing compared to what we saw in Galveston, when we found a place where gas was 0 cents a gallon. That's right—they were giving it away!

Vernie noted how upset I was that the car took only 6 gallons because I had recently filled it up.

It must have been our lucky day—they also gave us a free set of glasses!

BEN COOKSEY • WASHINGTON, INDIANA

WHEN TRAVELING WAS A BARGAIN

In our 1953 Studebaker Champion, my wife, Angie, and I traveled to California from South Bend, Indiana, in '55.

The first night, we stayed in a "ma-and-pa" motel in Omaha for $5. While there, we visited an old service buddy of mine and toured Boys Town.

We spent two nights in Denver at $5 a night, and visited Will Rogers' grave in Oklahoma. In the salt flats in Utah, we paid $6 for a motel. Later we played nickel slot machines in Reno, where the cost of a motel rose to $8. It was back down to $6 a night when we toured San Francisco.

Driving down the coast, we visited Disneyland and Knott's Berry Farm, where we were surprised to see workers bulldozing orange trees to make room for the amusement park.

We visited Hollywood and San Diego, drove into Mexico and then to Tucson. I accidentally left a scapular medal at a hotel in Tucson, and by the time we got home, it was waiting in the mailbox.

We saw the sights in Texas, New Mexico, Oklahoma, Missouri and Chicago before finally heading home. We drove 6,331 miles on $79.65 worth of gas and paid a total of $112.50 for lodging. And we still drive that beautiful '53 Studebaker Champion on occasion.

DICK CAMPOLI
SOUTH BEND, INDIANA

BEACH BUDDIES. Ben Cooksey (top photo) and his friend Vernie (above) stopped at Galveston Beach on a 1955 trip.

SUPER STUDEBAKERS. Dick Campoli and his wife drove a Studebaker Champion from South Bend, Indiana, to California. The car below, another Studebaker from the same era, is a Hawk.

THE KINDNESS OF STRANGERS

CHRISTMAS "SLEIGH" WAS A LITTLE CROWDED

I joined the Army on Dec. 15, 1959, when I was 17. Five days later, I had the choice of going home for Christmas or staying at Fort Carson, Colorado, and pulling KP duty for 15 days.

A fellow recruit and I wanted to go home, but we didn't have enough money for bus fare. We decided to hitchhike some 1,100 miles to San Antonio, Texas. From there, we could get bus tickets home. He was going to Nuevo Laredo, Mexico, and I was going to Aransas Pass, Texas.

On that first day, we got as far as Trinidad, Colorado, where we spent the night drinking coffee in a small café. The next day and night, we went all the way to Amarillo, Texas, in a semitrailer. From there, we had to walk across town to a spot where we could hitchhike.

It was late afternoon, and we were getting hungrier and colder. On top of that, it had started to snow. Our chances of getting a ride out of town were getting mighty slim.

Then our saving angel came by in a VW Bug, offering us a ride all the way to San Antonio.

In the Bug were the young driver, his wife, an infant, a toddler and a big shaggy dog. The backseat had been removed to accommodate a sort of bed for the mom, the kids and the dog. With the dad and two tired, cold, hungry young soldiers in the front seat, we were all going home for Christmas.

This family went out of its way to help us, buying us dinner and breakfast. They not only took us to the bus station, they even paid for our tickets!

I will forever remember these people and their kindness. May God still bless them.

RAFAEL VILLALOBOS • FULTON, MISSISSIPPI

POLICEMAN ALMOST BLEW A FUSE

After my sister and I bought a used 1947 Plymouth in 1951, we discovered the car's habit of blowing a fuse when the headlights were turned on. Our brother showed us how to change the fuse, so we had a supply of them in the glove compartment when we took two girlfriends along on a weekend trip from our home in Allendale, New Jersey, to Atlantic City.

We took the backroads, and we always traveled at night to avoid the heavy day traffic. While

GIRLS JUST WANT TO HAVE FUN. Jessie Gaskill (right) poses with her sister before the girls hit the open road to Atlantic City in their 1947 Plymouth.

driving over the South Mountain Reservation on a narrow, hilly road, the fuse blew, so I pulled the car off the road.

To change the fuse, you had to lie on your back under the steering wheel. While I was doing this, a policeman pulled up to see what the trouble was. When we told him, the officer insisted on changing the fuse himself. He put his cap on top of our car and struggled under the steering wheel with his feet hanging out of the door.

That's when another car pulled up, and we heard a man's voice ask, "What's going on here?"

It was another police officer. He had seen the first officer's cap on the roof of our car and a pair of feet sticking out the door.

We were stunned that within the span of mere minutes, two police officers had come by on that lonely mountain road.

After we told the second officer what was going on, we asked how it was that two policemen could appear in such a short time out in the middle of nowhere.

They explained that there was a Girl Scout camp in the area, so local police officers patrolled the road regularly.

After we got back under way, we had a good laugh thinking about what went through the mind of that second officer when he saw a policeman's cap on top of our car and the officer's legs hanging out the door!

JESSIE GASKILL • NEW PALTZ, NEW YORK

SOME FINE FOLKS

Her large family moved from Missouri to Florida, relying on the kindness
of strangers when things went awry. **ADA SMITH** • RICHLAND, MICHIGAN

Dad packed our family of six into his Marion-Handley motorcar for the long move from Springfield, Missouri, to Zephyrhills, Florida. It was 1924 and I remember that car quite well, with its soft leather interior, wood spoke wheels and two folding jump seats.

Following us in their old Franklin were my aunt, uncle and three cousins, who were also moving to Florida.

Our plan was to camp out along the way. Back then, there were no roadside campgrounds, so each evening we'd look for a suitable spot and then ask permission to pitch our tents there.

The first night we slept in a churchyard. But on our second day it began to rain, and by noon both cars were hopelessly bogged down in mud.

Fortunately, a farmer came to our rescue, pulling us out with his mule team. The farmer and his wife invited all 11 of us (and our dog, Bingo) into their home to wait for better weather. The roads were impassable for a whole week, so we all got to know each other pretty well!

Making More New Friends

When we finally left, the farmer and his wife had tears in their eyes. We waved goodbye to that dear couple and rolled out of their farmyard. It wasn't long before we reached the Mississippi River. We crossed by cable-operated ferry and headed southeast.

Then, near Anniston, Alabama, my uncle's car broke down. The Scott family, traveling in a homemade "house car," stopped to help and towed the disabled car into town.

After learning it would take several days for a new rear axle to arrive by rail, we were told that we were welcome to camp on the courthouse lawn.

The Scotts decided to stay and camp with us, and we ended up having a great time! During the evenings, many townsfolk joined our group to sit around the campfire and exchange tall tales.

After we left our new friends in Anniston, we crossed into Georgia. Easing into a small town, we stopped a gentleman on the main street and asked where we might find an inn. The man introduced himself as the local dentist and began chatting amiably with us. Soon, he insisted that we follow him home.

The dentist and his wife provided hot water, soap and towels so each of us could take a bath. They even let us bathe the dog!

Florida—at Last

After bidding goodbye to those kind folks, we traveled on until we finally crossed into Florida.

Citrus groves lined the road as far as the eye could see. It truly was paradise compared with the mud we'd left behind in Missouri.

For years afterward, everyone in our family remembered the trip, and especially the fine folks we met along the way.

FLORIDA OR BUST! Ada Smith (at far left in top photo) recalls the long trip to Zephyrhills, Florida, in 1924. Right: A postcard view of the town as it appeared in the same year.

COWED. Charles Terry (standing) tells of the day his pal Fred Durk (sitting) had his trousers snatched by a cow. Charles is holding the leash of his dog, Rush, in the 1927 photo.

ALL IN GOOD FUN

LIVESTOCK HORNED IN ON VACATION

Camping, fishing, mosquitoes and a troublesome cow are what I remember most about a family camping trip in 1927.

I was 10 years old, living in Chicago, Illinois, when our family and my best friend, Fred Durk, visited a 40-acre site my grandparents owned in northern Wisconsin, 3 miles from Spring Brook.

The older folks pitched two tents for themselves. Fred and I pitched ours in a low spot. The tent didn't have a base and I woke up in a puddle. To make matters worse, the mosquitoes were really thick.

Gull Lake, a weedy lake great for sunfish, bass and northern pike, was a couple of miles away. For $1, a farmer rented me and Fred a leaky old wooden boat and oars—and a bailing bucket that had to be used every 10 minutes.

One day Fred was wading in the shallow part of the lake and had hung his pants on a bush. The farmer's cows came to the lake to drink, and one accidentally hooked its horns on Fred's pants. Fred tried to get them back, but the cow ran off into the brush. Fred was barefoot and couldn't catch the cow. He said his wallet was in the pants, so we all searched the bushes where the cow had gone. We did find the pants but no the wallet, or the dollar or two in it.We did catch some fish, though, so the vacation wasn't a total loss.

CHARLES TERRY • ELGIN, ILLINOIS

THE FRUGAL FISHERMAN

In 1950, when my husband, Tim, was 7 years old, his parents, Emily and Leroy, bought a brand-new car. This was as good an excuse as any to drive from Greenfield, Ohio, to visit some of his Emily's family in Kingston, Ontario.

Off they went—Tim and his parents; his brother, Bill; and sisters, Terry and Barbara. It was summer, so it grew hotter and hotter in the car as the day went on. After a while, something started to smell very bad. Leroy got out of the car to check under the hood. Finding nothing amiss, he got back in and started driving again, but the smell got worse and worse— and so did Leroy's temper. This was a brand-new car, so nothing should've gone wrong.

Leroy stopped the car again, and this time he checked the trunk. Whew, that was definitely where the odor was coming from! A shoe box buried in the luggage caught his attention, and he opened it. Inside were the hot, reeking remains of a substantial quantity of night crawlers.

Turns out young Tim, trying to be frugal, had brought along his own bait for fishing in the St. Lawrence River with his uncle and cousins.

We've laughed about this story a lot over the years. Most of the pictures I have of my husband as a youngster show him with a fishing pole or a fish in his hands.

JEANNE FOLSOM-BERGEN • PHOENIX, ARIZONA

CATTLE: A.M. WETTACH/RDAEB

TUMBLING TO TEXAS

In 1931, my Uncle Earl convinced Dad to join him in a garage business in Bryan, Texas. So we packed all we could into the old Model T and left the rough job market and harsh winters of North Dakota.

We stopped for gas, and to relieve our boredom, my 7-year-old sister, Doris, and I (pictured below) ran and jumped around the service station. Doris broke into a series of cartwheels, backflips and splits. With her natural ability, she put on quite a performance and began to attract an audience.

To our surprise, as the people clapped and cheered, a rotund, cheerful man in the crowd swept off his hat, held it out and said, "How about a little something for the little lady?" Nickels and dimes dropped into the hat—enough for gas to take us to the next town! Of course, gas was only about 15 cents a gallon back then.

So we made our way to Texas, Doris performing at gas stations, me passing my cap and people laughing and enjoying a little break from driving.

Doris and I are now in our 80s, both living in Florida, and she can still do acrobatics. But with the price of gasoline today, she'd have to do a lot of cartwheels to get to Texas!

BILL JOHNSON • SARASOTA, FLORIDA

MISCHIEVOUS SMILES? Ramona (left), the prankster from the story below, posed with Jeanne Freeman on one of their Lake of the Ozarks visits, around 1965.

SETTING HIS TOES ABLAZE

While vacationing with a group of friends and neighbors at the Lake of the Ozarks, we relaxed beneath the shady trees surrounding our cabins. Stretched out on lawn chairs, the men were soon napping as the ladies chatted.

My friend Ramona had just finished polishing her nails a blazing red when she was struck with the idea of painting my husband's toenails as he slept. With the impish deed completed, we women could barely restrain our giggles while waiting for Sheldon to wake up.

Sheldon was a muscled-up cattleman of 6-foot-2 who worked a large Kansas wheat farm. After awakening, he stared down at his red toenails for a moment and then began to laugh loudly. Sheldon quickly identified the toenail artist, since Ramona was laughing just as loudly. He thanked her for the very professional job—the best and only pedicure he'd ever had!

The next day, while cruising around the lake, the men saw a ski jump at a private residence. Sheldon stopped the boat and walked up the dock to ask the owner's permission to use the jump. Her first remark was, "Your toenails are painted red!" She laughed and told us we were welcome to enjoy the ramp.

When we returned to the lake the following year, we asked to use the ski jump again. The owner laughed, exclaiming to Sheldon, "Sure. I remember you. You're the fellow with the red toenails!"

JEANNE FREEMAN • ABILENE, KANSAS

HOME AWAY FROM HOME. Mary Clark's parents (above) were trailer pioneers in 1949. Right: Dorothy Galley (far right) says it took her dad five months to build this camper, dubbed Silver Bullet No. 2, in '35.

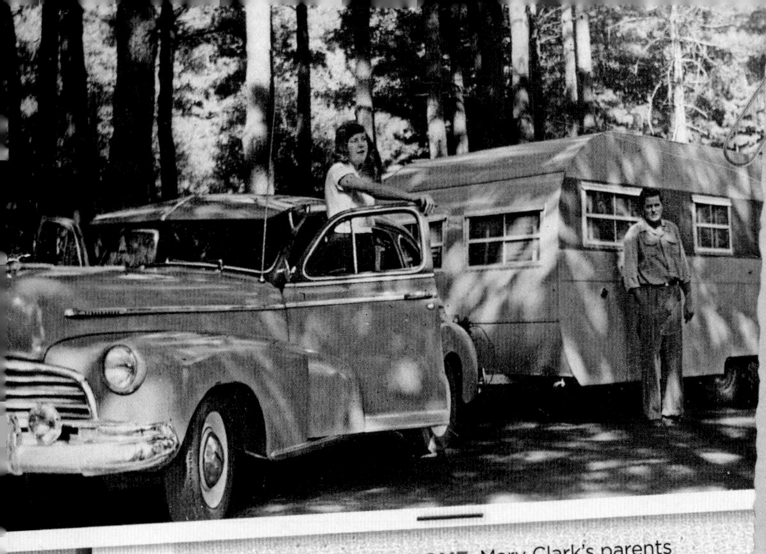

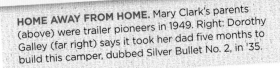

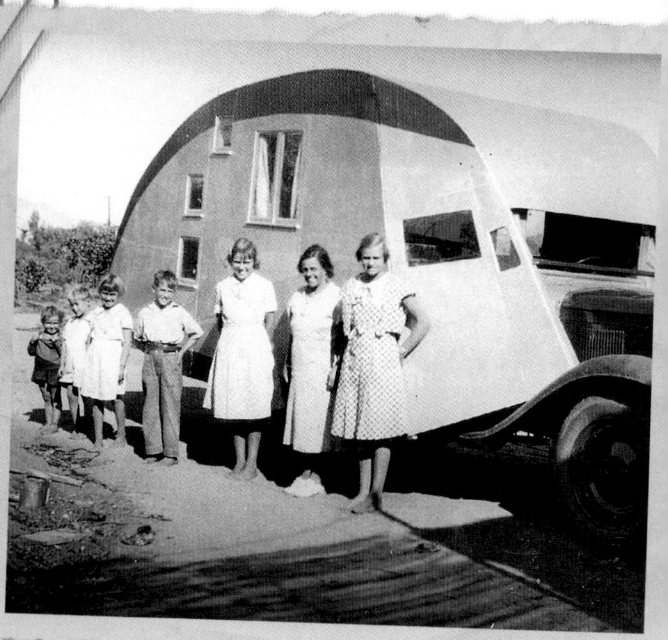

CAMPER **CHRONICLES**

TRIP MEANT A LOT

In 1949, my parents, Harold and Nellie Okerstrom, my sister, Sharon, and I traveled from Pasadena, California, to New York City and back with our house trailer (shown above left).

I was 4 then, so I don't have many personal memories, but my parents often spoke of that "trip of a lifetime," the amazing sights they saw and all that the trip meant to them.

Since RV parks were then nonexistent, we spent many nights in gas station parking lots, even using their facilities.

I do remember how people in towns would stop on the street to watch us pass, as trailers were so rare back then.

While some thought my parents' decision was foolhardy, my mother was so thankful that they made such a grand cross-country journey, since my father died at 45, only six years after the trip. They'd had dreams of many more trips and looked forward to retirement, but that was not to be.

MARY CLARK • JOHNSTOWN, COLORADO

THE SILVER BULLET NO. 2

My father built a series of homemade campers through the 1920s and '30s, and our family had some exciting cross-country adventures in his odd-looking contraptions.

Dad built his last camper in 1935, mounting it on a '29 Chevy truck chassis. He spent $85 for parts, and the project took five months.

We painted that camper silver with a turquoise stripe to give it a streamlined look, then christened it Silver Bullet No. 2. (Our first Silver Bullet was a '24 Essex pickup that we camped in for years.)

Late in 1935, Mom, Dad and we kids piled into our new camper for a trip from California to New Jersey. People laughed, gawked and stared at us all the way. But that strange-looking vehicle carried us 3,200 miles in seven days—and we rode in comfort!

Silver Bullet No. 2 eventually racked up more than 30,000 miles in trips back and forth across the USA.

Despite the stares and comments, we had a ton of fun in Dad's homemade RVs. And you could say he passed the travel bug down to us: Today, six of us siblings have campers or motor homes.

DOROTHY GALLEY • BANNING, CALIFORNIA

ONE-WHEELED WONDER

We had great plans for our family of five in 1960—we wanted to head east from our home in Elba, New York, and see New England and the Atlantic Ocean.

My husband could make anything, so he created a one-wheeled travel trailer (see photo, opposite page, top left) out of a small trailer from Sears, Roebuck & Co. On the road it looked flat, but when we reached a campground, it changed into a covered wagon.

My husband fashioned hoops that fit in holders on the sides that were then covered with a fitted piece of canvas I made on my little Singer sewing machine. A board could be clipped onto the back wall to use as a table for a camp stove and provisions.

A medium-size mattress just fit in the bottom of the trailer for my husband and me, and the kids slept on the back floor of our roomy 1957 Ford sedan.

Everyone was happy with the arrangement and

enjoyed those 10 days pulling that little trailer, but I said the way it rocked when we slept in it made me sick each morning.

It wasn't until I got home that I discovered the morning sickness was because I was carrying our fourth child!

BERNICE YUNKER • ELBA, NEW YORK

IS IT A TENT OR A TRAILER?

A hardtop travel trailer would have been a luxury in 1956 for my parents, Marion and Dave Carr of North Easton, Massachusetts.

So they bought a Higgins tent trailer (photo, top right), one of the first recreational vehicles made after World War II.

My siblings and I slept in the trailer while Mom and Dad slept on a double air mattress in the back of our Chevy station wagon.

The metal top of the trailer folded up and out to make beds on either side, and aluminum poles supporting the canvas unfolded to make the top.

Dad customized the rig with an icebox door accessible from the outside, painting the unit white and gray to match our car (see photo above right).

We spent hours practicing setting up and taking down the trailer. Each of us had specific tasks and learned to work quickly without getting in each other's way. We got so good at it tha nearby campers would stop and marvel at how we could pull up to a site, set up the trailer, and be sitting down for supper in 20 minutes.

Mom said we had Dad's World War II Navy training to thank for that.

DIANE CARR
SHREWSBURY, MASSACHUSETTS

SANDY ACRES. "This slide at one time belonged to my aunt Inez Reece, who traveled often in the area around Payson, Utah; she had family there," writes Jane Thompson of Morrisville, Missouri. "I don't know who the people are. The large trailer was being pulled by a 1955 Ford Fairlane."

Wyoming's Wide Open
WILD FRONTIER

When four Boston girls set out to visit a real ranch, they were in for an adventure.

AILEEN NILE • DUNEDIN, FLORIDA

Back in 1934, three co-workers and I embarked on a cross-country trip I'll never forget—especially riding through the rain in a rumble seat!

We four girls were in our 20s and living in Boston. A friend wrangled an invitation for us to visit his uncle's ranch in Wyoming. It was an offer we couldn't refuse.

All we had was my battered Model A Ford. But Dad came to the rescue, offering a monthlong swap for his Chevrolet coupe with a rumble seat.

Dad rigged up a green- and orange-striped awning to cover the rumble seat, and we were ready. We shipped a duffel bag full of ranch clothes ahead, strapped two suitcases to the running boards, and we were off!

We drove to Buffalo, took a ferry across Lake Erie, then drove to Chicago. We arrived right at the time they were hunting down the infamous John Dillinger. After an evening in the Windy City, briefly visiting the World's Fair, we headed across the dusty prairie states.

Laughing in the Rain

We changed drivers every hour or two, rotating inside from the rumble seat. When it rained hard, the water hung low on the awning, and those in the rumble seat had to slouch way down. It wasn't comfortable but, oh, how we laughed!

When we finally reached Colorado, we fell in love with the mountains. We rented a cabin at a fishing camp in Estes Park and stayed three days, climbing, fishing and enjoying the scenery.

We then headed north to Kaycee, Wyoming, to pick up the duffel bag. After miles of desolate country, there was the ranch, like an oasis in the desert. We limped in on a flat tire but received a royal welcome.

Our host was congenial, generous, amusing and very loquacious. He provided horses to ride, took us sightseeing, and regaled us at night with tall tales and local legends.

He also gave us nicknames: Faith, Hope, Charity—and Skunk Killer! The first three were interchanged daily, but the fourth name stuck, as that girl had driven over a skunk.

WHY NOT WYOMING? Vacations needn't include five-star accommodations to be first-rate travel experiences. These city girls were happy to trade the sleek skyscrapers of Boston for a rustic retreat—a ranch in Wyoming.

Dances with Ranchers

One night our host organized a dance for us at the schoolhouse, and ranchers came from miles around to meet and greet the "four Boston ladies." We danced, ate and made merry till the wee hours.

The week flew by, and soon we had to say farewell. We headed for Yellowstone, where we stayed at the lodge and saw Old Faithful erupt.

After a night in North Bay, Ontario—and a bout with bedbugs!—we sped through Ottawa and Montreal, making it home with a day to spare before we had to go back to work.

Total cost of the trip, including a new tire, came to $93 each. It was worth every penny, but we were sure of one thing—we never wanted to ride in a rumble seat again!

RUMBLE SEAT **ROUND UP**

BRAVING THE WILDS OF WISCONSIN IN A RUMBLE SEAT

In 1936, I lived with my parents in a Chicago suburb, but we had relatives 400 miles away in Michigan's Upper Peninsula. The long, difficult trip might as well have been a thousand miles.

That was the year my dad bought a new Dodge, a real beauty with a surprise rumble seat especially for me, he said.

When I learned we'd be going to Kingsford, Michigan, to visit our relatives over Thanksgiving, I was so excited I could hardly sleep.

I told all my friends about the dangers of going into deer and bear country, and how I'd have to ride outside in the rumble seat with lots of blankets piled high over me, since there wasn't enough space inside the car.

We set off in the cold early morning darkness, and when we got to central Wisconsin, it started snowing. I was excited and hoped for lots of snow, although I'm sure my parents were praying that it would stop. Each time I tapped on the window between us, my mother would motion for me to lie down and cover up.

Despite the cold, I finally got warm in my nest of blankets and fell asleep. Many hours later, I was awakened by the laughter of my Michigan cousins who, flashlights in hand, were pushing the snow off my blankets.

As we went inside to hot chocolate, my father told me all about the big black bears he'd seen while I slept. Little did I know that he'd made them up just so I could tell the story when we returned home—which, of course, I did.

We made our triumphant return with a deer on the fender of the Dodge (Dad did a little hunting, too) while I rode looking out for bears from my unique vantage point.

My grandsons sometimes visit me at my home in the Upper Peninsula, but I'm afraid they'll never know the fun of making the trip in a rumble seat.

JACK LARSON • KINGSFORD, MICHIGAN

TRAVELING IN THE RUMBLE SEAT

Oh, how well I remember a trip my parents and I took one summer long ago. We lived in a suburb of New York City in the early 1930s, and we decided to "go touring" to Michigan in our Marmon.

With my parents up front and me in the rumble seat, we set off for Grand Rapids on a route that took us through southern Canada.

Before we departed, I thought it would be great fun to be relegated to the rumble seat. I wore a pair of aviator goggles so I could make believe I was a flying ace. However, I hadn't counted on suffering from motion sickness. To make matters worse, the very smelly exhaust flowed right in the direction of the rumble seat!

I have had many and varied experiences in my life, but that trip from New York to Michigan and back—taking in the great outdoors in a rumble seat—does not stand out as one of the more joyously remembered!

FREDERICK SACK • MIAMI, FLORIDA

RIDIN' THE RUNNING BOARD

DOG WENT AWOL IN CAPITAL

I was 8 in 1922 when our family took a summer vacation from Somerset, Kentucky, to Washington, D.C., in our new Dodge.

My faithful friend Bobby, our black- and white-spotted, stubby-tailed rat terrier, rode on the right front running board with his body pressed against the hood of the engine and all four feet pressed against the fender.

He'd ride there as long as we were traveling at normal speeds or faster, but when we slowed down, he would jump off and race with the car.

When we set off on our tour of the nation's capital, Bobby started the trip in his favorite spot. When we slowed down, he sometimes jumped off the fender as usual and we had to coax him back on.

We made it to the outskirts of Washington, D.C. and found an unusual place to stay—an Army tent with a wooden floor and Army cots.

The next morning, we went to see the sights, with Bobby stationed in his favorite place. We slowed down several times looking for gas, but when we eventually found a station—no Bobby!

We searched for several hours. We told everyone we saw that if they ever saw Bobby, Dad would pay to ship him back to Kentucky and give a reward for their trouble.

After seeing the city's attractions, we stopped again in the neighborhood where we'd lost Bobby and repeating our offer. There was nothing else we could do but head home, where we settled into our routine and grieved our loss.

One day I went swimming with friends at a pond about a mile from home and thought I heard a familiar bark. I looked up and it was Bobby!

Barking excitedly, a black and white streak jumped into the water and swam straight to me. It was the best reunion of my life. When we got home, Mom said Bobby had been shipped back by people at the gas station where we'd searched for him.

When my family had opened the crate, Bobby ran in circles until he hit my scent, then off he went.

Bobby and I spent several happy years together before he passed away at the ripe old age of 15.

VETRICE DAY • WEST PALM BEACH, FLORIDA

UP IN FLAMES

The year was 1936, a summer in the middle of the Depression. For the first time in their 17 years of married life, my parents decided to take a family vacation. Was I excited!

"Family" included my parents, me and my eight siblings, and our grandfather, so this was no small undertaking. Our destination was the home of Aunt Hazel (Mother's sister) in Ludlow, Massachusetts—a 12-hour drive from our farm in upstate New York.

Father got behind the wheel of our 1929 Chevy sedan. Beside him was Mother with 1-year-old John in her lap, and Grandpa holding little Mickey.

The rest of us were layered into the backseat. What a spectacle we must have made as we rolled off!

In those days, suitcases were often carried on the running board. Grandpa had tapped smoldering ashes from his pipe out the window, and they got lodged in our luggage and caught fire! Fanned by the wind as we sped along, the conflagration was well under way before we noticed.

Father quickly pulled over and beat out the flames with the only firefighting equipment immediately at hand—3-year-old Cathie's new sweater! Her eyes filled with tears as she saw it reduced to a charred lump.

TRAVELING CLAN. The Day family in 1922 (from left): mother Mattie, Vivian, father H.P., Virgil, the author Vetrice and Vernice.

As the day, and our patience, drew to an end, our destination seemed just over the horizon. But wait—what did that sign say? Could we have taken a wrong turn somewhere? It turned out we were 25 miles off course.

When we finally reached Ludlow, one noisy, eager bunch tumbled from the car and quickly filled our relatives in on our burning adventure!

MARY COOPER • PITTSFORD, NEW YORK

THEY GOT "LUCKEY"

It was November 1920 when my wife, Minnie, and I set out with our two children, Wilber and Virginia, in our 1919 Chevrolet on a road trip from Brighton, Michigan to Florida.

Two days into the trip, as we were driving through Toledo, Ohio, we were blissfully ignorant of what fate had in store for us. We had planned to drive that day only as far as Bucyrus, Ohio, where we were to spend the night with our close friends the Graetzs.

Things went well as we pulled through Toledo, but we had not proceeded far outside the city when we discovered a handbag that had been strapped to one of the running boards had fallen off. It contained nightclothes, toiletries and some other necessities.

So we decided to turn the car around and retrace our tracks to see if we might be fortunate enough to find it somewhere alongside the road. No such luck.

The next best thing would be to advertise for the bag in the *Toledo Blade*. So we drove to the post office in the nearest town, which happened to be Luckey, Ohio. I immediately went in to put in an advertisement in the daily. While I was inside, a truck driver pulled over alongside our car. Noticing the luggage strapped to the running boards, he asked Minnie if we had lost a handbag.

He explained that he'd found a bag on the side of the road on his way into Luckey, and left it with the local authorities in case someone claimed it. Minnie was so elated that she actually wanted to kiss this kind stranger!

Arrangements were made to have the handbag shipped via express mail to the home of our good friend Tunis Hicks, whom we planned to visit in Washington, D.C.

We were afraid the bag might not make it in time, but it was there upon our arrival at Tunis' home several days later. After that, we decided that the town of Luckey definitely lived up to its name!

SETH B. JACOBS • BRIGHTON, MICHIGAN

BLOATED GOAT. "My brother Robert told me a great story of a camping trip he took back in 1929, before I was born," says Janice Dupree Smith of Grand Rapids, Michigan. "My father had to borrow a goat to take along on the trip because my sister Sally had to be fed goat's milk. Robert said Dad put the goat, Rosylee, in a crate on the running board of his Essex and faced her forward because he thought she'd like to see where she was going. (That's Robert and Rosylee with her in the photo above.) But she bloated up like a balloon. So the next day, Dad faced her in the opposite direction and all was well."

> " *Though we travel the world over to find the beautiful, we must carry it with us, or we find it not.* "
>
> —*Ralph Waldo Emerson*

SUMMER FUN. Estelle Lipp enjoyed her family's annual summer trip from Queens, New York, to the wide open spaces of New Jersey. She's shown at far right in this 1950 photo with (from left) her cousin Maxine, brother Michael and cousin Phyllis.

City Girl Escaped to
POMPTON LAKES

Driving into the country from New York City was almost as exciting as the vacation itself.

ESTELLE LIPP • WINTER SPRINGS, FLORIDA

Some treasured memories from the early 1950s come from the time I spent at the summer home of my Aunt Sylvia and Uncle Sol near Pompton Lakes, New Jersey.

Except for these trips, we spent every day in New York City, mostly within a few blocks of my home. So traveling to Pompton Lakes took us somewhere entirely different.

My parents, sister, brother and I would leave our home in Queens, New York, to begin the drive of several hours. Along the way, the scenery changed dramatically.

We left the city by driving through a tunnel and landed in a part of New Jersey that was old and dirty-looking. Steam rose in the streets, and fire hydrants were open to cool off kids in the summer heat.

As we drove, the streets changed from those with only apartments and brownstones to ones with houses and trees. When we saw Holstein and Guernsey cows grazing and roadside stands selling produce, I knew we were getting close.

When Clancy's watermelon stand and the sign reading "Pompton Lakes—9 Miles" came into view, I knew it wouldn't be long before Aunt Sylvia's chocolate cake with mint icing would be melting in my mouth.

Our relatives ran out to greet us with open arms. They were just as happy to see us as we were to see them.

One by one, Aunt Sylvia embraced us. First came the big close hug. Then she'd set whichever one of us she'd just embraced at arm's length and remark accordingly.

She'd note that my older brother, Michael, had gotten taller. Then she'd hug and look at me and say, "She looks just like Mama." Father would answer, "She's my Hungarian beauty."

Lynne, the youngest, was still a baby and was named for the child with the same name that

Aunt Sylvia and Uncle Sol had lost a long time ago. Whenever Aunt Sylvia saw my baby sister, something happened to her eyes that didn't happen when she looked at Michael and me.

In the meantime, Uncle Sol gave us another round of hugs and kisses as my parents did the same with my cousins Phyllis and Maxine.

Sylvia was my favorite aunt because she loved just the way my father, her younger brother, did—openly and with a full heart.

There were not enough beds, so we slept on cots. I never realized it wasn't comfortable to sleep on stretched-out canvas in a house with no air conditioning. It felt cozy and I slept well.

In the morning, Uncle Sol and my father took us five kids to Pompton Lakes. Once at the water, I floated inside a tire tube for as long as I could.

I haven't seen my cousins in many years, and my parents, aunt and uncle are long gone. But I travel back to Pompton Lakes whenever the waters in my life become turbulent. Those cherished memories take me to an oasis of peace, and will be ones I keep with me as long as I live.

ROLLING REUNION

In 1998, my three siblings, their spouses and I decided to get together for a road trip. This rolling reunion took place in a Dodge Ram van, various motels and fast-food restaurants. We agreed to meet at Carol and Ward's farm near Springfield, Missouri, and start out on a beautiful Monday in May.

With much anticipation, we set out toward Tennessee, crossed the Mississippi River and headed on into Memphis. From there it was a short drive to Tunica, Mississippi, and its casinos. We checked in to a hotel, did a little gambling and had some dinner before settling in for the night.

After lunch in Jackson, we headed southeast to Gulfport, Mississippi, and drove along the coastal highway, taking in a beautiful view of the Gulf of Mexico. This led us to Biloxi and the lure of a few more casinos.

On the road the next morning, Janis and Gene made a startling discovery: She had forgotten to pack his underwear! We set out for the nearest clothing store so we could all feel comfortable riding in the van with Gene!

Back on the highway, we headed for Mobile, Alabama, where we took a tour of the battleship *USS Alabama* and the submarine *USS Drum*. Both had seen service during World War II.

Then it was on to Pensacola, Florida, via the long Pensacola Bay Bridge, with another gorgeous view of the Gulf. A stop at a friend's house in Navarre Beach gave us the luxury of an ocean swim before the next leg of our journey.

Other highlights were stops at Georgia's scenic Stone Mountain and its Antebellum Plantation and Farmyard; the magnificent Smoky Mountains in North Carolina and Tennessee; and Big Spring, Missouri, where we had a memorable al fresco lunch in the Ozark Mountains before going to see the enormous springs, which are among the largest in the United States.

Our road trip was a wonderful way to spend a reunion. Someone had told us that a trip with siblings and in-laws would end in disaster, but we had the time of our lives! The memories will always be dear to my heart.

BEVERLY DAVIS • ARVADA, COLORADO

My Thumb Took Me
10,000 MILES

On June 10, 1936, I left Raleigh, North Carolina, on a transcontinental hitchhiking trip. At the time, I was 18 and a student at the University of North Carolina.

I'd attended a military school before college, so I had a uniform to wear while hitchhiking. Its neat appearance let drivers know I was no bum. The pack on my back (a small tent and an inflatable mattress) was also an attention-getter.

After I left North Carolina, my first stop was Nashville, Tennessee. Near Frankfort, Kentucky, I caught a ride with a salesman who was on his way to St. Louis, Missouri.

Most salesmen were good drivers—and fast, too. They had to be to cover their territories. Luckily for me, many of them liked having someone ride along.

The 300-mile trip to St. Louis was my first long hop. After a stopover in Springfield, Missouri, to visit a girl I knew, I headed south again.

The Texas Centennial was going on in Dallas. The huge celebration put a big dent in the $100 I had brought along. I later learned just how far a loaf of bread and a jar of peanut butter could stretch!

After three days in Dallas, I caught a Chevrolet going west to El Paso. We made the 500 miles in one long day. Then, after a visit to Juarez, Mexico, it was on toward Phoenix.

I have vivid memories of my encounters with migrating "dust bowlers." They were just as broke as I was, but they'd always stop to offer me a hunk of bread or a word of encouragement. It seemed the people with the least to offer were often the first to show kindness.

I was hitching outside Phoenix when a trucker pulled over and asked me if I could drive. I told him I guessed I could learn. With eight speeds, this truck was more complicated than I thought, but I must have done all right, since he soon fell fast asleep.

He was dog tired, and I ended up driving that truck through deserts and mountains all the way to Los Angeles!

From there, I caught a ride to San Francisco and spent July Fourth near the Golden Gate Bridge. The road up the California coast to Crescent City was the most beautiful stretch I'd seen yet. I spent that night on the beach with the stars overhead.

When I left Seattle, I had only $5 left—and I was getting mighty sick of peanut butter sandwiches! Again, luck was with me as I caught a ride all the way through the Rockies to Helena, Montana.

Outside Rapid City, South Dakota, I spent a

THUMBS UP! Kent Mathewson (above) hitchhiked his way across America back in 1936. He also packed along a tent for some low-cost lodging.

memorable night in the Stratosphere Bowl, where the Explorer II hot-air balloon had set an altitude record the year before for a manned flight.

I also visited Mount Rushmore (then being built) and got a kind reception from its creator, John Gutzon Borglum. He seemed impressed that I'd hitchhiked so far, and gave me a personal tour.

Just past Rapid City, on July 14, a big sedan whizzed past, then stopped when the driver saw my "Raleigh, N.C." sign. He asked if I knew any people in the hardware business there. I did, and we ended up riding more than a thousand miles together.

A hardware salesman heading home from the West Coast, he had a V-8 and knew how to use it! Four days later, I was back home in North Carolina with a whole $1.50 left in my pocket.

My 37-day trip cost $98.50. If I hadn't splurged at Juarez and the Texas Centennial, I could have done it even cheaper. But what's the use of going on a trip if you don't have a little fun?

KENT MATHEWSON • ADVANCE, NORTH CAROLINA

Out on the Open Road

Some of my fondest memories of growing up in the 1950s and '60s were the times my aunt and uncle, Da Da and Ray Hamby, took my sister, Nancy, and me on summer vacations.

Their Corvette trailer was painted turquoise and white to match my uncle's 1955 Chevy (above).

We'd spend several weeks on the road and go through several states. In the summer of 1957, we stayed at Yellowstone National Park, where this photo was taken.

I'll never forget the adventures we had and the places we saw in that little trailer. What fun it was!

SHIRLEY SCHUMAN • LAS VEGAS, NEVADA

> **The really happy man is one who can enjoy the scenery on a detour.**
>
> —Anonymous

CHAPTER 10

Are We THERE YET?

Taking a trip by car back in the good old days was often an adventure into the unknown.

The first "unknown" was the roads—early in the century, few were paved. Most lanes were simply dirt or gravel, rutted in dry weather and rivers of mud when it rained.

Often the biggest travel uncertainty was the car itself. Compared with today's autos, those old-fashioned flivvers could be mighty unreliable.

Flat tires, broken axles and sickly engines could put a lot of unscheduled stops into a trip. Thank goodness no one seemed to be in a big hurry then!

Directions were another unknown. In the days before published maps were widely available, motorists often "took the long way" to get where they were going.

Starr Dunn of Kent, Ohio, remembers a trip she took in the summer of 1920. Her parents and their five kids climbed into a 1917 Studebaker touring car in Gotha, Florida, and took off for Grafton, Ohio, more than 1,000 miles away.

"They used the *Automobile Blue Book* to navigate," Starr says. "It gave ambiguous instructions like: 'Leave Gotha going north. At 1.3 miles, turn left onto main road. At 2.7 miles, make sharp left turn in town of Ocoee. At 3.4 miles, make right turn at gas station."

Take a look back at some of the mishaps and mayhem weary travelers encountered en route to their destinations.

SHINY FOR NOW. The Model T at right was gleaming—but not for long. In the days of muddy roads, automobiles wore a good deal of dirt.

Tough Trip in a **MODEL T**

Home never looked so good after a crowded road trip filled with detours, muddy paths, car troubles and deep ditches.

DICK VINCENT • LOUISVILLE, NEBRASKA

Back in the '30s, we lived in Omaha, Nebraska, and every Thanksgiving, our family journeyed down to Topeka, Kansas, to spend the holiday with relatives.

It was a 200-mile drive, and normally it took several hours. But the trip we made in 1932, when I was 10, took all day and part of the night. It was almost the last trip of my life.

That drive was a disaster from beginning to end. It all started with the car itself—a Model T center door sedan. This was not one of Ford's better ideas. One door was centered on each side of the vehicle. Entering via the backseat, the driver and the front

passenger had to hunch over and creep through the narrow passage between the front seats to get up to the front.

The car also lacked a trunk. All luggage, tools, gas can, chains and whatever else the occupants wanted to take had to ride inside with the passengers.

Detours Were Doozies

That year, Highway 75 was under construction. There were a number of detours onto dirt roads, which became quagmires because it rained during our entire drive. To make things more interesting, the detours were marked only where they started. From there, we had to find our own way!

Once off the main road, we seemed to be lost most of the time, and because Dad ran the car in low gear and at the full throttle to ram through the mud, we frequently ran out of gas. Then Dad would slosh through the mud to a farmhouse to try to buy a little fuel and get directions to the next town, where we could fuel up and continue our journey.

Filling the tank in that old "T-Bone" was another experience. The tank was under the front seat cushion in my lap while the attendant snaked the hose through the driver's-side window.

Back on the muddy roads, we seldom made it up a hill without first getting stuck at the bottom. This was my cue to get out with a shovel to dig and push while Dad spun the wheels.

On the way down a hill, we'd try to build up enough speed to make it through the next mud hole. Dad went as fast as he dared, with the car sliding back and forth. It was all Dad could to do keep it out of the ditch.

By the time we reached Topeka, it was long past dark and everyone was tired and muddy. We stayed a few days, then loaded up and headed home. On that trip, if you can believe it, things got worse.

First, the car began to run poorly. We stopped in every town, and each local mechanic tried something, but nothing ever worked. It got so bad we all "helped" the car along by leaning forward going up hills, hoping we'd reach the top before the engine died.

At least we didn't get stuck on the way home—but that's only because it was so cold that all the mud froze. With the cold came snow, and by nightfall, Dad couldn't see where the road was.

All Downhill from There

Finally, we came over the last hill and saw the lights of South Omaha. It was all downhill from there. But that was the problem—the car started going faster and faster, and soon Dad was unable to control it. We crashed into the ditch! I was thrown into the plate glass windshield and was cut.

The car lay on its driver's side. Dad pushed me up and out of the passenger-side door, and a passerby grabbed me and stopped my bleeding by holding his hand over the wound. No one else was hurt, so the man loaded us into his car and took me a doctor. Later, he drove across town to take us home.

The doctor who patched me up said I would have bled to death if that man hadn't put his hand over the cut. It's hard to believe he was there so quickly— we hadn't seen another car for hours.

The Model T, however, was wrecked beyond repair—and I'm not sure anyone was upset about it!

> **"Travel is only glamorous in retrospect."**
> —Paul Theroux

We Survived 'Old Shaky'

Nowadays, cars whiz along on Interstate Highway 8, a modern expressway near Yuma, Arizona. Back in the '20s, though, things were quite a bit different on the same desert route.

Then, motorists were lucky to hit speeds much over 12 mph—and even at that pace, it was a tooth-rattling ride. That's because the original road was made of wooden planks. No wonder they nicknamed it "Old Shaky"!

In 1924, my family and I made a trip across the desert on Old Shaky, and I'll never forget the experience. Then called Route 27-B, this hardwood highway helped travelers negotiate the shifting sand dunes known as "The American Sahara" between 1915 and 1926.

Old Shaky was made of portable 12x8-foot sections laid end to end. The sections consisted of 4x12-inch planks bolted across heavy timbers. Three strong metal bands held each section's planks tightly together.

After sandstorms, a maintenance crew with a four-horse team would dig up any sand-covered sections and, if necessary, reposition the road to fit the new lay of the land.

"Real" Road Ended

I was 10 years old when our family moved from California to Arizona. Dad drove us in his 1920 Dodge touring car, pulling a simple homemade trailer behind.

The hard-surfaced highway we'd been on ended in El Centro, California. Ahead of us, Old Shaky waited to help us snake our way through the desert.

We stopped at a service station for gas and water. The attendant's tales of what to expect in the miles ahead frightened Mom, Sis and me. We were especially worried when he brought up the possibility of bouncing off the road and getting stuck in the sand!

Dad tried to calm our fears. "We're lucky today,"

SANDY SITUATION. Road conditions were difficult at best in Texas, Oklahoma and other areas of the Great Plains, as well as sandy spots in California and all throughout the Dust Bowl. Sections of wooden planks served as roads in such areas. The wood sections were often repositioned throughout the sandy areas as needed. (See photo below.)

he said soothingly. "It's cloudy and cool, so the radiator won't boil. And there's no wind blowing, so flying sand won't be a bother."

Mom sighed. "I'm glad for that," she said. "It's such a nuisance to put up the side curtains!" (Those were made of isinglass and heavy black leather. When the weather was threatening, we'd remove them from under the backseat to enclose the open touring car.)

Away We Went!

Worried but determined, the family set off. Dad's Dodge shook and rattled uncontrollably as its tires rumbled over Old Shaky's rough washboard surface.

Automobile springs just were not designed to handle such a hammering. No matter how slowly Dad drove, the up-and-down motion of the Dodge seemed to accelerate. Dad actually had to stop the car occasionally just to quell all the bouncing.

The road was only 8 feet wide, which meant oncoming cars could not pass each another. Turnouts at quarter-mile intervals allowed one vehicle to pull over and let another by.

"But what happens if we meet another car in the middle?" Sis asked in a worried voice when we passed the first turnout.

"One of us will have to back up," answered Dad. The fact that he had no experience backing a trailer didn't make us nervous Nellies feel any better about the situation!

Trouble Ahead?

Later on, we did spot an approaching car in the distance. Luckily there was a turnout just ahead, so Dad pulled over and waited.

Finally, a chugging Model T pulled alongside. Dad and the other driver discussed road conditions and weather—but mostly they just complained about the bone-jarring ride.

The day dragged on as we bumped our way across that desolate landscape, and it seemed as if the 10-mile trek to Yuma would never end.

When we finally reached town and stopped for the night, we discovered that a trunk filled with clothing had bounced out of the trailer somewhere along the way! We were so weary that no one even mentioned going back to look for it.

Not long after we settled in Arizona, Route 27-B was paved. Sections of the old plank road soon became historical relics—one was even displayed at the Chicago World's Fair in 1933!

Now Old Shaky is merely a curiosity in transportation history. But the memory of our bone-rattling journey continues to bounce around in my mind!

LUCILLE MACDONALD • RENO, NEVADA

WAITING OUT A DUST STORM

During the Dust Bowl days in 1934, I borrowed my dad's Model A, picked up three friends and headed for Canyon, Texas, about 18 miles south of Amarillo.

Late that afternoon, we saw a huge dust storm approaching. We knew that it was trouble and immediately turned back toward Amarillo. Soon it was so dark we had to pull off the road.

While sitting there in the blinding storm, we could feel wind-driven objects hitting the car. One was so loud it sounded like it might have been a runaway washtub!

Finally we decided that we had to drive on, but the car was so charged with static electricity that the ignition system wouldn't function.

Eventually we flagged down a car. The driver towed us back to Canyon, where a mechanic knew how to discharge the static. By nightfall we were again headed toward Amarillo.

The dust piled up so thick on the windshield it was impossible to see. We made it home by driving with the windows down—the driver kept an eye on the center strip of the pavement, and all of the passengers had their heads out, watching for any oncoming headlights.

By the time we arrived in Amarillo, our faces were caked with dirt and our noses and mouths were almost filled with mud. The dust storm was so big that fallout was still being reported on the Texas Gulf Coast two weeks later!

W.E. GARRETT • KERRVILLE, TEXAS

JEEP JAUNT. When the author (right) departed with his buddy Ray (on the left, above) on a cross-country trip in 1948, they drove a Jeep and pulled a trailer.

BIG JOURNEY
IN A TINY JEEP

Despite my service during World War II, I'd hardly been out of California. Neither had my friend Ray Schlick, who had also been in the service.

After graduating from college in 1948, we worked hard all summer long to raise money for our cross-country trip of a lifetime.

We bought a surplus Army Jeep and trailer. Ray made a metal top. We painted both the Jeep and trailer red, crammed it with old camping equipment and set off with $40 between us.

We left Westwood, near Los Angeles, in August and headed north up the California coast. The first night we camped overlooking San Francisco Bay, then followed the road into redwood country the next morning.

That was when it started to rain. Large silver dollar-sized drops splattered so hard against the tiny windshield that it became almost impossible to see the narrow highway winding through the twisting valleys and steep hills.

Refuge in Redwoods

By late afternoon we'd had enough. We pulled into a state redwood park and started wrestling with the secondhand tent, but it kept collapsing, and the Jeep was too small to sleep in. Then we spotted two enormous redwoods with hollow trunks. Ray and I sat cozy and dry, each in our own tree, munching on our dinner of cheese and crackers.

We continued driving north, to Vancouver, British Columbia, where we mooched off my aunt, watched Canadian football and were fixed up with two pretty girls for a dance.

Our $40 was almost gone, so we headed back across the border, drove over the Cascades in a raging hailstorm and finally stopped in Yakima, Washington, where we got jobs picking apples.

Wheel Eluded Them

After two weeks, we had enough money to head for Yellowstone Park. Unfortunately, halfway across eastern Washington the trailer threw a wheel that went rolling into a field of barley. We spent much of the night crawling around looking for the wheel, only to find it in the morning about a foot from our tent. It took two days and $15 of our precious money to repair the trailer. We were short of dough, but when we got to Yellowstone, we treated ourselves to dinner at the lodge.

That night we were back outside, and it was cold. We wore all of our clothes and stuffed ourselves into our sleeping bags. In the morning, we awoke to a temperature of 9 degrees.

The cold affected the Jeep, too. It wouldn't start! Ray built a fire, and when the wood had been reduced to coals, we pushed the Jeep over them. We were so happy when it started!

From Yellowstone we headed east and stopped in Cedar Rapids, Iowa, where Ray's aunt and uncle fed us some terrific meals while we found work shoveling soybeans into silos.

After 10 days, we moved on to Connecticut, where my sister lived. On the way, we slept under the stars. In Pennsylvania, we woke up under 2 inches of snow.

My sister opened her home to us, but we were unable to find jobs. A $20 check in the mail from Ray's folks saved the trip. We left with Thanksgiving turkey sandwiches in our pockets and motored south. We still had no luck finding work, as all the seasonal jobs had been filled.

Desperate for money, we had no choice but to sell the trailer. With everything packed on the roof of the Jeep, we became a mobile version of the leaning tower of Pisa.

The South was warm and wonderful, and mild nights made us forget about using the tent. We were unable to find work and struggled back home after 3½ months with less than $1 between us. We tried to get rid of the tent—but, golly, no one wanted it!

JOHN PERCY • SEQUIM, WASHINGTON

COMPASS POINTS. The author's buddy, Ray Schlick, stops to study a map while the two take a pit stop en route to Yellowstone National Park.

THREE FOR THE ROAD

With a cargo of critters, they set out on a grueling cross-country trek in 1954.

RONDA BREWSTER-WALKER • COOKVILLE, TENNESSEE

In August 1954, Father, a career Navy man, was transferred from Jacksonville, Florida, to Vallejo, California. Mom, Grandma and I were left behind to pack and drive across the country to meet him.

Mom and Grandma actually relished these adventures, including any challenges that they encountered along the way.

It was amazing how much Mom crammed into our two-tone 1950 Pontiac. The backseat was my domain, and it would be my job to tend to our pets during the trip.

There were two very large black cats named Anthracite and Bituminous (Ci and Bi), a cuddly cocker spaniel named Sandy, and a loud and very cantakerous parrot named Jose.

Texas Was Hot!

Mom and Grandma were a formidable team—their energy and enthusiasm were boundless.

I, on the other hand, was a typical bored teenager. I hated traveling by car and slept continually, day or night. If the car was running, I wasn't.

The first part of our trip was uneventful, but things heated up in Texas—literally. We couldn't believe how hot it was! It took five days and four nights to get through Texas, and the third day of our crossing was the absolute worst.

We were miserable and so were the animals—the cats and dog were gasping, and the parrot stood on his perch with his wings spread and tongue hanging askew.

Desparate, Mom stopped in a small town, bought a 50-pound block of ice and put it in the backseat with me.

I'd rub my hands over the wonderfully cold block and flick ice water on everyone (our menagerie included). The water evaporated immediately, but it saved our lives. I felt like a heroine that day.

After that, Mom decided we'd travel by night and sleep by day. I liked that plan! I could spend all day in a motel pool, then sleep while we were in the car at night.

Unfortunately, I forgot about sunburn. After one day in the sun, trying to sleep in the car at night was sheer torture!

Finally we neared the California border. There was a checkpoint ahead to prevent people from bringing in things they shouldn't—and we realized they probably wouldn't allow Jose.

Good grief! We had to think fast. Grandma piled anything she could find on top of his cage to make it look like a jumble of clothes. However, when Jose was in total darkness, he got nervous and clucked like a chicken. We figured chickens wouldn't be allowed, either.

When the inspector poked his head in the car and began asking questions, Grandma coughed, sneezed and wheezed into her hanky to drown out Jose's clucking. (After all, she was asthmatic and very convincing.) Meanwhile, Mom was screaming out the answers in order to be heard. What bedlam!

Finally, the inspector seemed satisfied and waved us through. Mom dropped the old car into low and stepped on the gas.

Up the mountain we climbed, with Bi and Ci purring, Sandy snoring and Jose breaking into song. Mom, Grandma and I joined in with a chorus of "California, Here I Come!"

WESTWARD, HO! The author's family vacationed in Key West, Florida, a few years before their trip West. Behind Ronda are her mother, Mary; grandmother Mildred Washburn; and dad, Ronnie Brewster.

BLACK HILL COUNTRY. The stunning hills of South Dakota served as a picturesque backdrop for a vacation trip the author took with his uncle. Camped in a pickup truck deep in the forest, the two soon encountered battling bulls and even a bear—or so they thought!

TOO CLOSE **FOR COMFORT**

My uncle, D.C. Eyler, and I ran a car company in Bartlett, Iowa, in 1950. Money was too tight for an expensive trip that year, so we decided to take a poor man's vacation to the Black Hills of South Dakota instead.

Our 1947 Chevrolet pickup truck had an open bed. We covered it with a borrowed old canvas top, which had a few holes to let in the rain. Our beds were two Army cots placed lengthwise in the truck bed. For meals, we invested in a two-burner gas stove.

One afternoon during our trip, we decided to camp in a national forest among some tall, stately pines. This was an open grazing area for cattle.

We stopped to admire the beautiful beasts, which were accompanied by a large bull. Off in the distance, we heard another bull coming toward us. It was a smaller bull intent on taking over the cow herd. As it approached, I knew there was going to be trouble.

Suddenly the two bulls charged each other at full speed. They smashed into each other head-on, like locomotives.

After several such collisions, the smaller bull retreated down to the lower valley, defeated. Uncle D.C. and I decided maybe it would be better for us to move on, too.

We set up camp near a small creek, had a bite to eat, then turned in for the night. The forest around us was black as coal. We tried to sleep, but it was very cold that night. All we could think about was the glorious daylight.

The sounds of forest critters surrounded us. One noise was particularly loud and close by—a gnawing noise, high up in one of the trees. It had to be a bear, at least!

Suddenly there was a loud crash in the truck bed, and the truck shook as if a bomb had gone off. My uncle and I each grabbed a pistol and a flashlight and found the culprit—a huge porcupine!

The porcupine had tumbled out of a tall pine tree, torn a large hole in the canvas top and then smashed to the floor of the pickup, right between our cots.

We jumped out of the truck, opened the tailgate and chased the critter out. Then we spent the rest of the night trying to sleep sitting up.

KEITH EYLER • EL CAJON, CALIFORNIA

STICKY SITUATION. In the early days of driving, folks knew that getting stuck was par for the course.

FAMILY TRIPS WERE
MIRED IN MUD

MISSOURI TRIP MEASURED IN MUD HOLES PER HOUR

One August morning in 1924, the young roosters woke me very early, their hoarse, immature efforts heralding the dawn of a new day. And what a momentous day it was!

My parents had moved to Lexington, Missouri, from Columbia, Missouri, in 1918 (I was born in 1919), and today would mark their first visit back home.

Daddy had just purchased a beautiful black and shiny Ford touring car with a self-starter, snap-on side curtains and a headlamp on each front fender. The timing was right, too—the corn was laid by, the wheat threshed and sold, the hay baled, and the summer fruits and vegetables canned and stored in the cellar.

Mama and my older sister, Clara, had prepared our dinner the night before and packed it into a galvanized pail that Daddy lowered into the well to keep it chilled overnight.

I was small, so I got to sit in the front seat next to Daddy, while Mama held baby Nellie in the backseat. Daddy was in such a jovial mood, and Mama was all smiles, too. She'd powdered her face, back-combed her long dark hair and fluffed it a bit over her ears. With her pretty jeweled side combs and hairpins, I thought she was the loveliest lady in the world.

From my vantage point beside Daddy, I was filled with wonderment. Until then, my travels had been a buggy ride to visit neighbors or the 3-mile trip into Lexington from our farm. I had no idea the world was so very big and beautiful.

There were few gasoline pumps back then and no restrooms. When the family needed to "rest," Daddy stopped the Ford between two cornfields. He and my brother Bobby went one way while Mama and we girls went another.

Somewhere between Waverly and Malta Bend, I watched Mama get out a wash pan and a gallon jug of water, then bathe and dress our baby sister for the day—right there in the backseat as we traveled along at 10 mph!

About the time she finished, Dad told me I'd better turn around and sit down because we were coming to a mud hole. A man with a team of mules and a heavy chain was waiting to pull us through the mud for $1.

We encountered many such men that day. There were even stories about farmers who hauled water to their mud holes every morning. For some of them, keeping that mud hole going was the best cash crop August had to offer.

At noon, Daddy stopped at a grassy spot under a shade tree. Bobby poured more water into the tin wash pan, and we all washed up for dinner. Nothing has ever tasted better than that meal—fried chicken, potato salad, deviled eggs, sliced tomatoes, fresh peach cobbler and lemonade.

In those days, a flat tire every 35 miles or so was normal (I can still smell that patching glue), but for me, the trip was marvelous until we crossed a bridge over the Blackwater River. The boards clattering under our tires made such a frightful noise that I was sure we'd fall into the water. No experience since has terrified me more!

Daddy was quick to comfort me. When we crossed the Missouri River, he told me to look at a nearby railroad bridge and pointed out that there were no loose boards on our bridge.

He also promised we'd reach Grandma's before dark. Sure enough, we pulled into her driveway around 6 p.m. We were 100 miles from home, and it had only taken 13½ hours. Our relatives marveled that we'd made such good time.

EMMA CALVERT FITCHETT • INDEPENDENCE, MISSOURI

ANGELS ANSWERED HER PRAYER

My father bought a car in 1918, when I was 6, which made it possible for us to visit my grandfather about 30 miles away.

During one trip to Grandfather's, we came to a low spot covered with water. Tire tracks led into and out of the spot, so my father assumed it was not deep. The car sank up to the running boards. For the first time in my life, I was aware that my father was helpless. Nothing he could do would get the car out of that mud hole.

In my childlike way, I prayed that God would send help for my father.

Very soon, a truck carrying all kinds of rope came along. My father took off his shoes and socks, rolled up his trousers, tied a rope to the car, and we were pulled out.

To this day, I believe the men in that truck were angels sent to answer my prayer. My faith was born in a mud hole.

ANNA BUCKWALTER • RONKS, PENNSYLVANIA

MEMORABLE MUDTIME MEAL

When I was a child, we traveled from Keokuk to Sandyville, Iowa, to see my grandparents. The last mile was a dirt road, and it was often muddy.

One time we got stuck. My mother took my brother and me to a nearby farmhouse while my father and the farmer got the car out.

While waiting, we enjoyed goat's milk and blackberry pie. I've never had that combination since. It was so good.

LORNA SPARROW • HAMILTON, ILLINOIS

STUCK IN THE MUD

In August 1926, our family was traveling back to our home in Chicago after our annual summer visit to an uncle's farm about 100 miles north of St. Paul, Minnesota.

Our 1925 Dodge sedan held Father, Mother, me (I was 11 at the time), my two brothers and three younger sisters.

Somewhere in the middle of Wisconsin, our car became mired down in mud on what passed for a highway in those days. My brother George and I removed our shoes and stockings, got out and pushed for all we were worth.

I still recall the flying mud and water as we did our best—to no avail. Dad had to ask a nearby farmer to bring his team of horses to rescue us. How tired and dirty we all were!

What we didn't know was that the arrangements Father had made would bring a happy ending to the whole affair. After we were pulled into the farmyard and had a chance to get ourselves cleaned up, the farmer's wife had a fried chicken dinner ready for us.

We all agreed that it was the best meal we had ever tasted!

LEO BRABANEC • NEKOOSA, WISCONSIN

DETOUR... MUDDY ROAD AHEAD. Back when most country roads weren't paved, there was rarely a detour, and cars—and sometimes people—came home caked in mud.

DANGEROUS DUO. Clyde Barrow and Bonnie Parker terrorized banks in the '30s, and caused some nervous excitement for a young Texas couple on what started out as a pleasant spring ride.

Benny and Joyce...Not
BONNIE AND CLYDE!

Her first turn behind the wheel led to an unforgettable case of mistaken identity in 1934.

JOYCE URRUTIA • LA GRANGE, TEXAS

In spring of 1934, when I was 17, a friend taught me how to drive. Benny was 19, and his secondhand Model A Ford roadster had a rumble seat and stick shift. After a couple of weeks' practice, I was getting the hang of driving.

Every Easter, Benny made a 180-mile round trip between San Antonio and the Austin State School to bring his disabled brother home for the holiday. He asked if I'd like to go along and try some highway driving.

I was tickled to pieces when Mama approved. She even packed us sandwiches and a thermos of hot coffee.

A late Texas norther had blown in, so the next morning, I bundled up in a jacket and old black beret, and Benny wore a brown suit and an old felt hat. Bluebonnets were blooming, and the sun felt warm even though the wind was cold.

Our open car was without a radio, so we had no way of knowing there was a massive manhunt under way in Texas, Arkansas and Louisiana for notorious bank robbers Bonnie and Clyde.

We drove along innocently, laughing and singing and enjoying the day. I was behind the wheel when we reached the halfway point, the little town of Buda, Texas.

Switched Drivers

A big wall of construction barricades across part of the highway scared me. "Better let me drive," Benny said. "You could run into something unexpected and land us in a ditch."

PHOTOS: H. ARMSTRONG ROBERTS

When we got into town, there were more barricades across the side streets. Benny turned and drove onto a narrow street between two large brick buildings.

"What the heck!" he yelped, braking so hard that he killed the engine. Straight ahead, police cars blocked the streets. A line of policemen, Texas Rangers and sheriffs advanced toward us, each with a rifle or pistol pointed at us!

"Holy cow!" Benny yelled.

"Hands in the air! Don't move!" came the command, as the armed officers cautiously approached us.

Benny's face was the color of frozen green pea soup, and I must have looked just as bad. I managed to glance over my shoulder, where I saw more lawmen approaching from the rear.

"Don't even breathe!" they growled, reaching into the car and searching for weapons.

"Don't shoot, officers!" we babbled. "Just please don't shoot!"

Was It Bonnie's Beret?

Then a big old potbellied sheriff strolled up to the car, holding a photo in one hand and a cocked pistol in the other. He looked me over. "You shore do look like Bonnie Parker, gal," he drawled. "Got any identification?"

"There's a letter from my granny and a library card," I offered, reaching out a shaking hand for my purse.

"Whup!" he barked. "Keep them hands high."

Pulling the purse out from between Benny and me, he went through it himself.

Meanwhile, another lawman questioned and searched Benny. Fortunately, Benny had a letter signed by his mother so he could pick up his brother at school.

We still didn't have a clue what all this was about. After the sheriff looked at Benny's letter, he handed it back with a $5 bill on top.

"Sorry, kids," he apologized. "We thought sure we'd trapped Bonnie and Clyde. Heard they were coming into Texas to rob a bank, and you two kinda fit their description.

"Real sorry we scared you so bad. Yonder's a cafe. Go get yourselves some coffee and pie and get settled down before you drive out of town. Be my guest with the five there."

With that, he holstered his pistol and strolled off, leaving Benny and me staring at each other in disbelief.

In the years since, I've seen movies about the end of Bonnie and Clyde—and I've been forever grateful that none of those Texas lawmen had nervous fingers that day.

BRAVING THE WILD WEST

In a 1951 Studebake Commander Starlight coupe, I traveled out West. It was 1957, and back in those days, with no speed limit in some places, you went as fast as you could go.

A sign just out of Tucumcari, New Mexico, said Last Chance Gas, and it was 15 cents a gallon. Man, that was expensive, so I turned around and went back into town, fueling up at a Whiting Brothers gas station for 5 cents a gallon plus 3 cents tax.

It was 100 miles to the next place, a Chevron station in the middle of nowhere. If you didn't make it before 9 p.m., you had to sit there until 9 the next morning. And if it was a weekend, the gas was 5 cents higher.

I got my very first speeding ticket while driving 25 mph in Kingman, Arizona, where the city speed limit was 15 mph. I spent the whole weekend in a cold jail in the courthouse basement. Fortunately, the judge let me go, warning me never to get caught speeding in his town again.

I went through Victorville and Eagle Rock, California, stopping to see friends I had known since 1950—Roy Rogers, Dale Evans and their son, Dusty. I stayed with them for three days.

I ended up in Hollywood, where I worked at the YMCA until heading back to Missouri. It was a fun excursion, and the Studebaker was the best car I ever owned.

RAY PITTAM • REDDING, CALIFORNIA

1961
▼

IT'S A MIDSUMMER
NIGHTMARE

THE MOVIES HAVE NOTHING ON THIS FAMILY VACATION

Last July, I witnessed a typical summer scene: Our neighbors, who could pose for a Norman Rockwell family picture, were busily preparing for vacation. Mom, Dad and three young boys packed the SUV with glee, then waved as they motored away. This triggered a memory of vacationing with my own family, but my feelings were far from gleeful.

The eldest of three sons, I was 13 that summer—hoping and praying that my parents would let me stay home when I was 14. After all, my aunt and uncle lived next door. I have always loved my parents and two brothers dearly, but spending a week with siblings in the backseat of a 1951 two-door Ford was less than idyllic. Driving around the country until 4 o'clock, when Dad finally found a motel with a vacancy, couldn't compete with playing baseball at home or meeting girls downtown.

Mom inevitably met any and all protests about going along on the trip with the same statement: "But boys, this trip will be educational!"

The pattern was repeated every summer. The Ford was packed to the limit, including a gallon container filled with lemonade, prepared for the boys who would be fighting each other in the backseat.

"He started it."

"No, he started it!"

Twenty miles from home, my brother Tommy had already gulped the container dry all by himself. Now, of course, he needed to use the bathroom. The delay was compounded by the need to refill the lemonade jug.

As though on cue, a stern warning followed: "This is the last time I'm doing this today! Don't ask for any more refills. We'll never get there."

These were the days before the interstate highway system. Major highways of that era ran

THE HOUGHTON MOTEL. "It was June 1958, and school was out in Yucaipa, California," says Geneva Houghton, who now resides in Hemet. "We packed our 1957 Chevy and headed for Three Hills, Alberta, where our son Milton had been attending high school. Every night, after we pulled into a new camping area, our '57 Chevy became our own personal motel."

through the center of the largest cities, and it didn't seem to matter if we were heading south through Baltimore and D.C. or north through Utica or Albany—Dad, God love him, always got lost.

We always seemed to find ourselves in the worst part of any town or city. While we struggled to find our way, with seedy characters gawking at the strangers with out-of-state license plates, Mom repeated the magic words: "This is educational!" We didn't agree.

Our family's excursion to Montreal in 1955 is etched in my memory. We had spent the better part of the day cavorting around a remote area of New Hampshire. Dad wanted to show us the farm where he lived when he was a small child. He had stopped several times to ask locals for directions and to slap the three of us around for fighting.

We found the spot where he thought the farm was, but only a rundown shack remained on the property. We crossed the Canadian border late in the afternoon and reached Montreal's outskirts around 6 o'clock. After searching for an hour for someplace to spend the night, we finally saw our dream motel. My brothers and I were jubilant: "Look, Dad, it has color TV!" That was a real rarity in 1955.
It also had a swimming pool, swings and slides—and a vacancy.

We all waited, scarcely able to contain our excitement, as Dad emerged from the motel office. "Well, they want too much money here, boys. But the guy told me about a more reasonable place just down the road. At least I think that's what he said. His English wasn't too good."

A few minutes later, that reasonable place appeared—cabins. After securing a cabin for the night, we drove into Montreal and cruised around the city long enough to discover that nearly everything was much more French than English.

Finally, the five of us settled down for a much-needed rest. The cabin had two double beds in one room. Since no cot was available that night, guess which three people had to sleep in one bed.

They say that three's a crowd, but "crowded" is a word that could never do that night justice. The car would have offered more rest.

Then I remembered the previous summer and our trip through the Pocono Mountains by way of Bushkill Falls. After the third day, a downpour kept us confined to the cabin. Floods blocked bridges and roads. Trapped, we had to postpone our return home for two more fun-filled days. I never dreamed that anything could rival such aggravation, but I was wrong! Are you listening, Chevy Chase?

BRENT PETERSEN • CRANBURY, NEW JERSEY

HAPPY WANDERERS. This 1950s Edsel ad might have been slightly misleading in depicting cross-country family travel as harmonious.

TENTING IN THE DARK

Seven of us piled into a 1961 Chevy Impala in 1964 and headed from Wakefield, Michigan, to Canyon City, Colorado.

There was my husband, Ernie, and me; Ernie's brother, Bill, and his wife wife, Liola; and Bill and Ernie's sister, Ingrid, and her two daughters. We were taking Ingrid and the girls to meet her husband in Canyon City. Then he'd drive them to California.

The first night, we were somewhere west of Omaha. We drove around the small town. looking for a place to camp. When we finally found a site, it was underwater. It was near midnight and pitch dark before we finally found some dry ground where we could pitch a tent.

We two couples slept in the tent, and Ingrid and the girls slept in the car.

We had no more than put down our heads when a bright light came right into the tent. Then came the whistle and roar of a train.

I thought it was coming through the tent! Ingrid thought it was going to hit the car.

The train passed without incident, and after recovering from the shock, we settled down. But we soon discovered we had set up the camp not only next to a railroad track, but also a highway.

All night long, the semis shifted gears as they prepared to stop at the railroad crossing. And another train went by.

After the experience was had that first night on the road, you would think Ernie and Bill had learned their lesson and would look for a campsite before dark. Not them.

On our way home, in Wyoming, we again pitched camp at night, only to be awakened at first light by the crowing of roosters and the quacking of ducks in an irrigation ditch. We had spent the night camping in a farmer's front yard.

JANICE KORPELA • CORNUCOPIA, WISCONSIN

DIARY OF A MOTORCYCLIST. The author (above) at one of the scarce gas stations. In Kansas (right), the road was more like a river.

They Pointed Their Motorcycles East
TOWARD ADVENTURE

Three buddies trekked acorss the U.S. in 1922, encountering mishaps and mayhem along the way.

GEORGE BAGGE • SUN CITY, ARIZONA

I *discovered a diary, written by my father, while I was cleaning an old trunk in the attic. I started reading and quickly found myself back in his world. The following is an excerpt from that diary:*

It was 1922. I was 18 years old, active and excited about doing something different—a motorcycle trip from Los Angeles to New York City.

No one I'd heard of had ever ridden a motorcycle across the country, and everyone thought I was crazy, except my two best friends, who were also 18.

I had a 1916 Harley I'd bought for $16. Some of the parts were missing, but I rebuilt it to top condition.

Although I'd been told there were few roads, gas stations were scarce, motels and restaurants existed only in cities, and water was next to impossible to find, my two friends wanted to join me.

Goodbye, Blacktop

Cecil Smith, quite aware of the hazards, had a Harley and a sidecar like mine. Bob Hill, full of life, went along as a relief driver. In one sidecar we carried supplies, and in the other, the passenger.

We started on June 24. The blacktop road from Los Angeles ended at Victorville. From here on, there was nothing but desert!

I had a dream of going back to my hometown of West New York, New Jersey, but little did I realize that doing it on a bike through the Mojave Desert in June was not the greatest of plans.

Later, we even traveled on the Santa Fe Trail, composed of rock, dust and two wagon ruts—plus scorpions, sidewinders and, overhead, vultures that seemed to be waiting.

In Barstow, California, my bike wouldn't start; the magneto had gone bad. We sent it back to Los Angeles by train to be repaired as we sat and waited. We took off as soon as the part came back and we got the bike running. We arrived in Needles, California, at midnight, and the temperature was 110 degrees.

During the desert ride, the brilliant sunshine, terrible heat, dust and lack of moisture began to take their toll. Our lips were dry and starting to crack and bleed. Our canteens were getting low; we had no idea where the next water would be found.

We crossed the desert into Arizona—picking up gas, food and water—and rode at night, hoping for cooler weather.

The spokes on the rear wheel of Cecil's bike began to pop. Finally the tire was rubbing the chain and wearing a hole through the side. With no way of staying out in the heat, we had to use our new spares. We used all three spares and put holes in all of them before we got to Flagstaff.

We found a motorcycle shop and respoke our wheels. We paid the owner, then burned the shop down to the ground, destroying its contents. It wasn't intentional! One of us lit a cigarette as we left the shop and threw the match into what looked like a tub of water. It turned out to be gasoline.

As we were frantically putting the wheel back on the bike, the shop owner caught up with us.

Left in a Hurry

"I saw you throw that match in the gasoline, but don't worry about it," he said. "I had it all covered with fire insurance and I'm glad it burned down."

Despite his assurances, the three of us left as fast as possible. We continued to look over our shoulders for three days and nights as we passed through Santa Fe, New Mexico, and finally stopped in Trinidad, Colorado. Our stop wasn't planned; someone had forgotten to tell the Purgatoire River not to flood.

We thought about removing our tires and riding the railroad track but decided to wait it out. When the water got down far enough so the engines wouldn't stall, we started through it. You couldn't see the road, but we used telephone poles as guides.

We headed for Kansas City, but our bikes stalled and we ended up pushing them through mud and water. It was nearly impossible to keep going.

Somewhere outside Columbus, Ohio, we crossed a river bottom, and the forks holding the front wheel of my bike snapped.

A farmer let me park the bike in his barn while I made the repairs. All three of us hopped on the other outfit and took off in search of parts. Eventually I found a pair of forks in a junk pile next to a small bike shop. I paid $12 for them.

Coming out of the Cumberland Mountains in West Virginia, we were driving along a long, straight grade with a small village at the bottom. I reached the bottom, looked back, and realized that my buddies had disappeared.

Apparently, the front clamps on the sidecar of Cecil's bike snapped. Out of control, with Cecil on the bike and Bob in the sidecar, they ran between a gas pump and a building, knocking down a fellow pumping gas and ripping a large hole in the rear fender of his brand-new touring car!

Soon a crowd of townspeople came marching up the street with the sheriff, who wore a star—and a gun large enough to shoot the tops off mountains.

Rescued by Salesman

The three of us were saved by a salesman, who told the sheriff the event was as accident. We made restitution and left the same way we did Flagstaff—as fast as possible.

From then on, it was easy. In Pennsylvania, the roads were paved again. When we got to New York, they ran two front-page stories in two days, and the mayor gave us the keys to the city. We felt like celebrities. My dream had come true.

As I closed the diary, I felt as if I had just ridden across the country myself. I was so proud of my dad and thankful to know a little more about his life.

The epilogue is simple. After their 3,800-mile journey, they crated the bikes and shipped them home. They had intended to ride back, but the bikes looked and rode like they'd been in the war. So the boys returned to California by touring car.

DEEP AND DUSTY. Think you've seen potholes? The Santa Fe Trail, still riddled with wagon ruts in 1922, was no easy ride on a motorcycle.

A Long Ride Home

FERRYBOATS AND SPLIT LIPS

I recall crossing the Missouri River on a car ferry with my mom, dad and sister. We lived in Sabetha, Kansas and took the boat to visit my aunt, uncle and two cousins in Mound City, Missouri.

This photo of the ferry (below) is from about 1917, before I was born. It crossed the river at Rulo, in the very southeast corner of Nebraska, just north of the Kansas state line.

A bridge was built across the river at the spot in the 1940s or '50s, but I couldn't look at it without thinking about those ferry rides as a child.

One trip I'll never forget was in 1929, when our car slipped off the road and ran into a ditch. I was sitting in Mom's lap, and my face went right through the windshield.

My lip and nose were badly cut. A doctor in Mound City met us at his office on a Sunday morning and stitched my upper lip back together.

It was quite exciting, and I got a lot of extra attention in my first-grade class. The wounds healed with only minor scars.

JACK REINHART • LA MESA, CALIFORNIA

ALL THE WRONG BUTTONS

We owned a 1960 Plymouth that we bought in 1964. It was blue over white, with push buttons on the dashboard to operate the automatic transmission.

In 1972, my husband, three children and I were coming home from a camping trip. We were all exhausted from swimming, waterskiing and other outdoor activities.

On the way, we stopped for gas. When we tried to leave, the push buttons wouldn't work.

My husband was finally able to get the transmission into drive. Then he told me I'd have to drive all the way home without stopping because he didn't know whether he would be able to get the car going again. Then he promptly fell asleep and left me to do all the driving!

What a nightmare. The children were asleep in the back and my husband was asleep, too, with his head in my lap. I couldn't wake him to save my soul.

I drove the nearly 400 miles home without any help, and we sold the car as soon as we got the push buttons working again.

VIRGINIA ADAMS • PEORIA, ARIZONA

THEY CHEWED THEIR WAY TO L.A.

Late one night in 1935, my son and I were returning to Los Angeles from San Francisco in my Hudson. About 2 a.m. on a lonely road, the cooling fan broke and the flying blades cut holes in the radiator, shooting steam in the air.

Fortunately, we weren't far from a roadside service station with a night-light burning. Under the light was a bell and a sign offering 24-hour service. I rang the bell, woke the owner and told him about my car trouble.

He said the closest town where I could get a new radiator and fan was 12 miles away—but the garage there wouldn't open until morning. He added that we could stay in his garage for the night, as there was nowhere else to go.

I looked around, pondering what to do, and spotted a rack of candy, cigarettes and gum.

With a husband in the Merchant Marine, I had learned a lot about fixing things myself. I asked my son if he wanted some gum. "Sure," he said.

I bought some, and we started chewing. Then I stuck the chewed gum into the radiator. Believe it or not, it took 56 packages (280 pieces) to patch and plug all the holes!

The owner filled up the radiator and gave me a 5-gallon can of water. I paid him $2.80 for the gum, and as we left, I could tell by the shake of his head that he didn't think we'd get that far.

Taking it slow and easy, I stopped often to check the radiator. We got home in time for me to get to work and for my son to go to school.

I bought and installed a new fan but left the radiator alone. Three years later, when I sold the Hudson, the gum was still holding it together!

ELIZABETH EASTMAN • CALISTOGA, CALIFORNIA

> "*Traveling—it leaves you speechless, then turns you into a storyteller.*"
> —Ibn Battuta

Car Conudrums

DUSTY DRIVE. "The road from Winnipeg, Manitoba, where we lived, to Saskatchewan, where we had family, was not paved when we went for a visit in 1954," says Ardath Effa of Edmonton, Alberta. "This picture was taken when my husband, Herman, and I finally managed to encounter a paved road. As you can see, we brought a lot of mud with us on our 1949 Nash. There were no car washes, so I used the pop bottle I was holding to wash off the windshield with water."

WATERING THE LASALLE. "On our way to the top of Pikes Peak on Aug. 14, 1946, the driver of this 1929 LaSalle touring car, Eddy Walsh, stopped at the Pikes Peak Ski Club headquarters for some water to cool down the radiator," says Carl Buckland of Los Alamos, New Mexico. "My wife, Mary Ella, seen in the car, and I were on our honeymoon, having been married four days earlier. We took this trip up Pikes Peak with a Denver touring service, as we had no car of our own."

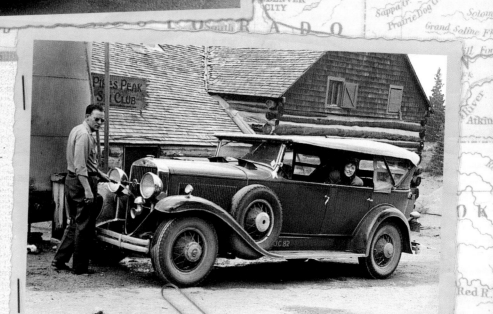

SUNDAY DRIVE DELAYED. "One of the 'joys' of car ownership in 1922 was being able to change your own tire," says Marion Fortier of Vacaville, California. "This snapshot, taken somewhere between Martinez and Oakland, California, must have been during a Sunday drive. My grandfather is in a suit with a vest and my Aunt Orna (at left) is in a pretty white dress. I'm next to Granddad. I'm pretty sure that changing a tire wasn't in the plan for the day!"

Tied Down to a 'T'

They say moving can be an exasperating experience. This was likely true for my parents, Charles and Eva Gilbert (seated in car behind truck), when they moved all their worldly belongings from Milton to Albany, Wisconsin, after their 1926 wedding. My grandfather Charles Burhans drove the fully loaded Model T truck.

It looks like everything was just thrown on top of the Model T. Notice the truck door held open by a rope tied to the radiator cap. And the stove is sitting on the car's running board! I guess folks were pretty ingenious back then.

PAT HERMANSON • EVANSVILLE, WISCONSIN

My Own **Memories**